Surviving Sexual Contradictions

MURIEL DIMEN

Surviving Sexual
Contradictions

*A Startling and Different Look at a Day
in the Life of a Contemporary Professional
Woman*

Macmillan Publishing Company

New York

Copyright © 1986 by Muriel Dimen

Grateful acknowledgment is made for permission to reprint excerpt from *The Gold Sell* by Sharon Olds. Copyright © 1986 by Sharon Olds. Published 1986 by Alfred A. Knopf.

Macmillan Publishing Company
866 Third Avenue, New York, N.Y. 10022
Collier Macmillan Canada, Inc.

Library of Congress Cataloging-in-Publication Data
Dimen, Muriel
  Surviving sexual contradictions.
  Bibliography: p.
  Includes index.
  1. Sex discrimination against women—United States.
2. Sexism—United States. 3. Sex role—United States.
4. Feminism—United States. I. Title.
HQ1426.D56 1986   305.4′2′0973   86-12600
ISBN 0-02-531620-6

10 9 8 7 6 5 4 3 2 1

Printed in the United States of America

For Sasha Mariel

Acknowledgments

In the matter of debts, I am fortunate to suffer an embarrassment of riches.

First, I wish to thank those who made possible my study of psychoanalysis. Ernestine Friedl, Robert F. Murphy, and Eric R. Wolf supported me early on, and Lucie Wood Saunders's continuing encouragement has been, in effect, unconditional. The Department of Anthropology of Lehman College, City University of New York, granted me extensive leaves of absence so that I could attend the New York University Postdoctoral Program in Psychotherapy and Psychoanalysis, as well as the New Hope Guild Program in Adult Psychotherapy, institutions to which I am grateful for having admitted a nonpsychologist to their ranks.

In a special class is my debt to Arthur H. Feiner for the second epiphany of my adult life. The first occurred at the beginning of college, when, in discovering social science, I also discovered a way to make sense of the world around me. The second took place much later, during my psychoanalysis, when I found a way to make sense of myself.

Although this book contains no reference to any person whom I have treated, I record here my gratitude to my patients, who, by sharing with me a portion of their lives, allow me to rediscover psychoanalytic theory every day.

Second, I am beholden to the feminist and other progressive social movements in which I have participated during the last twenty years. Much of what I say here synthesizes and serves up for more general consumption the pioneering ideas brewed in a myriad of study groups, consciousness-raising groups, conferences, and writings large and small. In particular, the Group for a Radical Human Science gave me the opportunity to write the paper out of which this book grew. Although fractious, often chaotic, and ultimately disappointing, GRHS provided, during its brief life span, a rare forum in which one could examine both the personal and the political, the psychological and the social, without being forced to select one or the other as the ultimate cause of human behavior.

Third, I may now turn to those individuals who helped me as I formulated and wrote this book. Elsa First, Howard Gadlin, David Lichtenstein, Sara Ruddick, Adria Schwartz, and Paula Webster read and criticized my earliest proposals. Conversations with others shed light on problems I encountered as the writing progressed: Jessica Benjamin, Peggy Crull, Robert Giard, Virginia Goldner, Edgar Gregerson, Adrienne Harris, Daphne Joslin, Carol Kramer, Phyllis Kriegel, Carol Lefcourt, Ricki Levenson, Abigail Norman, Adrian Rifkin, Seth L. Schein, Jonathan Sillin, and Lynne Zeavin.

Several friends and colleagues were kind enough to pore over various versions and portions of the manuscript: Carol Ascher, Donna Bassin, Ellen Cantarow, Harriet Cohen, Adrienne Harris, Katherine King, Maxine Margolis, Laura Martin, Robin Omata, Robert Roth, Adria Schwartz, Sue Shapiro, David Schiller, and Linda D. Wolfe. Adrienne Harris deserves special thanks for reading the entire manuscript a second time during a period of crisis.

Fourth, I am happy to thank those who have made the publication of this book possible. I am extremely grateful to my publisher, Hillel Black, for his unfailing enthusiasm, faith, and accessibility. My editor, Marion Wheeler, gave me the benefit of her fine sense of structure and language, as well as her early support. Edward A. Novak III smoothed the production process with thoughtfulness and patience, and Sharon L. Gonzalez was especially considerate about last-minute copyediting. And I could not wish for a better literary agent than Charlotte Sheedy, who believed in this book from its very beginnings and always came through in the pinch with generous encouragement, advice, optimism, and humor.

Finally, I thank my family and close friends, past and present. In particular, my brother, Michael Dimen, not only cheered me on but convinced me that it was easy as well as invaluable to use a word processor. And my cousin, Carole Fink, often kept me going with her deep belief in the value of my work.

I am grateful also to Carol Ascher for many years of literary and other mothering.

And, last of the last, there are those steadfast friends who have sustained me with their respect, honesty, and love. Harriet Cohen criticized my arguments and style even when it was hard to do so. Middle-of-the-night telephone calls with Katherine King saved many a day. Robert Roth, present at the birth of this project, has always confronted me in an extraordinarily productive fashion. And, despite the claims made by his work and family life, David Schiller not only read my manuscript with the care and challenge of an editor but was a fount of great-hearted comfort and counsel.

It gives me long-awaited pleasure to acknowledge all these contributions to whatever is good in this book, and to exempt all but myself from responsibility for the faults therein.

New York City, *September 1986*

Contents

Author to Reader   xiii

Prologue/A Woman on the Streets   1
   (Any Day, Any Time)

In Passion's Wake   13
   (6:00 A.M.)

The Strange Relationship Between Sex and Reproduction   31
   (7:30 A.M.)

Monkeys, Apes, and the Myth of the Ever-Ready Female   53
   (9:00 A.M.)

Power and Sex   73
   (11:00 A.M.)

Dependency and Empathy, or Autonomy's Better Half   91
   (2:30 P.M.)

Normal Envy   113
    (5:15 P.M.)

Women Alone   134
    (6:45 P.M.)

Women Together   154
    (9:00 P.M.)

Looking for Their Own Desire   177
    (Midnight)

Epilogue/On the Road   201
    (Dreamtime)

Bibliographical Discussion   216

Index   251

Author to Reader

In 1981, as a member of a panel whose subject of inquiry was "The Question of Feminism," I delivered a brief paper to a small group of psychoanalysts and social theorists, who were both my colleagues and my friends. My topic was women; my theme was the relationship between the personal and the political.

My paper wove together personal anecdotes with a commentary about their political significance. The stories I chose to tell were sexual ones. Recounting events that had happened to me and other women whom I knew, they were meant to demonstrate how even the most impersonal and distant social institutions and political constraints penetrate the most intimate and private core of personal experience. The commentary placed these stories in their psychological, social, and political contexts. Explaining the events as products of sexism, it argued against the idea that sexism is a conspiracy perpetrated by men against women. Rather, it insisted that sexism, like all social systems, affects men and women alike. Our participation in it is ambiguous, something in between playwright and puppet. Indeed, it was this ambiguity that fascinated me.

This book, modeled on that paper, consists of two voices. Each portion begins with the first-person story of one woman's day as she lives it. The other voice comments on that day. The first voice expresses the personal, the private, the individual; the second represents the political, the public, the cultural.

The first voice is a contrivance, that of an imaginary character whose day I have invented. However, I have plainly modeled my heroine's workday on mine, and she is, like me, both social scientist and psychotherapist. Her day is a series of episodes that serve as a hypothesis, a sort of experiment, for the second voice, which comments on her day. In a way, the narrative asks, What if? If a woman behaved and thought and felt as this particular woman in the course of a day, what would that mean about women's experience and social life in general?

The commentary answers in a voice that synthesizes several perspectives—anthropology, psychoanalysis, feminism, and social criticism. First, it examines the events of this day as an ethnographer would happenings in a foreign land, holding them up for scrutiny against the backdrop of the culture in which they appear. Second, the commentary speculates about these occurrences as would a psychoanalyst, wondering about the hidden, unconscious meanings of everyday life. Third, the commentary uses the narrative to explore the political problems of sex and gender with which women and men currently grapple. And, finally, the commentary argues that aspects of our culture, inextricably linked with patriarchy, inhibit personal freedom and social justice.

However, the commentary pretends to no omniscience about the protagonist, accepting that her inner being, like everyone's, eludes us. To put this in other terms, the commentary is to the narrative as theory is to life. The first may illuminate but can never exhaust the second, and the second is not reducible to the first. We may point to all manner of social and psychological causes for human behavior. We may be able to predict, with some confidence, what people will do, and chart, within limits, the future course of our society. But we can never eliminate the triangular tension between choice, causality, and chance in which our lives are suspended.

There is a profound relationship between the personal and the political, between private and public life, between individual experience and culture: If you go deeply enough into one, you come upon the other. In the heart of personal life lie the commonalities linking people who belong to the same culture. At the same time, the kernel of social life holds the premises, principles, and passions that give life to each individual. Personal experience is ingrained and contoured by culture; culture is reciprocally informed and maintained by individuals and their personal principles and passions.

This idea, that "the personal is political," is particularly feminist. What I have to say is part of the feminist attempt, now ongoing for over twenty years, to understand the personal/political problem as it influences private and public life. Indeed, feminists came to believe that this influence invalidated the conventional dichotomy between private and public life. They argued that what happens in the privacy of our homes, bedrooms, and hearts is welded to what happens in the streets, boardrooms, courts, and legislatures. And, conversely, they held that the most public of events are in part expressions, products, and buttresses of the most familiar details of everyday life.

Not unexpectedly, some things got polarized as the feminist movement probed this difficult and sometimes painful problem. Sometimes the personal was simply reduced to the political; the social context suddenly became the sole determinant of individual experience. At other times, the political was subsumed by the personal: Personal life—family, friendships, sex, therapy, personal development—was defined as the only viable reality, while the constraints of the social world were all but neglected.

The truth does not lie somewhere between these extremes. The extremes are as true as is the relationship between them. The psyche is not a microcosm of social life, nor is the world a psyche writ large. The political *is* political, the personal *is* personal. But neither exists without the other. Human life did not originate with a culture to which human psyches were added, nor with minds to which social life was appended. Mind and culture generate each other; neither is causative. If there are ultimate causes of human behavior, we do not yet know them. I believe, in fact, that the mechanistic conceptions of "cause" and "effect" are inappropriate tools with which to plumb human depths. But until we know better, we must try to talk about both the personal and the political, as simultaneously as possible but without collapsing the one into the other.

This book, offering up for general consumption a synthesis of recent feminist and other progressive thought, attempts to restore the balance between the extremes. Its two concurrent voices, expressing the personal and the political, examine feminine experience not in compartments but as it is lived in two coexistent realities—the inner, psychological one and the outer, social one.

I assume that the personal is always particular. I do not propose my heroine to be typical of anyone. There is no such thing, in any case, as a "typical" woman or man, black person or white, Jew or Christian—except in our minds and textbooks. The idea of "type" is a category of thought, not of life, the complexity of which eludes typology and single-cause explanations. Not every woman is, like my heroine, white, thirty-seven, and divorced. Not every woman lives in a city, teaches classes, sees patients, meets old lovers, or hovers on the edge of sexual experimentation. However, although she is not Everywoman, the experiences of her particular life are meant to convey something outside the particular that is elemental, that rings true to any reader.

The political is as general as the personal is particular. By definition, it joins us together outside our individualities, creating the cultural context that makes sense of individuality. Therefore, the commentary on the personal narrative, the second voice, relies heavily on the concept of "culture." Although this concept would seem to need little explanation, the definition can be misleading when applied to a complex society like ours. Commonly understood, *culture* refers to a more or less orderly and homogeneous collection of traditions, customs, and values. But this definition ignores the diversity of tradition and the differences of power within and among cultures and even subcultures. And, since variation is the raw material for cultural evolution, the concept erroneously tends to put forth harmonious stability as the norm, relegating conflict and change to that which is abnormal.

In order to do justice to a multifaceted, conflicted, and changing culture like ours, the commentary draws on four principal dimensions: the Judaeo-Christian tradition, the Western tradition, capitalism, and the state. *The Judaeo-Christian tradition* is the term for the religious and cultural heritage that serves as the source of many of our fundamental moral values. *The Western tradition* refers to the Euro-American intellectual inheritance that emphasizes rationality, objectivity, the mind/body dualism, and democratic values and philosophies. *Capitalism* means the American economic system, with its mix of free enterprise, government-supported industry, and social welfare; its linkage with imperialism; and its amalgam of upward mobility and a stubborn class division into rich and poor. And *the state* denotes the major political frame for society in the twentieth century. In it, political power, both coercive and mediated, is wielded primarily on behalf of the upper classes and is centralized in a bureaucracy that has tremendous sway over the life of every individual.

There are two points that I wish to make about the commentary. First, it does not pretend to "objectivity." Despite the firm Western belief that truth is discoverable without preconceptions, the twentieth-century notion of the relativity of truth suggests otherwise. At a minimum, observations and interpretations of social reality always start from an idea about the nature of reality, an idea that amounts to a point of view. And any point of view proceeds from the theories, social position, and interests of the viewer. Nor is appreciation of human reality "subjective." Those who observe and interpret human behavior do so in dialogue with friends, colleagues, the people whom they study, and cultural tradition (whether its grain is followed or cut against).

Just as the dichotomy between personal and political is false, so the dichotomy between objective and subjective, when applied to human beings, whose responses can influence what their observers see and think, is simply wrong. However, the stance of the observer of human beings still awaits definition. All that can be said at this juncture is that it occupies different ground from either subjectivity or objectivity. And this estimation, I believe, describes the position of my commentary.

The second point I wish to make about the commentary is a corollary one. The commentary speaks in the voice of a woman. It is not, however, "*the* woman's voice," a characterization that I dislike, although not for the usual reasons. There are "women writers," just as there are "men writers." How could there not be? But, as phrases, as ideas, as entities, *woman's voice, woman writer, women's literature,* and the like are dangerous because they skid into biological determinism. What women say and write no more results from the DNA that produces ovaries than does the thinking of black people come from the genes governing skin pigmentation.

Still, there is no doubt that each of us is gendered. Each of us is assigned to a socially significant, sexual category at birth and is from the start treated in accordance with or in opposition to it. Therefore, the voice of each person will be a gendered one, echoing both the political and the personal experiences of gender. That many writers, claiming the genderless "writer's voice," wish to deny the influence of gender should not obscure the silliness of doing so. The claim to speak in a voice uniquely capable of discerning the universals of human existence in the ordinary confusion of everyday life is very alluring. It would be wonderful to be able to speak so transcendently. But no one, short of prophets, does.

In this book, I build on the early, core feminist insight that our culture makes women into objects. But I also attempt to go beyond this perception. Accepting the proposition that "femininity" is a political creation, I nevertheless assume that women's subjectivity, like men's, is not a cloning from a cell of culture. Were our psychology the product of simple conditioning, neither feminism nor any political protest could ever come into being at all.

Rather, subjectivity is a dialogue between oneself and the surrounding world. This dialogue, which attempts to make sense of life in a way that makes sense to oneself, is simultaneously private and public, personal and political. Expressive of desire, of the unconscious longing that animates everything we do, it contains discord as well as harmony, for, although our world makes sense in some ways, in other ways it does not. Indeed, women's subjectivity is an endless process of refusing to make sense of patriarchal nonsense.

Feminism is therefore a logical exchange in the dialogue of femininity, one that, however, also begins a new conversation. Feminism turned our view of the world inside out. Exposing the cultural unconscious to public view, it made conscious what we had always known to exist but had ignored because it threatened the bedrock of our civilization. Feminist writings of the second wave that arose in the sixties argued that the second-class status of women was a product not of nature but of culture. Like "maternal instincts," male domination was socially constructed, not biologically programmed. Sexuality, family life, sex roles, the psychology of men and women—these were created by patriarchal social forces that could, because they were not innate, be changed.

Feminist activism set to work initiating the changes mandated by theory. Feminist writers and speakers rallied women to join feminist groups, where they raised their own and others' consciousness about their social domination. Through agitation, lobbying, and organizing, feminist groups effected important changes in social institutions. Affirmative action allowed women to get jobs previously denied them and made inroads on wage discrimination. The Supreme Court decriminalized abortions. In couples and families, men and women began to modify their traditional roles. Women, armed with contraception and a new respect for and knowledge about their bodies and longings, started to explore their sexual desire with awareness and dignity. Even language changed, as *he or she* occasionally came to replace the ubiquitous, universal third-person *he*. And, perhaps most astonishingly, feminism became part of the cultural landscape.

However, as the story and commentary of this book reveal, the problems persist. Indeed, in some basic way, they have changed hardly at all since the beginning of the second wave. Because some women, largely middle-class and white, have succeeded in ascending professional and corporate ladders, it looks to the rest of society as if the feminist revolution were over. Yet many women, indeed proportionately more, remain poor. Women of color still confront racism as well as sexism. Even abortion, the right to which is fundamental to women's control of their own lives, remains a battleground. And women, no matter what other work they do, continue to be in charge of rearing children.

Finally, the kind of success that feminism has had may be its failure. Once extraordinary and extreme, it is now routine. Having achieved political validity, it takes its place alongside numberless other interest groups and thereby becomes nearly invisible. Accommodated in the public mind as women's claim to economic emancipation, its radical edge is blunted. It may be that the price of accommodation, the pruning of feminism's truly radical promise of genuine equality and freedom for all, has been too high. For what has slipped into obscurity is feminism's core, utopian vision—a society, based on a humanitarian value system, in which all people have access to the material and spiritual necessities of life and are free to pursue their sexual desire, in which work is spiritually as well as financially rewarding, in which the care of children and of personal relations count as "work" and are shared by all, and in which neither race nor gender nor sexual preference can prohibit participation in the enjoyment of and running of society.

The present state of feminism is like the present state of women—ambiguous and laden with contradictions. Women are living in a time when, despite the gains they have made toward social equality, patriarchy retains a stubborn, if now more hidden, hold on all of our thoughts, feelings, and social institutions. The current problem is that women are supposed to live as if they were free when in fact freedom is still in the future. To live in such a particularly ambiguous circumstance is to struggle endlessly with contradiction. Ordinary life becomes a jungle on whose rooted floor it is easy to stumble, yet whose tangle is so comfortably familiar that one is often reluctant to hack away a single strangling vine. We want to shape our own lives to satisfy our own desires, yet find ourselves conforming to familiar social rules and institutions that imprison rather than free us. Still, at the same time as we collude in patterns and rules ingrained in us by childhood and tradition, we also try to resist the temptation to follow them. That we must endlessly battle against a gravity pulling us simultaneously in two directions explains why contradiction is the central metaphor for women's experience in the middle of the feminist revolution.

Certainly the determining acts of her life were not ideally beautiful. They were the mixed result of a young and noble impulse struggling amidst the conditions of an imperfect social state, in which great feelings will often take the aspect of error, and great faith the aspect of illusion. For there is no creature whose inward being is so strong that it is not greatly determined by what lies outside it.

GEORGE ELIOT
Middlemarch

Finally they got the Singles problem under control, they made it scientific. They opened huge sex centers—you could simply go and state what you want and they would find you someone who wanted that too. You would stand under a sign saying *I Like To Be Touched And Held* and when someone came and stood under the sign saying *I Like To Touch And Hold* they would send the two of you off together.

At first it went great. A steady stream of people under the sign *I Like To Give Pain* paired up with the steady stream of people from under *I Like To Receive Pain*. *Foreplay Only—No Orgasm* found its adherents, and *Orgasm Only—No Foreplay* matched up its believers. A loyal Berkeley, California, policeman stood under the sign *Married Adults, Lights Out, Face To Face, Under A Sheet* because that's the only way it was legal in Berkeley—but he stood there a long time in his lonely blue law coat. And the man under *I Like To Be Sung To While Bread Is Kneaded On My Stomach* had been there weeks without a reply.

Things began to get strange. The *Love Only—No Sex* was doing fine; the *Sex Only—No Love* was doing really well, pair after pair walking out together like wooden animals off a child's ark, but the line for *38D Or Bigger* was getting unruly, shouting insults at the line for *8 Inches Or Longer,* and odd isolated signs were springing up everywhere, *Retired Schoolteacher And Parakeet—No Leather, One Rm/No Bath/View Of Sausage Factory.*

The din rose in the vast room. The line under *I Want To Be Fucked Senseless* was so long that portable toilets had to be added and a minister brought in for deaths, births, and marriages on the line. Over under *I Want To Fuck Senseless—* no one, a pile of guns. A hollow roaring filled the enormous gym. More and more people began to move over to *Want To Be Fucked Senseless.* The line snaked around the gym, the stadium, the whole town, out into the fields. More and more people joined it, until *Fucked Senseless* stretched across the nation in a huge wide belt like the Milky Way, and since they had to name it, they called it the American Way.

SHARON OLDS
The Solution

Surviving Sexual Contradictions

Prologue:
A Woman on the Streets

(Any Day, Any Time)

I am a thirty-seven-year-old, heterosexual, white woman from a middle-class, upstanding, nonchurchgoing, half-WASP and half-Jewish family. I am a sociology professor at a New York City college and a psychotherapist. My life-style would be defined as "bohemian" by my mother's friends, and my concept of fashion can only be described as New York eclectic. I am divorced and childless and live with my cat and my plants in New York City.

I am walking home, and a slightly drunk and slightly disheveled man is following me, saying, "Mamma, oh mamma, baby please, I wanna fuck you, I give good tongue, oh sweetheart, *please.*"

1

I am annoyed. "Oh, leave me alone. Haven't you anything better to do?"

He sniggers, then turns away.

After I enter the lobby of my building, I wonder, *What was that man trying to do? Did he want to degrade me, attack me, stimulate me sexually, flatter me, or simply tease me? Should I be angry or feel sorry for him?* And I ask, *Why me, anyway?*

The voices in my head immediately provide answers:

What do you expect when you dress like that? My mother responds rhetorically.

But it happens even when I'm wearing my down parka and my overalls, I explain in bewilderment, adding with some outrage, *How dare he talk to me? He doesn't even know me.*

Let me at him, I'll kill the bastard, growls my father.
Oh Daddy, stop it, I reply, embarrassed by his passion.

You know you love it, insists my own analyst.
Maybe, I admit grudgingly, like a patient cornered on the couch.

You must have a pretty poor opinion of yourself if you get turned on by someone like that, comments an advice columnist.
I guess so, I say, feeling a little humiliated.

You can't ignore what's going on around you. You have to hear what's directed toward you on the street, because it's dangerous out there, the indignant, rational feminist in me asserts in no uncertain terms. *One out of two women is the victim of rape or attempted rape at least once in her life. You have to be alert.*
Maybe, I posit. Soothed and vindicated, I stand a little straighter.

I think your reaction is disgusting, pronounces the politically correct social theorist in me. *This man is a product of his environment, his class, race, ethnicity. He is attacking not you but your middle-class privilege.*
I'm sorry, I'm sorry, I plead, filled with guilt.

Perhaps he's compensating because he feels so weak himself, the psychoanalyst side of me counsels empathically. *He gets rid of his self-*

hatred by projecting it onto you, and at the same time he can make verbal love to the all-powerful mother whose comfort he longs for.

Yes, yes, okay, but still . . . , I argue in increasingly louder tones to these contradictory voices, *Still, I don't know him. He doesn't know me. Is the noise coming from a person like the noise of an ambulance siren? Do I have to hear it so that I can get out of the way and not get run over?*

Don't let it upset you, dear, temporizes the voice of the next-door neighbor of my childhood and adolescence (who used to get me or one of my teenage friends into his den on some pretext or other to engage in intense, flirtatious discussions with the door closed). *Just ignore him. Don't give him the benefit of your attention. Don't dignify men like him with a response. You'll only encourage them.*

You don't understand, I shout back at him, frustrated almost to tears. *My brain hears, my desire is stirred, I lose control of my body. My body is no longer mine. On the street my body is theirs. I can define myself all I want, but in their eyes I am a body on the street, two tits and no head and a big ass. My body becomes a cunt, and although I'm not physically raped, psychically I am, and I ache from it.*

And yet, and yet . . . , I go on more quietly to all the voices in my head, *I am moved, touched, even aroused by a man who I think is a creep. I don't understand how this can happen, and neither do you.*

WOMAN AS SUBJECT-AS-OBJECT

A woman walks down a city street. A man whom she does not know makes an obscene noise or gesture. She counters with a retort or ignores him and walks on.

This is a common enough sequence of events. It happens every day of the year. It is happening this year, just as it has happened during each of the last twenty years, indeed, as it has happened every day of every year since human beings began to build cities. Superficially, this is a simple, ordinary encounter. A stranger rudely intrudes with sexual innuendo upon someone minding her own business who manages to ignore him and go on her way.

But beneath the surface is a complexity of feeling, thought, and intention that, despite two decades of feminist theorizing and two millennia of women writing about women, we have just begun to decode. Hidden in this complexity are the personal and political contradictions of women's lives, making the experience of street hassling the quintessential moment of femininity in our culture.

What femininity gives with one hand, it takes away with the other. Here's the knot: On the one hand, a woman wants, simply, to be. On the other, she wants to be who she is—a woman. To be a woman, however, makes it extremely difficult simply to be, that is, to be a human being, because women live in the heart of a contradiction. They are treated as unconscious, passive objects but are required to respond as sentient people who acknowledge and participate in a transformation into something that is other-than-human. They become negatives, not-men, and are therefore less than human, a condition that is linguistically, ideologically, and socially construed as masculine. *Mankind* encompasses all human beings; *he* is the abstract, genderless individual, the self. In this construction, "man" becomes Self, and "woman" Other, a self who does not belong to herself.

To be Other is to be the Subject-as-Object. In our culture, social arrangements put women in a perpetually un-self-possessed state, and they are never allowed to forget that both their psyches and their bodies are always liable to trespass. Street hassling is a characteristic example of the predicament of the Subject-as-Object: A man can, without invitation, approach a woman, because the social interaction between women and men is premised on the belief that biology determines behavior. Someone who has a penis has the power, the unspoken privilege, to say anything to—even to touch—someone who lacks a penis and who consequently lacks reciprocal power. Were a woman to initiate a sexually toned conversation with a man she does not know, she must expect that she would be taken seriously. In contrast, the street hassler expects her to ignore his intrusion, to act as if she were not aware of him. Yet her very awareness is what makes her not a mere Object, but a Subject-as-Object.

Despite the success women have had in the corporate world, despite the public acknowledgment of the legitimacy of women's complaints about sexist attitudes, despite women's increased assertiveness and pride in their femininity—despite all the achievements of women's liberation—women are still the Subject-as-Object. Indeed, in the light of feminism's achievements, their status as Subject-as-Object becomes visible. In our culture, men have traditionally been regarded as Subjects, women as Objects. However, if any evidence had been needed to convince the public mind that women were not passive, inert things but active, conscious human beings, feminism has provided it. Not only feminist activists but feminist-inspired women in all fields of endeavor, and of all classes, races, and sexualities, have come to public attention for their activity, will, and independence of mind. The events of the last two decades should therefore have made it impossible for the public eye to view women as Objects any longer. That women continue to be so viewed despite their manifest subjectivity is demonstrated by their unabated vulnerability to street hassling, which in turn reveals the essential contradiction of their lives: Neither Subject nor Object, they are, paradoxically, both.

Regardless of feminism's impact on our culture, women remain conscious that whether they are wearing sheer summer dresses or bulky winter clothes, whether they swing their hips or march tightly compacted, any man may still choose to invade their personal space, physically or psychologically or socially, if he feels like it. Sometimes the intrusion is merely fatuous—the man on the street who says, "Smile," to the woman hurrying along preoccupied by concerns about work, a sick child, or the latest nuclear accident. Or it can be pleasantly if irritatingly possessive—the husband who, on passing through the kitchen, grabs his wife's breast. Men's intrusiveness may be only titillating or unsettling, like the excessive flirtatiousness of a neighbor or relative. It may at times be traumatic, as in the case of sexual abuse inflicted by a father or uncle or brother. And, finally, men's privileged invasiveness can take the violent form of rape.

Women are not men's slaves, nor are they presently at the beck and call of their fathers or husbands. Their position is far more ambiguous than that. They know, as subjects, that they must recognize that they are treated as objects, into which they must sometimes also transform themselves. In order to live from day to day, they must both accept and reject what they know, that they are and are not people. A person is someone whom others treat with a respectful awareness of personal boundaries and dignity, to whom an address, for example, is a request, not a demand, for attention. According to this definition, then, a woman is not a person. At the same time, this is what she is supposed to be, and this contradiction is what she is supposed to swallow with a smile on her face.

The experience of being the Subject-as-Object is an ordinary one in our society. Men have it as well as women. It happens when they go to work for someone else. For at least eight hours a day, they are directly or indirectly subordinate to another's decisions, even while they are supposed to exercise their own judgment about their work. Although this prosaic experience is culturally defined as an anomaly for men and thereby as altogether anomalous, it is taken as a matter of course for women. Women who work for wages find themselves in the same predicament as men, but, unlike men, they do not escape it when the workday ends. They are the Subject-as-Object everywhere they go.

POWER, GENDER, AND DESIRE

Women's perpetually contradictory existence is based on the way that our society constructs power and in so doing informs desire. The power that women and men have, like the power of any social group, is of two sorts, political and personal. The first is based on the material things of existence, on the economic and political wherewithal to satisfy the demands of physical and social survival. Political power comes from having both a livelihood and a part in the running of society.

The second sort of power rests on the ability to give meaning to life. Personal power requires the symbolic and psychological tools—ideas, a set of values, a sense of entitlement, and forms in which to express these, such as language, music, or art—to define what the world is, what one wants from the world, and how one will get what one desires.

Both sorts of power are vital. The lack of political power is more immediately threatening to life and limb than is that of personal power, but the absence of personal power can destroy the soul. To be without one or the other kind of power is, then, to be relatively powerless. And neither can be fully attained without the other.

Like the other major social systems that distribute power in our culture—class, race, and sexual preference—gender does so inequitably, giving more power to some people and less to others. Gender makes men into first-class citizens and women into second-class citizens. Women in general have less political power than men, even though differences of class, race, and sexual preference empower some women more than others. Women frequently have to be twice as good as men to get the same job, and, in many industries, they are the last hired and the first fired. Women receive less pay than men for comparable work and move through the salary ranks more slowly. They have not only had to fight for the "universal" rights of "man," such as suffrage and the minimum wage, they have yet to establish the unquestionable legitimacy of rights deemed particular to women but in fact of universal significance, such as reproductive and sexual freedom.

Nevertheless, even when women's political power seems in hand—when they hold down jobs or move up in corporate hierarchies, run for office or win class-action suits—their personal power is still compromised by the way that gender defines their desire. Our culture has two patterns for desire, one for males and another for females. The first pattern honors, masculinizes, and makes adult the felt experience of "I want." The second demeans, feminizes, and infantilizes the state of being wanted, the felt experience of "I want to be wanted," an experience that is in fact active—to want anything at all is to assert a desire—but that slips easily into a sense of passive, dependent need.

Man then comes to mean the active one-who-wants, *woman* the passive one-who-wants-to-be-wanted. Even though both men and women experience—consciously or unconsciously—both patterns for desire, "man" is conceptualized as the subject of his own desire and master of the other's. In contrast, "woman" is thought to have no desire of her own. Rather, she is desirable, the one-who-wants-to-be-wanted-by-the-one-who-wants.

Gender fits a pattern to each person at so early a time in life—from birth onward—that one can neither give nor withhold consent. At birth, each child is assigned a sex and receives a name thought appropriate to that sex. The baby is then treated in accordance with the assigned sex, not only through such familiar customs as giving blue blankets to boys and pink ones to girls but in ways that unintentionally express cultural expectations. Some hospital nurseries reflect and re-create the idea that boys will embody the active Subject—the "I"—and girls the passive Object—the "it." In them the blue plaques on the boys' cribs display the words "I'm a boy!" while the pink plaques on the girls' cribs are inscribed "It's a girl!"

The behavior of all adults, including parents, is based in large part on these fundamental cultural expectations of gender difference. Many parents would like to believe that they behave identically with their sons and daughters. However, despite their conscious efforts to do so, they will tend to differentiate between them in subtle, unconscious ways. A mother may consciously think that she treats her infants as neuter. Yet she may nevertheless be more anxious when her daughter takes her first foray into another room than when her son does. Equally unintentionally, a father will be more likely to demand that his children behave in ways appropriate to their gender. He may, for example, speak more frequently to his son than to his daughter, thus communicating his expectation of active subjectivity to the boy but not the girl. And there are even less observable but still systematic differences in muscle tension, in how closely parents hold sons and daughters, and in the tone and pitch of voice in which they speak to them. These small variations in parents' treatment of sons and daughters transmit the pattern of desire appropriate to the gender of each child.

Children take in both patterns, for every human psyche contains images of both Self and Other. Merely from the conscious and unconscious behavior of the adults around them, infants sense these two patterns long before they can be said to "know" or "learn" anything at all. However, they do not simply learn a one-dimensional message to the effect that they are either male or female. In the course of socialization, children absorb the *contrast* between male and female. Through twinned processes of identification and disidentification, they come to know both that they are one gender and that they are not the other. Absorbing adults' behavior and language through interpenetrating waves of consciousness and unconsciousness, each child identifies with the pattern appropriate to the sex assigned at birth and disidentifies with the other. Each recognizes the assigned pattern as belonging to Self and the pattern not assigned as belonging to Other.

The consequences of this doubled process of self-recognition differ for girls and boys. Through socialization, the boy comes to experience "I want" as Self and "I want to be wanted" as Other. The girl comes to connect being wanted with Self and wanting with Other. In response to the surrounding culture, the boy will tend to train himself to be the active Subject who initiates his own desire and to minimize any wishes to be the Object who longs to be desired. The girl, in contrast, will tend to make herself into the receptor of others' desires, the Object who waits to know what other people want of her, all the while holding in reserve the Subject that she is also expected and longs to be.

The reason he forgets his wishes for objectification and she remembers hers for subjectivity is that the pattern for boys is more highly valued than the pattern for girls. In our culture, it is better to be a Subject who wants than an Object who wants-to-be-wanted. Subjects are first-class citizens, while Objects are second-class. First-class citizenship is accorded those who, impelled by their active desire, create things that transcend mortal existence, which is what Subjects are thought to do. Second-class citizenship is the lot of Objects, those whose existence is seen to be as unproductive and uninteresting as dead leaves.

And here the gendered pattern for personal power and the gendered design for political power fit together. Men's first-class political power enables them to create things that endure and thereby validates their first-class personal power. Thus, in the public domain outside the home where they are dominant, men earn hard cash, make material things that last a long time, and conceive ideas that outlive them.

In contrast, women's second-class political power ensures and ratifies their second-class personal power. In the home, where they are thought to belong despite whatever money they earn outside it, women create products, such as breakfast, lunch, dinner, and people, which are perishable and are therefore thought to be inferior, even though, like the fallen leaves that furnish the nutrients for new trees growing in the forest, they are essential to the round of life.

While men's first-class citizenship seems to afford an unambiguous pride in their gender that is so unremarkable as to seem "natural," women's second-class citizenship forces them to find honor in a dishonored form of self. For women, gender and self-esteem become dissonant—except in matters reproductive. No experience of "I want" is as harmonious with feminine identity and self-worth as wanting to have a child. For a woman to act as the desiring Subject in any other way is to risk the anxiety of degendering, a feeling that is tantamount to losing personal identity and personal power. Yet a lifetime defined by motherhood systematically undermines the sense of self-worth it confers. As figure and image, "mother" is desexualized, her desire subordinated to her children's.

THE COMPLETION OF THE CIRCLE

Being in the heart of the contradiction, being the Subject-as-Object, is a constant struggle to keep desire from being buried alive. When a woman is street-hassled, for example, the battle proceeds on two fronts: a private, personal one inside her mind and a public, political one on the street. When the street hassler speaks to her, he says, in effect, "I want it." Through speech, he takes what he wants, and she cannot stop him.

The woman, who thinks of herself as an "I," as a Subject, becomes, for an instant, the "it" that he wants, an Object without a will of her own. Her sense of "I" begins to disintegrate, and feeling like an "it" becomes more comfortable. She may feel good to be wanted-by-the-one-who-wants, because she feels good about fitting the cultural definition of "woman."

However, feeling good about being a woman can also be unsettling, because to be a woman is also not to be a person. If she tries to resist feeling good about being a woman, she feels bad about herself because then she cannot feel good about who she is. If she tries to recall her subjectivity, she may feel just as bad, because being the one-who-wants is to be a man—which she is not and does not really want to be. All she wants is to be a human being.

Being the Subject-as-Object is maddening. It is to be both Self and Other, and to be torn between them. In such a divided state of mind, one's perceptions of others, of one's relations to them, and of oneself become untrustworthy. This chaotic moment can seem like madness, to which one responds with a desperate struggle to understand and explain. When, then, a woman turns into the Subject-as-Object, as in street hassling, she can feel as though she were losing her mind. As if to prevent her from going crazy, thoughts and feelings rush in, materializing into a ghostly chorus, each voice shrieking a contradictory explanation for what just happened or a conflicting instruction about what to do about it.

Thus maddened, the street-hassled woman gets mad. Although she may not initiate, she can certainly retaliate. She may talk back to the street hassler. She may mock him and, in the stories she tells to herself and to others, caricature him.

Yet her retaliation is Pyrrhic. Just as the street hassler strips her of her presence and dignity, so she strips him of his. If she becomes like a toy, a piece of wood, a penny, something he can fool with to amuse himself as he stands on the corner, then he becomes to her just another one of the many anonymous dangers of life. His human possibility is as lost on her as hers is on him. The circle is complete. He becomes as much an object to her as she is to him. The street hassler may be poor—although some are well-to-do. He may already be partly petrified by an indifferent society that treats men as well as women like pieces of wood. But, rich or poor, he dies a little more because of the very patriarchal system that bestows male privilege on him in the first place.

Behaving in kind, being active—and the only other choice at the moment is to do nothing at all, to be passive—means to support a society in which no one can be a full human being, in which all men and women become objects to one another. When human experience is split between wanting and wanting-to-be-wanted, which are two sorts of longing that every person feels, and when the first part of the division is seen as masculine and good, while the second is feminine and bad—then every life will, overtly or covertly, be a struggle to be the first, not the second. Anyone who embodies the first seems admirable; anyone embodying the second merits contempt. When the street hassler emits obscene noises, he spits out and onto the woman any trace of the despicable state of wanting-to-be-wanted. Any female can, simply because of her gender, be a proxy for him. And he, in turn, proxies for all those other men whose socialization or subculture disallow such direct expression of masculinity-by-rejection-of-femininity. In street hassling, the man retains a semblance of humanity, albeit a violent version of it, while the woman loses even that, rejects her dangerous femininity as well, and becomes as if inert, absent.

It is in this very context that the woman's seemingly passive turn-on turns out to be active. If femininity prevents a woman from asserting "I want" directly, she will do it circuitously. Through the tortuous path of tuning in to and identifying with the street hassler's wants, she can recognize and recapture her own. For even wanting-to-be-wanted is, finally, a form of wanting. Her silenced but living desire resonates with the street hassler's sexual noises, as rude as they are. Her answering arousal to his lewd playfulness speaks past their mutual disavowal. It addresses what they share, their desire, the genderless longing that each feels, the "it" that each wants.

Here, then, is where feeling "like a woman" is a sign of life, not death. When all the voices in a woman's mind tell her to become Other by distorting her appearance or her knowledge of social reality or her experience of her own will or her feelings about her lust, her arousal tells her that she is a Self who lives and breathes. Her turn-on tells her that, despite every pressure to become an Object, her subjectivity nevertheless survives. She continues to want, she is an "I." Her desire reminds her that the man who objectifies her is not a piece of wood but is as human as she. And, finally, her arousal certifies that her anger is also alive and well, for both lust and ire are fueled by desire, without which there is no feeling at all.

In Passion's Wake

(6:00 A.M.)

We roll around in bed, I younger and smoother-skinned, he older, once fat and soft, now trim and hard but still fleshily sensual. Perhaps the champagne of the night before is the reason our spirits still bubble and fizz. Moments of pure delight. Finally I climb on top and rock into the black-silver inner spaces of realized desire where I forget what I'm doing and for one dizzying, bubbly, sunny second do not know whether he is male or female or if he is my mother or my father, and I know that I don't know but that I really do know that he is who he is, and I climax into this moment of laughing madness.

A tin can rattles down the street. I wonder how such a small noise can penetrate the windows closed against the March wind, and then it comes to me that what I hear is just the heat beginning to wake the pipes. Suddenly my eyes are open, fixed on the clock I forgot to set.

Ten minutes late. My mother's voice hovers in my consciousness: *That wasn't so smart, to make love in the morning when you have to go to work early.*

I push myself up on my elbow, which has gone slightly to sleep. I feel a bit woozy. My father's voice admonishes me now: *I told you to get one whiskey sour and nurse it all night.*

Oh, please, just leave me alone, I beg them both.

I look over at my lover's face, so innocent in sleep. There's a damp, chilly spot on the sheet beneath my hand where it rests just next to his back. Worrying that he might be cold, I reach across to pull the blanket up over his shoulder, subduing my lightninglike sexual arousal, taking care not to slip my hand under the sheet and wake him and start again.

As I pass the telephone on the way to the bathroom, I wonder if I can call in sick. No, I can't. I'd feel guilty, and the class is already behind schedule.

I stop in the kitchen to put on the kettle for coffee.

I flush the toilet, let the shower run so that it will get hot, smear toothpaste on the brush. As I scrub my teeth, I wonder, *What will he do for a toothbrush?* And I ask myself, not for the first time, *Should I have extra ones around for this sort of occasion? Or maybe it's time he left one of his own here.*

Capping the toothpaste tube, I imagine our good-bye kiss at the subway entrance. But then I remember that his morning is free until noon. It seems a shame to wake him. Should I let him sleep? If I do, I'll have to leave him a key. Should I? Does he want me to? Do I want him to have a key to my apartment?

I don't have time to stand here figuring that out. Perhaps the answer will just come to me. Right now, I have to take a shower and plan my outfit for the day.

Steam finally softens the air. I step into the tub, pulling the curtains behind me so that water won't splash onto the cat litter the way it did yesterday.

I could wear the dance skirt. No, it's too sexy for a teacher. Maybe a fifties look, beaded cardigan and straight skirt? How about the preppie grays and beiges down at the far end of the closet that I save for interviews with grant officials, deans, and new supervisors? No doubt my two-o'clock psychotherapy patient will find something wrong with whatever I choose.

And now here's something else to decide on. As I pass the soapy washcloth efficiently over my body, I feel, between my legs, a wetness wetter than water. Slick semen and contraceptive jelly are sliding out and down. Well, that will all disappear if I remove the diaphragm. But if I do, am I likely to get pregnant?

I massage the shampoo into my hair and try to remember when my last period was. My menstrual cycle is so irregular that I never know. But, still, even if I remembered, it wouldn't do me much good. I'd still worry. Maybe it seems silly. But look at it this way: If you knew when you were ovulating, then you would know when it was safe to take the diaphragm out, wouldn't you? But, if you knew that, then you wouldn't have to use birth control at all, would you? That's called the rhythm method, and everyone knows how safe that is. That's why they tell you to use the diaphragm all the time and to wait for a full six hours before taking it out. Isn't it? So it follows that if you take the diaphragm out, you might get pregnant.

According to this line of reasoning, you think you can get pregnant at any time, even though you can't. Except, of course, that you can. Take my friend Karen, who, twenty years ago, conceived the first time she had intercourse, during her period, when she thought she was safe.

So the cramps I had yesterday could mean either ovulation or menstruation. Or maybe they were just plain old intestinal cramps. Or maybe they're all in my mind. I don't know.

Now, if my period is really on the way, I had better have a tampon with me when I go to work. Unfortunately, the box in the cabinet underneath the sink is empty.

Images of the upcoming day crank, frame by frame, across my mind: I am passing the still-closed stores on the way to the subway. A between-class trip to the bathroom reveals blood on my panties. And a broken vending machine. Back in the office, neither of my two female colleagues nor the secretary has a tampon. I am walking past abandoned stores and used-car lots to the nearest supermarket.

I'd rather leave the diaphragm in.

Which means moisture. Well, this is what I'll do, I plan as I rinse my hair. I'll wear pants, since they might be a bit more absorbent than a skirt. If I feel too wet later on, I'll just roll up some toilet paper and tuck it into my vagina. And that should get me through the day.

Now, which pants? Oh, forget it. Let it be blue jeans again. Considering all the messages my clothes might broadcast today, a uniform is safest anyway, even under my analyst's scrutiny.

I reach for the huge bath towel.

But suppose I'm pregnant? Excitement, fear, and despair race around in my solar plexus. If I am, this would be the first time that I've conceived. How wonderful!

Or is it? Is pregnancy safe at my age? Can amniocentesis harm the fetus? How long will it take for my body to get back into shape? Am I making enough money to raise a child? When did I take the diaphragm out too soon? Is this the diaphragm failure that no one ever believes in and that makes you feel utterly helpless?

I can't think about it now. My life is too busy: a promotion coming up, some papers to write—the timing is bad. I'd have to get an abortion. Which, at thirty-seven, I don't want to have to consider.

Fed up with clothes and contraceptives and conceptions, depressed that my erotic haze has dissipated only to become a dumb hangover, I try to clear the steamy full-length mirror. But the mirror keeps misting up, blurring the outline of my body. All the better. If I saw my reflection clearly, I'd only want to go on a diet.

Once I told William, whom I'm supposed to have dinner with tonight and then accompany to the Devil's Delight, that he was getting a bit of a potbelly. He went to the bathroom to look at himself, complaining as he did that I had made him self-conscious. I complained that I was permanently self-conscious.

I pull the towel tighter, protecting myself not only from my own critical gaze, but from that of the other people in my mind—my mother, father, brother, women friends, fashion photographers, men.

BETWEEN

Erotic experience is extraordinary, existing somewhere between fantasy and reality, dream and daily life. It knows no shame and no bounds. It effortlessly encompasses pleasure and pain, power and love, mind and culture, conscious and unconscious. The variousness of eroticism makes it intrinsically ambiguous. Ambiguity endows the erotic with novelty, creativity, and mystery to make it exciting, pleasurable, and fearsome all at once. Sex opens doors to unknown inner recesses, defies reason and invites confusions, blurs physical as well as psychological distinctions between self and other, even between parts of the body. Although the experience may be sometimes pleasurable, sometimes painful, sometimes disappointing, it is always unsettling.

Sex is extraordinary because it bridges adult and child. In women and men alike, it juxtaposes the reality-orientation of maturity with the fantasies of infancy. It mixes the rational distinctions made by adults between self and other, mind and body, with the boundlessness of infantile feeling. The crossing of these divides likens sex to an altered state of consciousness. The ordinary speech of waking life sounds awkward in the context of the strangeness of sex—of the faces made grotesque by lust, of the genitals whose smell is a weird mix of urine and bread and sweat and perfume and whose texture is somewhere between the tough dry skin fit for public viewing and the secret, tender wet lining of organs. During sex, it feels far better to grunt and moan or to voice fantasies that speak in the language of consciousness about the passions of the unconscious.

Once it is time to get up and one is back in ordinary consciousness, however, adults may see in passion's wake a relatively shocking mess. Bodies and bedclothes are wet and sticky. One feels anxious to restore the genitals, now front and center in the imagination, to their normal place at the backstage of consciousness. Adults, thus reminded physically of the weird things said, done, and felt in the night, of the rules and boundaries breached in the darkness, are inclined to redraw the lines crossed by sexual passion. This inclination is the reason that, on the bright morning after, they may feel what children do to grow themselves up—disgust, which, as the inversion of pleasure, becomes the means to reject the things of childhood.

WOMEN'S RITUAL OF PURIFICATION

Both men and women contribute to this sexual disorder. But, while men appear to be free of it, women and their bodies incarnate it. Even though semen is surely as sloppy as vaginal lubrications, the penis, with all its bumps and hairs and odd curves and foreskin and discolorations and unpredictable erections, is thought in our culture to be a rather neat and straightforward organ. The vagina, in contrast, looks like a complicated mess. Wet, creviced, and dark, it seems to harbor the unknown, the repellent, perhaps the dangerous.

Yet the vagina is mysterious more in cultural symbol than in biological fact. The vagina's dry, symmetrical outer folds are easily visible; its moist, delicate tracery of inner folds and clitoris, easily accessible. Only the inner part of the vagina can be reasonably said to be out of visual and physical control. The symbolic omission of the vagina's visibility and accessibility suggests that its dangers are products of culture and imagination, not biology.

In our culture, the vagina threatens us because, as the passageway to life, it forebodes death as well. Its softness and receptivity intimate not only tenderness but engulfment. Its powerful muscles capable of both contracting and expelling can force life out of the womb, but they also hint at the power to take life away. The vagina's ambiguous connotations transform it from an organ, a structured mass of functioning tissue, into a symbol of the order of life and the disorder of death. Representative of the ultimate contradiction of life and death, the vagina and, by extension, the female body, come to signify all disorder, while what women do with their bodies symbolizes the restoration of order.

The contradictory symbolism of the vagina therefore has a lot to do with the way that women treat their bodies. Embedded in cultural mythology, the vagina's mystery and danger influence how women feel about themselves. It is difficult for women to avoid internalizing the conclusion that, since the defining part of their anatomy is believed to be contradictory, disorderly, and therefore dangerous, their entire bodies are equally wayward. There exists hardly a woman in our culture who is not ashamed of or embarrassed by at least one part of her body because it threatens to escape her control. The offending part may be weight, usually too much but sometimes too little. It might be blossoming outer and upper thighs. It could be a behind. It might be a large nose, or thin lips, or blotchy skin, or body aroma. Perhaps it is height, or the proportion of head or shoulders or torso. Or maybe it is hair on the head or hair on the legs or hair under the arms or hair on the eyebrows.

All human beings draw part of their self-esteem from the care of the body. But an unforgiving attitude of discipline, even punishment, punctuates the care that women often lavish on their bodies. When one part of the body goes wrong, let us say, the thighs are rippled and flabby and dimpled, it is as if the whole self had gone rotten. A woman striving for the perfect poundage or dress size might not be able to weigh herself because one number on the scale could fill her with so much self-hatred as to make her distraught for the next two weeks.

Since it is less painful to hate one's body than oneself, women can use their bodies as scapegoats. They make themselves Objects to their own Subjects. Even now, when feminism and the counterculture have made cultural notions of beauty more various, women still study themselves like ethnographers in a foreign culture, stealing glances of themselves as they pass a shop window or occasionally examining a particularly meaningful segment of their own, or other women's, anatomies. Like bookkeepers, they search out their assets, single out disfiguring liabilities. Then they go to work. They douche, spray, wash, powder, tweeze, curl, straighten, bleach, color, separate, push up, support, shave, hold in without breathing, tuck, cut, polish, cream, tense and release, flex, point, bend, jog, dance, swim. And, of course, they diet. They order salad when their men have steaks, or appetizers instead of main courses. They nibble but never eat a square meal. They make certain to eat less than everyone else at the table, especially their women friends. They starve themselves, or take diuretics, or binge and throw up, or chew food and spit it out.

To be sure, women's body care is not the penal servitude that it used to be. Our present standards of feminine beauty have been indelibly marked by the dozen years or so called "the sixties"—actually straddling both the 1960s and the 1970s—when the stays of beauty were literally loosed. In that era, bras, girdles, and makeup came off, weight got put on, clothes were either "unisex" or shapeless, and, following the revolution in black consciousness, hair went "natural." Indeed, bodies went natural as hair grew out on women's legs, under their arms, and on their faces bare of makeup—and on men's cheeks and chins as well. High heels were thrown away, flat shoes donned. Everyone's clothing became more informal. Dungarees became as much a national uniform as "Mao suits" seemed to be in China, while sportswear resembling the outfits of colonialists on safari evolved into togs elegant enough for cocktail parties.

In a two-steps-forward, one-step backward way, this revolution has been permanent. If, in the 1950s, women wore high heels almost all the time, and, in the 1960s, they wore flat shoes even to the office, now they split the difference: They wear running shoes on the subway and exchange them for high heels once they get to work. Some women still feel comfortable with body hair. But others who stopped shaving in the 1960s are hairless once again, having found their hairiness a personal discomfort or a social liability. To women's great relief and comfort, pants are now acceptable on almost any occasion they desire. But, even though women can now keep warm in winter, "unisex" still means that women cross-dress. Men do not wear skirts, except in some sectors of the avant-garde fashion and sexual communities. They have, however, begun to carry purses, wear makeup, get facials and face-lifts, and dye their hair, developments perhaps a bit more revolutionary than the cosmetics that help women to achieve the "natural look."

Still, there is, overall, more choice for those who choose to choose. Before the 1960s, when "fashion dictators" told everyone what to wear, no subculture existed that validated variety in physical appearance or diversity in adornment. But the insurgent counterculture, once so culturally prevalent as to dominate the fashion industry for a very brief moment, bequeathed permanent, albeit small, radical communities, particularly those of the gay and feminist subcultures. Even though these subcultures, like any culture, create their own conformism, they nevertheless still challenge mainstream women's fashion. These days, one may walk into a feminist bookstore and see a range of physical and sartorial types—the woman in a business suit who looks as though she had just left the office, the woman in jeans or a skirt wheeling a baby in a stroller, the woman wearing plaid shirt and overalls, the woman who lets her chin hair grow into a downy goatee, the woman sporting the leather chaps and studded bracelets of homosexual men who practice sadomasochism. Disorienting and unnerving though such variety may be, its visibility is thrilling. Some portion of the spirit is liberated when portions of the body are freed. The relative freedom to choose along the continuum spanning nature and artifice granted to all of us by the countercultural revolution depends on the continued existence of these communities tolerant of the extremes.

In mainstream culture, however, body care is still considered so fundamental to femininity that an item about women legislators can appear in the fashion section of *The New York Times*. What women do with their bodies remains everybody else's business. Something peculiarly and alarmingly uncontrollable seems to be happening deep inside women's bodies, which the public world reads as though it were written on their surfaces. Therefore, people stare at women with an intensity rarely accorded men. Women's clothing receives an attentive inspection that exceeds its intrinsic interest. And most women remain preoccupied with their real or imagined physical imperfections, obsess about dress, and make impossibly fine discriminations between otherwise similar shades of makeup.

Yet, like any human action, women's physical housekeeping means more than it appears to. Like dreams, it has both surface and hidden meanings. When a woman washes and dries herself after sex, it is as though she were carrying out a more complicated task than simple hygiene, a task that men do not seem to share at all. She is conducting a cultural ritual of purification whose function it is to preserve her culture by eliminating disorder.

All cultures depend upon such rituals to celebrate their core values and maintain their society. Sometimes these rituals are individualized, like those of the New Guinean Káfe culture, in which men as well as women scrub themselves of semen, believed to be dangerously polluting, on the morning after they have had sexual intercourse. Sometimes these ceremonies are collective, like that grand public ritual of our culture, the Miss America contest, which validates the daily private rituals carried out by individual women.

In any case, these rituals seem to be essential to the working of society. Their function is often economic. Káfe people believe that, without their morning-after ritual cleansing, people would fall ill and no longer be able to raise their crops, thus destroying their society itself. And perhaps this ritual does indeed ensure that other parts of the body are washed as well, thus serving as preventive antisepsis in fact as well as belief. Even though we, in our culture, believe that women's ritual of purification serves femininity alone, it is, on reflection, also of economic use, supporting not only the cosmetics, fashion, advertising, and diet-food industries but health clubs and clinics and doctors who specialize in weight loss as well.

But the rituals have psychological and cultural functions too. They serve to maintain order. Among the Káfe people, semen, like menstrual blood, is regarded as dangerous only when out of place or improperly channeled. Similarly, in our culture, sexual lubrications threaten disorder when they appear anywhere but in bed, because they signal the disorderly passions of infancy allowable in sex but nowhere else in adult life. Sexual substances are, in our culture, polluting because they reveal the clay feet of adulthood—childhood. Women's ritual of purification serves to restore the order of adulthood by ridding it of the pollution of childhood.

When a woman in our culture attends to her body, her care resembles that bestowed by a mother on her child. She washes, dries, powders, and dresses herself with the same sort of tenderness, or impatience, or concentration as a mother bathing and diapering her baby. It is as though she herself were an infant once again and, at the same time, her own mother. Her activities, therefore, evoke the symbolic meaning of maternal nurturance. When mothers care for their babies, they are not only keeping them clean and healthy, they are also readying them for the adult world. A baby wearing a dry diaper is not only comfortable but presentable. Mothers thus inaugurate the long process in which infants are transformed from disorderly little animals into orderly human beings. Although there is much more to socialization than baths, ointments, and garments, these ministrations and decorations initiate the transformation of nature into culture that characterizes personal growth. Each step in this evolution signals, and makes possible, the departure of childhood and the arrival of adulthood. The transformation is evoked, reflected, and ratified by women's ritual of purification.

In order to mature, we must do for ourselves what our mothers did for us. We must put ourselves in order, for the evolution from childhood to adulthood everywhere entails an increasing control of body and mind. However, in our culture in particular, adulthood is in effect defined by this control. We believe that adults are to be totally rational, never swayed by their emotions from the course set by logical thought. Adult interests are meant to lie with a Self that is sharply distinguished from Other. We expect adults to organize their lives along lines as clear-cut and accountable as the minutes in an hour, the hours in a day. We trust that such unyielding control over the self will yield firm control over life.

Infancy is the antithesis of adulthood thus defined. It begins as an undifferentiated state in which the boundaries between self and other have yet to consolidate. Not only are self and other merged, there is no distinction between mind and body. Joy is erotic, and a stomachache can feel like rage. There is no difference between clean and dirty. Infants loll in their urine and feces, relishing them as much as mother's milk and their own skin. Finally, infantile time is measured only by desire. The infant's calendar is not ordered by an objective grid of years, months, weeks, and days, but by the vagaries of longing born in the moment of frustration when the infant's oneness with the world first proves illusory. Satisfaction and frustration, each eternal in the moment, are the minutes and hours of the infantile day. The passage of time is clocked by the alternation between the boundless and omnipotent bliss felt when, at the very moment of hunger, mother provides the breast or someone brings a bottle, and the bottomless terror and helplessness felt when the milk is thirty seconds late.

The achievement of orderly adulthood depends on denying the messy, subjective diffuseness lingering since infancy in the unconscious. As babies become children, adolescents, and, finally, adults, and as the sense of separateness between self and other grows and refines, formerly undifferentiated experience is partitioned into compartments, its pleasures permitted only in play or sex, its terrors only at three in the morning. Desire, once a compound of want and need, comes under the sway of thought and culture, by which it is divided. Want, defined as a source of strength, becomes associated with maturity, the power of the will, and the transcendance of the spirit. Need, experienced as a feeling of imminent death unless someone or something arrives, is relegated to the mire of infancy, dependency, and biology. Yet this adult denial works imperfectly, if only because sexual desire reunites want and need, bringing infantile diffuseness right back to the present.

Women's rite of purification fills in where repression fails. Sexuality, in general, is very well suited to represent the undifferentiated, boundaryless passion of infancy. Women's cleanup after heterosexual intercourse, in particular, is peculiarly fit to symbolize the process by which disorderly, contradictory children grow themselves into orderly adults, and by which adults forget childhood. The ejaculation of semen into vagina transforms the disavowed psychological disorder into the body and responsibility of women, who, being the Other to the masculinized Self, are its logical recipients.

By cleaning up the unwelcome, sticky, sexual aftermath, the ritual of purification then pretends that the psychological "mess" has been altogether eliminated and that everything is under control. After a shower or a douche, the drip and slime of passion disappear and so, apparently, do the contradictions of selfhood. Women's now-dry bodies reinforce a principal cultural dictum, in which adults are expected to concur, that mind and body are separate, and that the mind can always control the body. Women, by remembering to buy tampons or sanitary napkins, keep enough contraceptive jelly on hand, and ascertain that the diaphragm or IUD is functioning properly, help to banish infantile diffuseness from daily adult life, thereby fostering the focused attention necessary to get through it. The body obeys the mind, the Object yields to the Subject's will, and all's right with the world.

In performing this ritual, women repeatedly reenact adulthood's iron control over the remains of childhood. The problem is not so much that women become enslaved to fashion—all human beings are subject to rules for appearance—but that, in removing parts of their bodies, they cut off portions of themselves. They thereby incarnate what each of us must do in order to grow up. To be sure, there are occasions when we must accustom ourselves to getting rid of parts of ourselves. We are all toilet-trained and even learn to enjoy the loss of noxious excretions that, in infancy, seem at one with body and soul. But adulthood in our culture also requires us to learn disgust for the delightful disorder of body and imagination that is the source of poetry and desire. Women, by happily eliminating parts of their bodies and selves that are in no way noxious, make this great effort appear to be a pleasure. They thereby mime and validate both their own subordination to patriarchy and any adult's acquiescence to a culture demanding order of expansive minds and bodies.

When women shave their legs or underarms or crotches or even faces, for example, they obliterate the Western sign of will and sex and power and gender that reads true on men, but on women signifies dirt and disorder and degendering. Hairless, women look as they are supposed to look—childish, prepubertal, "pure," blank, obedient. They embody the Subject-as-Object, the person who agrees to use her subjectivity against itself, who creates of herself a blank screen on which the demands of adult life may be imprinted. Their ritual signifies the constraint of self and loss of personal power that are often thought to accompany adulthood in all civilizations but in fact do so only in our own.

Therefore, when hair shows up where it should not, it is a sign on that blank screen. Announcing rebellion, it not only tells us that women are powerful, sexy, and self-willed adults. It also says that self-objectification, indeed, any objectification, is unnecessary. Its presence reminds us that we can refuse to do what we are told. At the same time, however, the consequences of nonconformity, such as the startled glances sometimes received by the eccentric woman who will not shave, risk the lonely ostracism that resembles and recalls the infant's terror when left alone. The hidden power that we have, the dangers of using it, and the safety in remaining the seemingly blank Subject-as-Object are the reasons that the sight of a woman's underarm hair shocks like an electric prod, her ugly stubble reassures onlookers that at least she has tried to conform, and all the women in the countercultural movie *Hair* had shaved armpits.

*

As I lick a drop of coffee that has rolled over the lip of the thick white mug, I think about Anna, Doris Lessing's heroine in *The Golden Notebook*, who rinsed and perfumed her neck and hands repeatedly during the first day of her period, so that no one could be offended by the odors that she alone, only when naked, could smell, but that she imagined could seep through her clothes and skin like a garlicky meal.

Perhaps, I speculate, we are both mad. Only mad people imagine that other people know what's going on inside them. Surely a problem of ego boundaries.

Coming from the bright kitchen into the darkened bedroom, I am momentarily blinded, but, not wanting to wake him by turning on the light, I rummage in the closet for the old, reliable, designer blue jeans and fit myself into them. They hold my backside in almost as tightly as the girdles I used to wear before so-called liberation. I pick out some bad-girl accessories to offset the look of conformity: black sweater; beatnik, ethnic earrings; high-heeled boots.

I tug the pointed-toed black boots onto my square-ish feet and return to the bathroom, where, standing in front of the mirror, I blow-dry my short, flyaway mousy hair (which I am thinking of henna-ing), slip my earrings into pierced ears, and brush on mascara, enjoying this peaceful little moment of self-absorption, a sort of pleasure that I would never have allowed myself ten years ago, at least not without guilt.

TEDDY BEARS FOR GROWN-UPS

Care and adornment of the body are not necessarily oppressive. As much satisfaction and delight may come from decorating one's body as from crafting a work of art, making a lovely garden, raising a child, or creating a satisfying community of friends and kin. The transformation of the natural to human use is intrinsic to human culture. Human beings derive much pleasure from making their bodies beautiful, in part because their body care expresses self-love and self-respect, in part because cultural notions of beauty represent the shared beliefs and values without which human communities could not survive.

The human creative dilemma, however, is to effect these transformations while minimizing the destruction they necessarily entail. The tension between creation and destruction emerges in every dimension of life. There must be ways to shape landscapes while remaining true to the rhythms of plants, animals, stones, and rivers, but, at least in our culture, they manage to elude us more often than not. We are perhaps not so obviously destructive to our children. But raising them involves a similar problem. On the one hand, we must provide them with a civilizing shape that enables them to mature into adults who can fit into and thus make their way through society. On the other hand, this social form ought not to cramp them but rather free them by enhancing their unique gifts and qualities. Often enough, however, their originality and freedom are mangled by the social machine through which they must pass on the way to adulthood.

An analogous, unresolved contradiction between conformism and freedom appears in regard to our bodies. We want to look good so that we can feel good about ourselves. In order to do this, we follow rules according to which our untransformed bodies look bad, therefore require modification, and, thus, reduce our self-respect. The ten pounds of "ugly fat" one wishes to lose belong, after all, to one's own body. In other words, we have to think we look bad in order to make ourselves look good, a kind of double-think that destroys the self-esteem it is meant to create.

The tension between creation and destruction may be inherent to human life. But it is magnified in our culture. Ours is a culture of omnipotence whose central value is absolute control. And our way of seeking total control is to treat as dead objects those living things which cannot be objectified without the risk of total destruction—nature, people, society, the mind.

This attempt at total, objectifying order inevitably creates disorder, which is, however, regularly denied in language and thought. The disorder may be ecological; in the name of "progress," strip-mining guts the earth, while mining companies profit. The disorder may be political; in the interests of "keeping the peace," conventional and nuclear weapons are manufactured, while the thirst for world dominion continues unslaked. The disorder may be economic; under the aegis of "free enterprise," "labor-saving" technology is invented, while people are commanded to captain their own ships yet are thrown out of work and blamed for their own wrecked lives by the same government that bails out failing banks and automobile manufacturers.

And the disorder may be psychological. In search of "self," adults are encouraged to believe that they can do anything they want, have whatever they want, be everything they want. Urged to reach beyond their grasp, they sometimes achieve, as individuals and as a culture, extraordinary feats. But for all the Horatio Algers and all the trips to the moon, the cost of such psychological overextension is a permanent, inchoate sense that something somewhere is wrong. At work, play, or love, people are apt to feel that they are less than they can be, but, at the same time, that they want too much.

Nor is it any wonder that, as orderly adults obligated to trim the disorderly passions of infancy, they feel they have failed. They cannot avoid failing if they are asked to be as greedy as children and yet to banish childhood from their minds. They cannot but feel incompetent when job security is as little under their control as the weather. They must feel inadequate when, made to believe in their own omnipotence, they can only feel impotent as their lives and that of the planet hang in the nuclear balance.

Faced with the contradiction of having to let their desire rip while keeping it in check, adults commonly pull in their belts. They try to desire less not by wanting less but by cutting their desire in half: They try only to want and never to need. When, for example, they feel a longing that is presently frustrated, they often try to relieve their pain by deciding whether they really "want" or merely "need" that for which they long. Should the answer be the latter, they then argue to themselves that they will survive the frustration of the need, convincing themselves to forget their yearning.

As useful as such rationalization is in negotiating the hazards of adulthood, it inevitably fails. According to this solution to the dilemma of desire, dependency feelings—the longing for love, for someone to provide care, food, and shelter—are weak, childish, "womanish." Even sexual needs, and the need to make meaning of life, take on an unwholesome or frivolous cast. In unavoidable consequence, life begins to make less and less sense. Life is meaningless without wanting, but there is no wanting without needing, and therefore no desire without need. As need drains from desire, so does meaning bleed from life. To eliminate need is to kill desire and therefore any appetite for living.

As desire wanes, despair flares up, perhaps no more so than at three in the morning when need, breaking its chains, often wakes us. The persistent uncertainties of daily life interweave with unconscious, infantile fears to create the dark feelings of doubt and anxiety so common in the adult night. Although the bursting out of need in fact proclaims the renewal of desire, it usually feels like a terrifying loss of control, like the return of dreaded infantile weakness and dependence. At these moments, one longs for—wants and needs—someone else to be there who can banish all that frightens. One yearns for the magic once provided by teddy bears, for a sign of hope, for a sign that someone else is there, and, therefore, for a sign that one is really in control.

Women, their bodies cleaned up and prettified, provide that sign. They are magic mommies who perform tricks with their bodies and minds that appear to prove that one can kill off need and yet continue to desire and thrive. The epitome of their performance is anorexia. Anorexic women demonstrate total objectifying control of mind over body. They quash the need for food so as to realize the want to be thin, thereby sending the following message: If they can want without needing, then so can you.

Women working on their bodies thus become the image of "pure" desire, active desire minus dependent need, the magic maternal omnipotence that the infant believes is its own. The contradictory logic of women's body care makes them embody wanting, even though, as the Subject-as-Object who wants-to-be-wanted, they are unable to appropriate wanting for themselves. And needing gets tidied away along with the destruction of the body and of the earth. Therefore, the anorexic woman, the Subject-as-Object in its extreme, takes to extremes the starvation of the spirit, in which our culture routinely asks each of us to collude as we simply try to live out our lives.

Women's sexual housekeeping keeps order in the public house. Their bodies in particular are likened to the cyclicity and spontaneity of the green world that nurtures life. Yet, while their bodies may represent nature, their bodywork represents culture. Women's body care tacks a happy ending onto the story of culture and nature, appearing to demonstrate that nature, and therefore human life, can survive the destructive aspects of the omnipotent mastery that is our culture's version of creativity. Although women sometimes handle their bodies as benignly as farmers cultivate their land, they are often as callous as agribusinesses intent not on growing food but on making profits. Still, while women may deform their flesh like colonialists hacking their way through jungles, they nevertheless survive intact, looking good, even managing to feel good. Their equanimity may be replaced the next day by the self-hatred that impelled them to work on themselves in the first place. But the moment of looking good seems, to them and to onlookers, as permanently blissful as the infant's experience of satisfaction after being fed on time. In the symbolism of women's bodywork, then, culture does not destroy but rather enhances nature, and, by extension, its ruinous omnipotence is validated by the beauty of its creations.

Each woman, in trying to look and feel her best, unconsciously bears the cultural burden of seeming to resolve insoluble contradictions. This burden contributes in no small way to the destruction women experience as they try to live up to prevailing standards of beauty. Men face similar pressures of having to pretend that the contradictions of adult life do not exist. But women wear this pretense in and on their bodies, as they are supposed to, and it makes some of them mad. To the extent that they are angry, they will rebel. They may refuse, consciously or unconsciously, to be either the sex objects who embody desire or the efficient housekeepers who neaten the erotic mess by storing, somewhere in the attic, the boundlessness of infancy and the disorder of culture. They may disdain high heels, makeup, razors and shaving cream. Rebellious women may disobey rules for slenderness and eat what they want when they want. Self-defeating though it may be, they may even sometimes forget the date of their last period, or omit buying tampons or contraceptive jelly, or take the diaphragm out too soon, or neglect to put it in at all. Or they may collaborate to create the feminist outcry that disturbs the sleep of adulthood. Whatever its form, their rebellion expresses the outrage that all adults feel, consciously or unconsciously, in a culture promising and then withholding the illusion of omnipotence that makes adults nearly as weak socially as infants are physically.

I take my raincoat from the front closet, then return to the bedroom and stand on the threshhold in slight paralysis, looking at him. Should I leave him the key? I don't know what he wants. I don't know what he feels about me. I feel scared. I hate him for making me afraid, for being able to sleep later, for not being quite so preoccupied about his clothes, for being a man, for making me want him nonetheless. I go to my desk, where I hastily write a note, asking him to hold onto the key, which will fit neither in the mailbox slot nor under the door, until the next time. I sign it "love" and leave note and key on the hall table on my way out the door.

The Strange Relationship
Between Sex and Reproduction

(7:30 A.M.)

*M*y usual subway, fortunately three minutes late, is just pull-ing into the station as I rush down the stairs to the platform. I push through the turnstile and step through the momentarily opened doors into the train, feeling relieved and slightly disor-ganized. The doors close behind me.

I take inventory. The car is about one-quarter full. No one looks dangerous. Three men, two black and one white, wear scarred blue jeans, scuffed boots, and the serious, inward expres-sions of men about to start a day of hard work. A dark woman, wearing a rose-patterned scarf babushka-style and a heavy beige

31

coat, knits rhythmically from a skein of purple wool in the tote bag at her feet. I fantasize that she operates a sewing machine in a sweatshop. A man and a woman, both dressed in business suits, sit together with their attaché cases next to them on the seat. She wears sneakers. A tall and very thin black woman reads her paperback book. She wears her army fatigues with such style that I assume she works in the fashion industry.

My father, riding the slightly decaying commuter line from our suburban home to his job in the city, says offhandedly, but provocatively, *I told you to be careful, not do a sociological survey.*

Oh, Daddy, I say, sighing, *you have no social conscience.*

I continue to look around and spot, at the end of the car, a "bag-lady" layered in skirts, blouses, sweaters, coats, and leggings. She forages a bit of doughnut from a dirty sack in one of her multiple shopping bags. Some of us glance at her, then away. I cannot imagine living the way she does. Or, rather, I can imagine and am horrified. She must be escaping from something pretty awful if she finds the tension of endless movement bearable. Or is her day like any other, different only in the sorts of decisions she must make, such as the choice about where to sleep instead of what to wear?

I lean back and close my eyes for a moment, then stare sightlessly at the advertisements. During this interval between the languourous night before and the day of nonstop action ahead, I am not yet required to be alert, even though I dare not quite relax. I float in a sensual cocoon, feeling a little wistful, as if on the brink of tears. But I also feel peaceful. Even happy. Am I in love? Or is my imagination just projecting those familiar steps toward marriage and family that occur after each pleasurable sexual encounter? I'll have the children named before I know it.

I think of the boyfriend I had at eighteen, whom I loved very much—and whom I held in awe—two not unconnected emotions. In those days, he and his friends were great fans of *The Ginger Man*, by J. P. Donleavy. So naturally I thought I should be, too. I tried, but it was very hard for me to see myself as the freewheeling, woman-served, and woman-leaving protagonist, a great individualist who loved planting his seed but didn't like kids or wives or any form of constancy. No doubt I took the book too literally, too personally. Perhaps I should have tried to identify not with the character but with the spirit he represents.

This was not the first time I had had difficulty with literature that portrayed the glorious life of adult freedom in male terms. In high school, when I read *On the Road,* I wanted to be a beatnik and go on the road too, but I could never figure out what I would do when I got my period. Where would I be able to buy sanitary napkins or tampons in rural Mexico? Were you supposed to carry a supply with you? How much could you carry and still travel light? If you took all you needed, there wouldn't be any room for all those nice jugs of wine in Jack Kerouac's car. The only beatnik I knew of who even dealt with this question was a woman, Diane di Prima. In her novel, *Memoirs of a Beatnik,* her heroine describes her first big orgy and recounts the moment in it when she pulled out her Tampax and flung it across the room. A grand moment, that.

Are you thinking, how gross? I ask the imaginary eavesdropper in my head. *Or, how irrelevant?*

Gross, yes. Irrelevant, no. Not to me. The obligation to worry about the gross mess became a part of life from puberty on. A nagging, seemingly stupid worry became a fact of life, not quite as unnoticeable as my skin. The same nagging worry included wondering, *Do they have any contraceptive jelly in Mexico? Just when during the seduction am I going to put in my diaphragm? Once it is in, will it stay in? And when the time comes to take it out, how, where, and with what will I wash it?*

Needless to say, I never went "on the road." But I often wonder what it would have been like to have come of age a bit later on. What would I have thought about movies like *An Unmarried Woman, Julia,* or *Norma Rae?* Books like *The Color Purple* or *Woman Warrior* or *Rubyfruit Jungle?* Television shows like *Mary Tyler Moore* or *Cagney & Lacey?* Would Isadora, the heroine of *Fear of Flying,* have been a role model for me? Maybe she would have inspired me to go hunting for the perfect "zipless fuck." But then again, look what happened to Theresa, the heroine of *Looking for Mr. Goodbar.* She got murdered. Of course, Isadora was married, and her husband takes her back in the end. Theresa was single. Maybe you have to be married to a well-to-do psychiatrist to have sexual liberation without losing your life, at least in novels and movies.

No, probably my role model would have been Ingrid Bengis. As she told her story in *Combat in the Erogenous Zone,* you could be a single woman and have lots and lots of sexual adventures, but you had be willing to roll with the hard and sometimes discouraging punches.

REPRODUCTION, RELATEDNESS, AND SEX

In Western mythology, men often pursue an adventure that becomes a journey to self-realization, a rite of passage to the neatly bounded, orderly adult self. This adventure-journey to individualization exposes the hero to all kinds of dangers and challenges that provide him with repeated occasions to prove himself and emerge a self-reliant, self-defined being with a sense of autonomy and agency. Works of literature possessing the force of cultural myth, such as *The Odyssey*, express the rule that only men may go through this process of self-discovery. Odysseus is sent by Zeus, after the fall of Troy, on a series of marvelous, life-threatening, oat-sowing, and character-testing escapades, while his equally resourceful wife, the quiet, clear-eyed Penelope, faithfully keeps the home fires burning.

In *The Odyssey* and other such heroic epics, the journey that women take is only implied. Present by near-omission, its route and destination are sketched in by the lightest yet most definitive of strokes. The only successful adventuresses in *The Odyssey* are the goddesses; mortal women, like Penelope and her servant, Eurykleia, stand and wait. Not for them the dazzling feats of daring and courage, the intensity of amorous encounters. While the hero has adventures, women seem to tread a winding path that often doubles back on itself. Theirs is the work that is both honored, because the dog-tired hero depends on being able to benefit from it, and denigrated, because it is never done. This is the emotional housekeeping of human life, whose purpose is to ensure that others have what they need so that they may be what they want. Like cleaning up rooms and clothes and dishes, only so that they can be used and dirtied anew, this maintenance work of "relatedness" is repetitive and endless. While Odysseus weeps for Penelope by day and revels with the goddess Calypso in nightly pleasure, Penelope steadily keeps his social place for him. Each day, she weaves a shroud. Each night she unravels it so as to delay its completion and thus put off the subsequent selection of a successor for Odysseus' bed and throne.

The cultural truths portrayed in myth have a way of becoming personal ones. The journey toward individualization and the path of relatedness, genderless in principle, are attached to men and women by myth and thereby made to seem as though given to them by nature. But individualizing and relatedness are in fact ways of being that are mandated by culture and influential in personal life. Linked to masculinity and femininity, they inform both social institutions and cultural expectations. They filter into the individual experience of real men and women through traditional mythology and books, movies, and television as well, which give us the mythology of our present culture.

These mythologies, by seeming to describe what *is*, manage to prescribe what *ought to be*. The ways of being assigned to men and women thereby exert an almost irresistible, ineradicable moral influence on personal experience. Even when women are depicted as setting off on the journey toward individualization, as is increasingly the case in books and movies, they are portrayed as doing so in reaction to, or in spite of, the path to relatedness that is still regarded as their traditional life course. That this realism reflects women's actual experience of liberation in no way diminishes the prescriptive force exercised by the notion of men's and women's proper ways of being.

In real life, even though men may not always embark on actual travels, their voyages to adulthood are endowed by cultural values with the glamour of the heroic, lone traveler, from Odysseus on. Their passages to adulthood celebrate independence, singularity, and the discovery and creation of subjectivity. They honor the "self-as-individual" who is responsible for himself and no one else, the adult self of our culture that all adults are supposed to be. They contain the thrill and excitement of sexual encounters. Whatever their content, they are linked in principle to the universal and the transcendant, creativity and achievement, abstract reason and tangible, enduring results. In consequence of this glorification, men identify primarily with the individualizing journey, just as they do with wanting and subjectivity. They forget the domestic path, just as they do wanting-to-be-wanted and the process of "objectification," of being stripped of desire and transformed into an object without will or life.

This is not to say that in real life women cannot make this rite of passage toward personal agency. They can and, indeed, are required to become individualized adults. Nor are they denied sexual adventure in the process. However, their route to self-realization is a little more complicated and a little less exciting because of that. Just as women are Subject-as-Object, so they must individualize yet simultaneously tread an additional path, that of connectedness. Women's self-realization entails becoming a self

that is connected to other people, an inherently contradictory
situation in our culture, where adults are supposed to be self-
sufficient. Just as women become the-one-who-wants-to-be-wanted,
so they become the "self-for-other," a "self-in-relation." And the
path of relatedness they take winds through the mundane par-
ticularities of personal life, the pragmatics of caring and nurturing, and the ambiguously shifting light of emotional fireworks,
everyday halftones, and private darknesses.

Unfortunately, the meaning given by our culture to sex and
reproduction makes the individualizing journey somewhat hazardous for women, and the path of relatedness the one of least
resistance for them. Sex is sex for both men and women, but it
is something more for women. The sexual act ends, for men, in
orgasm. For women, it either does or does not end in reproduction. Reproduction is a fact of life that women may never forget
because, according to our culture, they are responsible for it.
Their responsibility is, however, not only for babies. They are
bound as well to see to warmth and intimacy and shared history,
to weave a soft bed of intangible connections on which the weary
traveler, and all human beings, may come to rest. Reproductive
responsibility is an accountability for the connective tissue of
human existence, a political burden that women must bear personally.

Women are responsible for babies and children, not so much
because they give birth to them, but because our culture puts
them in charge of relatedness itself. Reproduction is not merely
about conceiving and giving birth to a child. It is about raising
that child. A newborn child is not only a biological organism; it
is a creature in need of other people on whose care it depends,
for which it will eventually be able to reciprocate. A baby requires
to be fed and cleaned by someone else. But it also needs to be
held and loved, for when a baby is born a relationship flowers as
well. Each infant depends on being connected to someone else,
because human beings are social creatures. Relatedness is the web,
usually woven by women in our culture, in which all adults live
out their lives.

The accountability for relatedness makes sex a very different
and often more sober affair for women than for men. Women,
burdened by this extra baggage on their attempted journey toward
self-realization, tend not to be as lighthearted as their male counterparts. It is impossible to be casual about the challenge and

danger of getting pregnant. Although pregnancy may prove womanhood to both women and society, its mooring in relatedness has profound psychological and physical effects on the course of a woman's life that may fall quite short of the conventionally heroic.

For every woman—heterosexual, lesbian, young, old—sexuality is inextricably entangled with reproductivity, that is, with procreation and relatedness as felt and socially instituted. Either female travelers will be thinking about boring things like condoms and diaphragms, which interfere tediously with heroic self-realization. Or, if they are lesbian, postmenopausal, voluntarily sterilized, or fertile and wanting to get pregnant, they will be feeling relieved at not having to think about it. Some may regularly stop their masturbatory sexual fantasies long enough to figure out what kind of contraception will best fit the scenes they have constructed. Others may have to halt their passion for a moment in order to insert a diaphragm, if they haven't already initially damped it by inserting the diaphragm in advance. Still others may risk their health by taking a pill or wearing an intrauterine device. Finally, those who decide to take a chance can have the thrill of forgetting about having to remember not to get pregnant.

"Hi, darling, are you practicing TM or what?"

I look up to see Andrea, settling into the seat next to me and unwinding her robin's-egg blue cashmere muffler. "Hi," I say in surprise, "what are you doing here?"

"You mean why am I riding these damn dirty subways?" Andrea responds. "My car broke down again, that's why. So, I'm sitting over there wondering how I am going to pay for a new alternator, and then I see you, looking like someone almost knocked you out and maybe you're on your way to recovery."

"Hah," I cackle briefly. "No, I just got drunk last night. I've been having an affair that I think might be turning into a relationship. And then this morning my mind naturally proceeded to how you can't just enjoy fucking because getting pregnant is always a possibility and how different it all is for men. . . . " I trail off.

"My, how introspective we are at this early hour. It's all I can do to remember my briefcase. So who's this person?" She undoes the top button of her navy down coat.

I move over to give her more room. "A painter I met a few weeks ago. He'd just sold a painting, so he bought champagne."

Her eyebrows arch. "Nice to be a member of, what do you sociologists call it, the leisure class?"

"You know very well what they call it," I retort. "You took Introduction to Sociology, didn't you? Or was it another black woman I became friends with in college?"

"Not likely, being that there was never but one in each class back then. Things have changed, I hear. Or so they say in the newspapers," she says wryly. "But how're you going to teach with all that on your mind?" She shakes her head in mock dismay the way she always does when she thinks mine is getting stuck in the clouds.

"Fortunately, today's lecture is on gender. I can always talk about reproductive responsibility." I raise my voice almost to a shout, for the train has started up again after an unusually long delay at the station where Andrea got on.

"Repro what?" Andrea shouts back.

"Reproductive responsibility—you know, we give birth to them, then we're responsible for raising them, sending them to school, keeping the house clean, being pretty and cheerful and sexy for our husbands, going to work if necessary, and never getting a headache. And when things go wrong and the kids grow up unhappy, we get blamed."

"Who is this 'we'? I didn't know you ever gave birth to anybody," she snorts.

"Cut it out. That is not funny when someone has just passed her thirty-seventh birthday."

"Well, okay, sorry," she says, looking away from me, "but some of us can afford to spend time thinking about, as you call it, reproductive responsibility. Others of us actually have to do it, darling."

"Okay, I didn't mean any offense, you know that. So, tell me, how's LuAnn?" I ask, feeling slightly guilty for being white and privileged, yet slightly nettled as well.

"Better, thank you, just over a bad flu. Thank goodness my mother came to stay. But she's on the edge of something else, I can smell it. You've heard of the terrible twos? Well, what's coming up is the terrible teens."

"And James?"

Her smile glows. "He's been flourishing ever since he started in private school. I couldn't have asked for more." Then her eyebrows peak again and she shrugs. "We can't afford the tuition, but he wasn't going to get a decent education in public school. Maybe by the time he reaches high school he can get into one of the good public ones. That gives us five years."

"Is Roger still driving the cab?" My vocal chords are beginning to ache, and Andrea inclines her head toward me.

"Uh-huh, and not doing too bad at all." Her lips purse, then her mouth turns down. "What am I saying? He's always worried about money and thinks that he's a failure because he's worried. I hope his ulcer doesn't act up again. To make it worse, the Human Resources Administration is creating a new department for the homeless, and I'm probably going to be asked to run it, which means a raise. Since he thinks he's supposed to bring home more money than me, I'm going to have to do something about his terminal inferiority complex. But I really can't complain. He treats LuAnn like she was his own, better than her no-good, so-called real father. . . . Uh. Sometimes I think I need a desert island all to myself."

We lapse into silence, overwhelmed by the subway thunder. I look over at her tense but self-contained face and marvel at her ability to make a living from nine to five and a family from five to nine. Once I brought up the subject of how she and Roger divide the housework. She made so many jokes that I knew not to inquire again. She wants to ask him to do more of the dirty work, like washing dishes or cleaning the bathroom, but feels it's not fair to ask him because he wasn't, as he says, brought up to do "women's" work. And, anyway, he helps out a lot with the children. And since it's second nature to her, but not to him, to think about what has to be done, she would have to remind him, and they would both think she was a nag and would end up squabbling.

THE DOUBLE DAY

Although the work that has to be done in society is divided by our culture into two kinds, "men's" and "women's," women frequently do both. The work that women are supposed to do takes place in the household, in the private, domestic domain, and consists of reproducing adult workers and the next generation, physically, socially, and emotionally. The work assigned to men is located outside the home, in the public domain, and consists of producing goods and services that are sold for money. However, just as women are expected to be selves who are also in-relation, so it is generally true that, more often than not, they work the "double day." Each day, they do two days' worth of work, one at the office, factory, or studio, and one at home.

The fact that women's real work is the double day is not so readily perceived in our culture, where women's dominant role model is the "true woman." Although "woman" might suggest any one of many different roles women play in society—wife, daughter, lover, or, as among the Mpondo of Africa, sister—in Western thinking, "woman" means in the first place the Madonna, the "mother." And if the central meaning of "woman" is "mother," the primary meaning of "mother" is "self-in-relation-to-other," which is the primary psychological skill required for doing both emotional housekeeping and actual housework. "Mother" is the one who thinks first not only of children but of the other in general, which is what the housewife needs to do if she is to be at all effective.

However, although the work assigned to women thus comes to seem like housewifery, and by extension "true woman" comes to signify "housewife," the woman who specializes in housework has in fact had only a bit part in Western—and human—history. In most epochs—and most cultures—all but the richest women have worked the double day. They have labored in fields or raised livestock or woven fabrics for sale or helped out in husbands' shops or taken goods to market or worked in factories at the same time as they have brought up children and kept house. Indeed, the work that women have done outside the home has, in many cultures, afforded them substantial public power.

The middle-class housewife of our culture is an exception and, to the surprise of many women, an ever rarer one at that. Feminist demands for the end of sex discrimination would suggest that few women were ever in the public work force at all. However, even as these demands were being made, women were constituting a larger portion of the employed. Not only was the economy expanding, but more women were finding that they could no longer afford not to work. The by-now-common two-income family is evidence that, apart from independently wealthy women or the wives of corporate executives, most adult women must now work for wages at some time in their lives.

Nor is this participation in the work force entirely the voluntary matter that the complaints of middle-class housewives made it seem. Certainly, women make choices about what they do. In the long run, however, women enter and leave the labor force depending on the vagaries of the market. Although many more middle-class women took paying jobs during the 1960s and 1970s than during the previous decade, their number had dropped off slightly as the recession set in during the early 1980s. In general, then, when the economy needs more cheap labor, women, like minorities, get jobs, but when it needs less, they are laid off and sent back to what is culturally considered their "natural" place.

No matter to which class or race they belong, whether their job has the status of a "career" or is simply a way of making money, women's culturally prescribed lot is the double day. While they are expected and expect themselves to be "true women," they must also always be prepared to earn money should economic circumstances so dictate. Yet they must also be ready to give up the public world and return to the private domain should they be called upon to do so.

The double day generates a set of complementary contradictions that operate like a vicious cycle, shuttling women back and forth between the two halves of the day and allowing them no apparent escape except perhaps to a desert island. What a woman gains in one part, she loses in the other. At home, her self becomes submerged in others' needs and wants; at work, she is, in principle, on her own, but she finds that she, like everyone else, is objectified in such a way that her home comes to seem like a dream of autonomy—which it is, but only when there is no one else there.

As housewife, a woman has, on the one hand, considerable personal power, because she is the one who can and does see to it that others' needs are satisfied. Success at her work depends not only on housewifely crafts, but on intelligence and psychological skill. Her skill, learned and practiced like all skills, consists of constant attunement to signals, large and small, that other people send about what they need and want. This special sort of attunement, or "intuition," is what impels her to exclaim with pleasure when her children bring paintings home from school and to hang them on the refrigerator. Intuition enables her to know, before her husband tells her, that he is worried about how much money he brings home and to head off a crisis by giving him the special treatment he needs. And, finally, this attunement to the needs and wants of the family also gives her an overview of what chores have to be done around the house, what should be bought from the grocery store, who is to do these things, when, and how.

On the other hand, even though the housewife may believe she is in charge of the household, the household often takes charge of her. Indeed, her intuition is the sort of skill developed by anyone in a subordinate job or social position. The woman who is busy thinking about others' wants and needs frequently finds that she forgets to think about her own or cannot recall what they are. Nor is there anyone who can spell her so that she can remember—unless, of course, she has a housekeeper, a privilege reserved for women with rich husbands or very high-paying jobs. Even when her husband is willing to share domestic work with her, she still has something extra to do. He will tend not only to shirk the duller, treadmill tasks but to require supervision in carrying them out—frequently not without umbrage. At home, then, women can find that they have no time for themselves because their selves have gotten lost in the thicket of others' interests. They can come to believe that true self-realization lies elsewhere, outside the household, in the public domain, where cultural myth says it is.

However, the self-realization that paid work promises is often illusory. As men and working-class women have always known, and as middle-class women are now finding out, life in the public sphere does not conform to the individualizing journey. Although the public domain affords an exhilarating freedom that contrasts with the frequently claustrophobic private sphere, the search for the self can actually be deadening. In public, women are treated not as individuals with particular skills, capacities, wishes, and needs but as objects required to fit categories of work.

The marketplace that women enter is supposed to be a free one, but they find that their job choice and mobility are limited. Women seek jobs in order to earn money but receive less than they ought. Although some women in the professions, the media, and the executive ranks earn high salaries, the average wage earned by women remains absolutely lower than what men are paid, and women of color have the lowest average incomes of all employed people. Women in general receive less for jobs whose worth is comparable to men's. And if the elderly are the poorest adults in our society, elderly women are the poorest of all.

Moreover, regardless of women's individual qualifications, their work is often seen as or felt to be demeaning. Most men do unskilled and semiskilled work. But proportionately more women are employed in jobs that smack of relatedness and are, as well, predominantly female—teachers, nurses, secretaries, fast-food cooks, waitresses, hotel workers. Since such occupations are seen as feminine, they offer lower wages and merit less social esteem, which makes not only women's income but their self-esteem less than it might be. At the same time, however, women who do such service work earn the resentment of unemployed, unskilled men, who lack the skills of relatedness, which women come by largely through socialization, that get them some of these jobs. And, finally, women holding management and other positions in industries where advancement in the hierarchy is possible still find, often enough, great obstacles, ranging from being passed over in promotions, to having to excel where male competitors must merely do well, to being harassed sexually by co-workers or superiors.

The objectification that women experience in the public domain conforms to the rules of the marketplace, whose operation tends to transform the pursuit of anyone's self-interests into the selfish disregard of others. An interest in self is essential to get a job or make a profit, but when one obtains a job or makes a profit it is, in principle, at the expense of someone else's self-realization. Job seekers who defer to competitors do not get work, and entrepreneurs who worry about the finances of those from whom they buy cheap or to whom they sell dear do not make profits. Moreover, everyone's self-interest is at the mercy of the self-interest of those in charge, the people who run things, be they the small shopkeepers or professionals with one or two employees or the presidents and owners of corporations employing thousands. Finally, both objectification and hierarchy make life in the public domain more often monotonous than adventurous.

Therefore, for the same reasons that the lonesome traveler in the public domain finds the domestic domain a refuge, women may also find it a pleasure, when they are not in need of a paycheck, to return to or stay in it. For in fact it grants a kind of autonomy that the public world of time clocks and hierarchies promises but never delivers. The home really is a woman's castle, even if she has to play queen to her husband's king. Alone, she can do what she wants at her own pace and can take immediate pleasure in what she creates: She can sit on the chair she has slipcovered, admire the cowgirl outfit she has just sewn for her daughter for Halloween, or try on the coat she has made for herself. But if she works, let us say, as a sewing-machine operator, she may never see, let alone wear, the garments in whose completion she has had a crucial role. The home is the domain of "true women," not only because cultural beliefs make it so, but also because there they, and men, can in some ways be more true to themselves than anywhere else in our culture.

"So what about this guy?" Andrea asks as the train stands silent again at the station.

"What's more immediately important is that I don't know if I'm pregnant or just late." I sigh.

"That too? Have we been taking chances?" She speaks a bit more loudly as the train takes off.

I stare at her. "Me?"

"No, I guess not. Well, if men got pregnant, birth control would head up the Bill of Rights, I can tell you that." She giggles, then puts her arm around my shoulder. "Sorry, darling. What do you plan on doing?"

"You mean, if I'm pregnant? Get an abortion." I turn my palms up and shrug in turn.

Picking up her briefcase, she responds. "Yeah, well, I'm going to get myself sterilized."

"Are you sure you want to do that?" I inquire in concern.

"Listen, I've had all the kids I want. And," her voice dropping as she leans over, "if I don't have to worry about getting pregnant, sex'll be what it's supposed to be. At last. Just like you say." Laughing again, she stands up. "This is where I get off. Look, let's continue this over a belated birthday drink, okay? I'll call you."

The train slows and stops, and she vanishes as abruptly as she appeared, leaving behind only an echo of her jauntiness.

I try to figure out what it feels like just to consider sterilization. I haven't even had an abortion. *Maybe,* I think with some anxiety, *that means I can never get pregnant.*

The train screams to a halt in between stations. Worried that

I'm going to be late for class, I look around, then spot a girl (*I know*, I say to the feminist in me, *I know, I'm supposed to say "woman"*) who looks to be no more than sixteen, studying a biology textbook that she holds in front of her pregnant belly.

Mentally, I ask my habitual questions. *Did she mean to get pregnant? And, if so, why so soon? Or was it an accident? Did she think of getting an abortion? Will she be able to finish school? Who will support her and the baby? Is she married?* I try to see if there's a wedding ring, but her left hand is hidden.

The possibility of having to have an abortion has always unnerved me, partly because of what happened to my high school friend Maggie shortly after my first real love became my first real ex. During the first semester of college, while I was in the throes of long-distance romance, she was enjoying her romance on the spot. Halfway through the first semester, as she romantically told the story in her letters to me from her college in Vermont, she got "carried away." (Cynically, I always thought she let her boyfriend talk her into it.) Soon she was throwing up every morning into the empty coffee can that she began to keep by her bed. Since this was prior to the Supreme Court's legalization of abortion and since she was afraid to tell her parents, she decided one day to take care of her problem herself. She sterilized a couple of knitting needles in her percolator on the common-room hot plate, wrapped their points in adhesive tape, then carried them back to her room and closed the door. She sat down on the bed and, as she was removing her panties in order to insert a needle into her vagina, she saw, to her relief, a spot of blood on them and happily concluded that she was menstruating.

By the time that she realized that she had only been spotting and really was pregnant, it was too late to do a self-abortion, and she didn't have enough money to pay for an illegal abortion or travel to a country where it was legal. So she dropped out of school, got married, and had a little girl. Two years later, her husband, who had just finished college when the baby was born, became aware of feeling oppressed by the responsibility of a wife and child before he'd had time to "find" himself. So they split up, and Maggie moved back home for a few years, then returned to Vermont and joined a hippie commune. She started a small bakery that she later expanded into a nationwide mail-order business and even finally put herself through college on her earnings. Her daughter, Dinah, is now the lead guitarist in a punk-rock band; they're called Dinah and the Dinettes. I don't think Maggie regrets anything. But she's the first to admit that her life wasn't easy. And I wonder what her life would have been like had abortion been legal, as it is now, or contraceptives so readily available, at least to middle-class white girls.

DAMNED IF THEY DO, DAMNED IF THEY DON'T

Since the 1960s a new kind of cultural mythology has sprung up, in which the revolution in contraception has freed women to determine the course of their reproductive lives. Like all mythologies, this one tells only part of the truth. Certainly, the relationship between sex and reproduction is no longer as enigmatic as it was for women twenty-five years ago. The remarkable changes in the technology of reproduction, paralleled by the increase in women's knowledge about their own health and by shifts in the law, have substantially altered women's sexual options and reproductive responsibility. Where women once had to search carefully and shamefacedly for doctors willing to prescribe birth control, they now can choose to go to clinics serving their sexual and reproductive needs exclusively. They can consult books replete with accurate and useful information about women's reproductive anatomy, pregnancy, genital diseases and remedies, and sexuality. In part because the medical industry has become more responsive to consumer demands and in part because feminists raised the issue of women's special health needs, gynecologists, too, are more informed and amenable to women's wishes to participate in decision making about their own bodies. Birthing has changed as well; natural childbirth and midwives have become an accepted part of the medical scene.

Contraception has amplified both women's sexual and reproductive choices. The range of birth-control methods, the availability of which was mandated by legislatures, adds the pill, intrauterine device, and sterilization to the diaphragm, cervical cap, and spermicidal foam. The pill, in particular, has permitted many women to sample the fear-free immediacy of sexual gratification always available to men. Contraception also permits women to decide when, if at all, they will conceive. The legalization of abortion grants those who can afford it some flexibility in deciding what to do should they become pregnant by accident. Women can now find out for themselves whether or not they are pregnant by buying a simple, over-the-counter kit. And amniocentesis offers them the opportunity to decide in advance whether they wish to bear a child who is genetically damaged.

However, the mythology of women's reproductive freedom omits the truth that the basis on which they exercise such choice is shaky. Part of the problem is that women do not control the manufacture or sale of the technology of reproduction, nor is it made entirely in their interest. Methods of birth control remain either awkward, dangerous, or unsightly. Foam continues to be as completely untrustworthy as ever. Diaphragms are unaesthetic and clumsy, as well as occasionally unreliable. Birth-control pills and intrauterine devices may be physically harmful, and they do not always work.

Furthermore, the degree of availability of such technology suggests that reproductive choice is still more an ideal than a reality. Not all women can afford it. The most reliable forms of birth control are still available only with a prescription, which adds the cost of a doctor's visit to the cost of birth-control devices. Sexually active teenagers depend on their parents' money to pay for contraception. Financial constraints also apply to amniocentesis and abortion, which are presently privileges of the middle and upper classes. In many states, welfare payments serve none of women's reproductive interests. In some, they cover the cost of abortion but require parental notification for girls under the age of eighteen. In other states, welfare may fund sterilization but not abortion, an exclusion that subtly encourages, if not forces, women receiving welfare to forgo by selecting a permanent form of birth control. Many critics have castigated this trend as a subtle form of genocide, insofar as disproportionate numbers of black, Hispanic, and Native American women receive welfare. In any event, these inequities mean that reproductive choice belongs primarily to middle- and upper-class women.

Yet increasing numbers of young middle-class women who have never borne a child are selecting sterilization as their form of contraception. In this generation, as in others, there are women who simply wish not to have children. But it may also be that the expense, unreliability, and ugliness of presently available contraceptive methods for women underlie this trend. And it is also likely that some young, fertile women are "choosing" to make themselves permanently incapable of having children because the basic structure of reproduction and relatedness has not changed. They may feel, consciously or unconsciously, that their responsibility for relatedness continues to be a burden that, in effect, allows them no choice at all.

The problem of reproductive freedom is not merely the material one of technological innovation, as the mythology simplistically has it, but rather the complex, psychological, and cultural one of relatedness. Now, as in 1960, unexpected pregnancy presents women with all the contradictions they experience in the rest of their lives. Here a woman is truly Subject-as-Object. The pregnancy happens in her body, but her decision to see it to term or terminate it is not entirely her own. She is held personally responsible for being pregnant, but any decision she makes is so hedged by cultural values and social institutions as to be taken out of her hands. An unplanned conception may disrupt other parts of her life. But, once pregnant, she is thought to have no other life. She is defined as a self-in-relation whose work is domestic work, even though she is expected to earn a living as well.

Therefore, despite the contraception revolution, if a woman decides to abort, she can still feel estranged from herself and be cast out from society. Even if she plans eventually to have a child, the decision to terminate her pregnancy can make her doubt her femininity. For any decision against child bearing excludes her from the category of the "true woman." Like the woman who has never been pregnant, she may wonder whether she is really a woman. Like the woman who chooses to make her career her life, opts to live alone, or does not wish to marry at all, she has decided against defining herself as primarily a self-in-relation. This choice, however, can make her feel as though she had ignored someone else's needs. She may thereby come to feel as guilty as she is thought to be by others who criticize her decision. Indeed, the presently most vociferous critics, those who exercise their politics by bombing abortion clinics, are responding in part to the threat that her choice poses to the bedrock of our culture, to the division of labor that assigns men to individualizing and women to relatedness.

If she decides to have the baby, she earns others' praise and relieves her guilty conscience, because she has become a "true woman." But then she runs into other problems. Having the baby means not only giving birth but raising it, which involves her in the never-ending, tangled tasks of relatedness. Having the child can interfere with the rest of her life, with, among other activities, wage earning and self-realization. Pregnancy, childbirth, and the care of a newborn may decrease her income should she lose her job because of them. A new child may divert energy from other already-born children who need attention and nurturing. Or new motherhood may slow and even stop the progress of her career.

Finally, although the revolution in technology makes more visible the moral ambiguities always implicit in any decision about reproduction, the mythology of reproductive freedom makes them as impossible to discuss as they have always been. Pregnancy, its prevention, and its termination are weighty and complicated matters. But traditional Judaeo-Christian ethics simplify them: Conception and birth are right; contraception and abortion are wrong. In reaction to this rigid morality, liberal thought, which underlies the new mythology, has taken the opposite but equally simplistic position: Any choice is right.

But no reproductive decision is, on a moral plane, either absolutely right or absolutely wrong. Any decision, not only to terminate a pregnancy but to conceive, is ambiguous. The personal dilemmas faced by young women in trying to determine the course of their reproductive futures require an ethic. Women deciding whether and when to have children, to carry to term, to abort, or even to adopt require guidance in making their way through the thickets of personal and political exigencies and values. They must sort out their own wishes and needs from those of their families and religion or subculture. They have to evaluate the relationship between the traditional bases of femininity and motherhood, masculinity and fatherhood. They must figure out how to understand their self-interest apart from the selfishness with which they have been charged upon deciding not to have children. Neither set of ethics, that of the traditional, moralistic position nor that of the liberal position, helps to resolve these and other dilemmas, all of which challenge the meaning of life as traditionally given for women.

Nor does either position offer any illumination on how women may negotiate the contradictory social arrangements for their decisions. Since, in our society, every adult is expected to be the individualizing self, women appear, when they decide to conceive a child or to terminate a pregnancy, to make the decision as independent people. However, since women are defined as the self-in-relation, they never, in principle, act totally independently. Already defined by connectedness, their decisions are, in effect, always made in tension between what they want and what others, including society itself, have already decided for them. In other words, their personal choices are entirely contingent on political decisions already made by the laws curtailing their reproductive freedom.

This double bind is graphically illustrated by the now apparent inequity of liberalized divorce laws in a still patriarchal culture. By and large, women remain responsible for children yet are prevented from discharging their responsibility adequately. Divorced women awarded custody are, in effect, either granted insufficient child support or unable to collect the payments from errant husbands. Since many do not receive reimbursements for the labor and income that they have contributed to their husbands' career success, they have difficulty making ends meet. Moreover, their postdivorce economic chances are substantially fewer than men's, for they confront stubborn sex and age discrimination in the marketplace as they attempt to go it alone. As a result, children, whose interests are neglected by no-fault divorce and who are assigned to women by default, constitute an increasing proportion of those living below the poverty line, a political shame for which mothers, unfairly, bear personal blame.

Paradoxically, the freedom to determine whether and under what conditions a woman will bear a child is the one area of relatedness in which women are freed from, or better, deprived of responsibility. They lack full rights to control their own fertility. They have the right to conceive, but they can get reliable contraception only with a medical prescription. They have the right to childbirth. However, their right to abortion is presently defined in terms of a doctor's right to privacy, not in terms of theirs to their bodies and selves. They have the right to sterilization, but sometimes the operation is performed without their informed consent, as when they agree to it after its reversibility has been falsely guaranteed. They have the right to social praise for motherhood, but they lack the right to the financial and other social resources that will allow them to mother adequately, such as prenatal and postnatal care, day care, good schooling, adequate incomes, and equitable divorce judgments.

Life without reproductive freedom is like taxation without

representation. If women were defined as full Subjects, as first-class citizens, then, given the premises of our society, whatever they did with their bodies would be their own affair. The only legislation on reproductive freedom would be that designed to protect it, as legislation protects freedom of speech. The ethics and morality of reproductive freedom would be based on society's need for women to be able to make individual, responsible, reproductive decisions.

As things stand, however, women are, in this matter as in others, Subject-as-Object, having to shoulder their responsibility for relatedness as best they can, while recognizing that they are hindered from doing so. They are second-class citizens at the mercy of the state, of those who make the laws about what they will do with their bodies. Their rights, such as that to abortion, are taken for granted by many young women who came of age in the 1970s. But, in fact, these rights are treated merely as privileges that can be rescinded at any moment. They are presently under governmental attack and have been ever since the conservative political backlash arose against the very feminist success that secured them in the first place. Feminist activism, taken by many to be dated, is therefore still necessary to protect these rights until women finally have first-class citizenship in law. Only then will their reproductive freedom be firmly anchored, and only then will they be able to discharge their reproductive responsibility with full competence, confidence, and pleasure.

The bottom line of women's double bind is that they have no escape. If they choose to do only domestic work, they are dismissed, and may dismiss themselves, for being "only a housewife." If they take paid jobs and try to be the self-as-individual, they are labeled as, and may feel, unnatural. As women, their only choice is relatedness in a culture where adulthood emerges through individualization, which is no choice at all. And if they refuse this impossible situation, then they put themselves outside the boundaries of their society. They become familiar strangers, internal aliens, madwomen, in short, the "bag-lady," neither here nor there, homeless, always wandering.

The train is slowing down. Now the car is filled mostly with students, some of whom read their textbooks. Others chatter and horse around, a few flirt, and one or two stare back at me, making me self-conscious about trying to see through their skins to their thoughts. Are they ever as obsessed as I am with this "repro-sexual" stuff?

When the train stops, most of us get off, including the pregnant young woman, apparently on her way to the college.

Monkeys, Apes, and the Myth of the Ever-Ready Female

(9:00 A.M.)

*T*he empty corridors with walls painted in neutral shades of brown on bottom and beige on top convey a familiar, reassuring sense of order and reason. Every question has its answer, every problem its resolution. Top is top, bottom is bottom, yes is yes, no is no, it's all as simple as that.

I wish. I smile ruefully in silent answer.

To work. I hesitate as I pass the elevator, then decide to march up the stairs and get some oxygen into my system.

I appear to be the first faculty member in today. Perhaps they have all taken off early for spring vacation.

53

I hang up my coat and look around my small office for my coffee cup. I do not see it on my desk, which is littered with memoranda from the dean, long-forgotten (by me and them) students' papers, instructions for fire drills that take place on July 4, invitations to retirement parties for people I've never met, insurance forms.

My mother criticizes, *Don't you think you should keep it a bit neater, dear?*

I ignore her. Now that the day is really about to begin, I have less time for inner shenanigans.

I go to the departmental office, shouldering my purse, because, if I left it in the office, someone might rip it off. I fill the aluminum saucepan at the water fountain and put it on the hot plate. And finally, on the table under the mailboxes where I left it two days ago, I spot the cup—more a bowl than a cup—with my name on it; I bought it in Normandy on my honeymoon.

While rinsing it at the fountain, I remember that I've got to get a tampon, just in case. I walk down to the second-floor bathroom and put a dime in the dispenser over the sink. Nothing.

I go into the stall. No blood. I pee, pull up my pants. They zip snugly around my crotch. The last wisp of erotic hangover drifts by.

When I return to the office, the boiling water is spattering onto the electric coil. I mix the instant coffee and, warming my hands on the bowl, go back to my desk. After I put on my granny glasses, I open a folder marked "Social Sciences 100" and concentrate on the material for today's lecture with an intensity that will banish all irrelevant thoughts and will induce a kind of amnesia. I'll have trouble recalling what happened before I got to school, even the conversation with Andrea, even the morning's passion.

After an hour, I head for the classroom, where the students have already taken their customary seats. As I enter, some are reading newspapers, others talk quietly or stare out the window. I place my folder and textbook on the desk, then close the door and begin.

"Let's start, everybody. I'd like to remind you that the midterm will take place a week from Monday, that is, the day we return from spring vacation. As I told you last week, it will include everything we've covered since the beginning of the semester—reading, lectures, discussions, and films."

I see winces and hear groans and feel like apologizing. "The format of the exam will be short answers, multiple choice, and true-false." I smile and breathe more easily when I hear the sighs of relief.

"Okay. Now I want to talk to you about two topics dear to my heart—sex and gender." I open the folder.

Kathy, who wears overalls, a plaid flannel shirt, and glasses like mine, leans forward, resting on her bent elbows on the desk, her chin in her clasped hands. Felice removes an infinitesimal mote from the left cuff of her flawlessly pressed, burgundy gabardine pantsuit, then pulls her notebook out of her burgundy leather briefcase and places it on the desk. Mason, who, in his late twenties, is slightly older than most of the other students and is dressed in black sweatpants and gray sweatshirt, folds up his newspaper and slips it into his portfolio of pen-and-ink drawings.

"Well," says Dennis, who wears extremely tight designer jeans (a different label from mine) that show a modest crotch bulge and who sports several gold chains that tangle in the chest hair curling through his open-necked shirt, "I guess I don't have to do any studying for that."

Some students giggle. Kathy glares. Joe, next to him, elbows his ribs. A few latecomers who just crept in look bewildered.

I'd like to giggle too. But, although his sexual pride is actually rather endearing, I don't want to seem to condone what is possibly intended as mockery. If I were a man, maybe I could smile along with him. But I doubt that he would have said the same thing to a male professor. On the other hand, it could be that his behavior has nothing specifically to do with my gender. Maybe my blue jeans invite familiarity. Or maybe my high-heeled boots are a little hookerish.

So I simply look at him without a change of expression and continue. "Yes, they're both juicy topics. But it's easy to mix them up. So, to be sure we know what we're talking about, let me define them." I write *sex* and *gender* on the blackboard.

The thirty-five students are settled in now, and some of them are beginning to take notes.

THE VARIABILITY OF SEX

Human sexuality, a complex and variable mix of biology, culture, and psychology, escapes the absolute distinction between "nature" and "nurture." The words *sex* and *gender* represent only endpoints on a continuum of human sexual experience. Biological sex and culturally constructed gender meet in the psychological middle span of the continuum, which is where sexual desire appears as well. However, human sexual experience involves the full range of the continuum; sexual passion, for example, engages body, mind, and culture simultaneously. In matters of human sexuality, the borders between biological underpinning, social conditioning, and psychological significance are equally indeterminate and their placement just as subject to fashionable ideas as is a woman's waistline. This leaves sizable room for variation, flexibility, choice, and ambiguity in the expression of human sexuality.

Human sexuality is complex and ambiguous because, although human beings are biological organisms, they are simultaneously creatures of culture and psychology. Like other forms of organic life, human beings survive by reproducing themselves from one generation to the next. However, human survival takes place within a psychological and cultural context. Indeed, culture and psychology give human behavior in general and human sexuality in particular their distinctiveness. Human sexuality is therefore the product of the interaction of biological, psychological, and cultural factors, each of which makes the others come to life, but none of which rigidly determines the others. From biology come ample capacities and wide limits. The capacities include procreation and sexual arousal. The limits are those of the reproductive organs, which dictate that someone with a penis and testes cannot carry a fetus, while someone with a uterus and ovaries can carry eggs but not sperm. From the psyche comes desire, which is inherently expansive and is the means by which sexuality receives symbolic significance. And from culture come social and political forms for the recognition, articulation, and action upon desire, forms given meaning by the psyche.

This diversified base allows human sexuality to vary greatly. Although most cultures, like ours, have only two genders, male and female, some have more. While our dual-gender system, assuming that all people have unambiguously male or female reproductive organs, emphasizes mutually exclusive male and female roles and styles, Navaho culture has three official gender roles. This three-gender system legitimizes biological ambiguities, such as hermaphroditic genitals, as well as individual variations in erotic preference. Genitally normal females and males make up two genders. A third gender consists of genital hermaphrodites, called "real *nadle*," and genitally normal individuals who choose to pretend they are *nadle*. Real *nadle* never marry; other *nadle* may select either a male or a female spouse, may perform all tasks except hunting and waging war, and are in some respects treated as women—who have a higher legal status than men.

Even cultures with two-gendered systems differ in the roles they assign to men and women. While our society officially excludes women from public life, the matrilineal culture of the Trobriand Islands of the Pacific makes them spiritual guardians of the cycle of life and death. Men's work includes working in the fields, long-distance trading, managing village political affairs, and keeping oral histories of land ownership and clan genealogy. Women keep house and cultivate fields, and while they can never be chiefs, even though this is a matrilineal society and kinship is therefore traced through women, they also have an important public presence. Through the valuable objects they make and ritually exchange following funerals, women are thought to exercise cosmological power, regulating the rebirth of ancestors in the new generation.

Attitudes toward sexuality, too, diverge from what our culture takes to be normal limits of propriety and feeling. Among the Tuken of Kenya, for example, sexual activity is not the simultaneously profane and holy activity, overfilled with pride and shame, that it is in our culture. Rather, it is matter-of-factly integrated into daily life. In each other's presence, men and women may discuss what they like to do in bed and who their favorite partners are, as long as there are no people within hearing who, because of kinship, political alliance, or age, would be inappropriate bedmates. Additionally, an unmarried woman, with a view toward becoming a man's second wife, may ask a married woman for her husband's sexual services; the wife would happily agree so as to gain the labor of a co-wife but would be angry were the intentions of her husband and the potential wife strictly erotic.

Just as sex varies culturally, so is it diverse psychologically. Even though there are cultural patterns for sexual practice and fantasy, individual experiences within each culture differ enormously. The intrapsychic dynamics that are a product jointly of personal and family history, culture, ethnicity, and religion, on the one hand, and genes, hormones, and anatomical structure, on the other, make any given person's experience of sex and gender so unique as to defy categorical explanations. It is tempting to explain sexual desire by reducing it to heterosexuality or homosexuality, to male or female, to class or ethnicity or race or religion, to culture. But individuals consciously and unconsciously compose their own erotic rhythms by shuffling culturally constructed sexual patterns, their own developing personality, and their unique temperamental and physical endowments.

In the mix of biology, culture, and psychology of which human sexuality is composed, reproductive anatomy and biological capacities serve as the raw material, culture and psychology as its sculptors. Yet, just as the sculptor responds to the form in the stone, so the elements of sexual desire are inextricable from their endless, mutually informative communication. Sexuality, as socially instituted and individually experienced, is therefore a highly ambiguous matter. Culture endows biology with political meaning, while sexual desire gives culture and biology personal meaning. Political and personal meaning are woven together by social institutions, in the context of which individuals learn the socially appropriate, and inappropriate, forms for gender, reproduction, and sexual desire, and use or reshape these forms to suit their own purposes.

Jerry, whose appearance oddly combines long hair, a gangster suit, and a single earring in his left ear, raises his hand. He never takes a note. If he did, there's no doubt he'd get an A, but, as it is, I'm not sure he'll pass. "You know, once I saw a TV show about apes. There was one male, bigger than all the others, and he was the one who got, well, to do it with all the wo—." He stops.

"Oh, yes, I know," adds Felice, "that's survival of the fittest, because they mate only when the females can get pregnant."

Made enthusiastic by their engagement with the lecture, I amplify and correct. "Well, you've got it partly right. The sexual behavior of nonhuman primates has regular patterns, and it does have something to do with evolution. But, you know, sometimes things are a little more colorful on TV than they are in real life. Apes and monkeys are rather more complicated and various than that. Sometimes the smaller males succeed in inseminating the females, and mating is not always synchronized with fertility."

Rosa is a woman of forty-five in a pale blue suit who returned to school as a nursing student after her kids were grown and out of the house. She makes a note, and then asks, "Professor, I don't understand how the timing of mating can vary, given that intercourse among nonhuman primates is regulated by the hormones, taking place only at estrus."

"I'd like to say more about that," I reply. "But first, can you define *estrus* for the class, please?" Like many other women who have picked up their education later in life, Rosa participates in class discussions with exemplary thoughtfulness and extraordinary competence.

She answers readily. "Estrus is the fertility cycle of females among most nonhuman primates. It occurs with varying periodicity among different species, overlapping with the monthly menstrual cycle. When a female is in estrus, she's fertile. If conception doesn't occur, she then menstruates, as humans do. Estrus is also the time when she's sexually receptive."

"Thank you, that was very clear. By the way, sometimes estrus is observable, sometimes it isn't. In some species, it may include visual signals of fertility and sexual receptivity. For example, the skin around the female chimpanzee's genitals and anus balloons and turns bright red when she is in estrus."

Dennis grimaces; Joe mimes a gag; Felice sticks out her tongue but keeps on writing.

Kathy frowns. "Isn't it uncomfortable to have your genitals swell every month? It must be hard to walk."

"Yes," I explain, "it would be difficult if the genitals were between the legs. But you have to remember that the genitals and excretory organs are placed more to the rear in nonhuman primates, as in cats and dogs. In fact, the change in their placement probably came about only when our apelike ancestors began to walk erect."

"In the show I saw," offers Jerry, "the apes had intercourse from behind."

A few of the students laugh. Felice covers her smile with her hand, her long, delicate fingers and graceful nails looking like an advertisement for an impeccable manicure. Jerry and Kathy exchange glances.

I smile, too. "You mean, I think, that the female receives the male from behind. The male enters her from the rear. Yes, dorsal-ventral intercourse," I say, hoping that this clinical language will cool out the giggles, "is the usual position for intercourse among nonhuman primates. And it is also the position for homosexual play and intercourse, at least among males." I write *dorsal-ventral* on the board.

Someone somewhere titters.

The worst problem in teaching this spicy material is the contagion of the students' hilarity. I restrain my own grin and proceed, as I always do at this sort of juncture, in as neutral a voice as possible.

"Yes, like other animals, human and nonhuman, nonhuman primates have homosexual relations, and they masturbate. In other words, their sexual activity does not seem always to be regulated by ovulation. Indeed, they are rather experimental, even playful. It has also been reported that gorillas and orangutans occasionally have intercourse face to face and side to side. Chimps, who are, according to blood and hormone chemistry, our closest kin, vary not only their positions but their courtship behavior. Either sex may initiate intercourse by, for instance, 'presenting,' that is, by sticking a rear end in another's face, which is also a sign of deference to an individual of higher rank. Either sex may decline such an offer. And, during estrus, a female does not necessarily take on all comers. If a male starts to follow her, she may accept or ignore him. She doesn't always accept the most aggressive or the highest-ranking male either. Sometimes, to attract a female's attention, a male may shake tree branches and make noise. Or he may stand up, thus showing off an erect penis."

Felice, whose memory is as precise as her burgundy nail polish and who is therefore sure to get an A for knowing all the answers, raises her lovely hand. "Professor, is this going to be on the exam?"

"No."

She puts down her pen.

THE FEMINIST CRITIQUE OF SCIENCE
AND THE AMBIGUITY OF SEX

What we see in monkeys and apes, indeed, in all of nonhuman animal life, is in large part a function of how we see ourselves. Monkeys and apes, or nonhuman primates, are for us convenient surfaces on which to scribble visions of human nature. They become blank screens for us because they occupy a special place in scientific discussions of human sexuality. According to Darwinian evolutionary theory, apes and monkeys are human beings' nearest living relatives in the animal kingdom, and therefore their anatomy, genetics, biochemistry, and behavior are thought to be able to cast some light on human behavior as it existed at the dawn of humanity.

In consequence, monkeys and apes have also occupied a special place in the popular imagination of the West as examples of what human nature would be without benefit of culture. There are three versions of this "pure" human nature. In one, we, like apes and monkeys, are driven by instinct to be lascivious, violent, and anarchic King Kongs. In the second, monkeys, apes, and human beings are impelled by their sexual biology, in which males are innately promiscuous, possessive, and aggressive, and females are innately monogamous, nurturing, and submissive. And, in the third, we are all biologically programmed to "pair-bond," to create the monogamous, heterosexual nuclear family.

These ideas, deep in the popular imagination, find their way into the scientific imagination through the theory of biological determinism, a line of thought that for the last century has influenced all Western secular thinking. This theory holds that biology is destiny, that biology is both the cause of and the pattern for behavior. Although biological determinism rejects the first, crude King Kong version of human nature, it has overtly or covertly put great stock in the second and third versions. According to "sociobiology," the leading school of biological determinism, male and female, each with inborn characteristics, behave as they do because innate sexual and reproductive differences are connected to other inborn differences in behavior and psychology. Males and females are biologically programmed to ensure that their genes live on in the next generation. Males do this by promiscuously spreading their seed, females by latching onto males to support them and their offspring. For different motives, then, each contributes to the reproduction of the human species.

However, biological determinism is not entirely "objective." Upon examination, the pure, natural, cultureless creatures depicted by biological determinism bear a remarkable resemblance to the roles expected of men and women in our own culture. Biological determinism transforms the Western cultural and psychological patterns for masculinity, femininity, and the family into biological givens by linking them to hormones and reproductive anatomy. Because the biological factors are genetically determined, the variable sexualities and social forms of nonhuman primates and human beings come to seem as fixed as the amino acids that make up DNA.

Ever since feminist scholars began to reexamine the evidence on monkeys, apes, and human beings, however, the story began to change. Feminism proceeds from the anthropological assumption that what is considered most natural by Western culture—the structuring of personal life, reproduction and childrearing, love, and sexuality by the patriarchal, heterosexual nuclear family—is in fact most cultural and therefore alterable. As feminist politics legitimated women's complaints about their second-class citizenship, women began to examine their own lives and wonder how to change them. Feminist scholars, many of whom found greater acceptance in academia, began to study the position of women from many different disciplines.

Feminists who were anthropologists, among the first to study alternative arrangements for family, sexuality, and gender in different cultures, influenced the work of those anthropologists studying nonhuman primates. Feminists who became primatologists, now informed by the new skepticism about the universality of male dominance in nonhuman primates as well as in human beings, demolished the conventional assumptions of female passivity, maternalism, and powerlessness. Their work demonstrates the centrality of females to primate social life, as well as an enormous range in male and female behavior.

Research on apes and monkeys by feminists reveals great variation in male dominance. In some nonhuman primate groups, males are dominant, in others they are not. The Ethiopian hamadryas baboons live in harems presided over by a dominant, jealous male who does not permit other males to mate with the submissive females. Among the Ethiopian gelada baboons, however, the closely related females who comprise the harems will unite to attack the dominant male should he try to dominate one of them. And rhesus monkeys, studied in North America and elsewhere, have equal dominance because of the separate but equal male and female hierarchies that structure their communities. Each troop is composed of females born within it and males from other troops who have been accepted by the females. Because males leave their natal community at puberty to form new troops as adults, adult females are the center of the community and organize food collecting.

The studies show that sexual behavior and family are also diverse. Some species of apes and monkeys are primarily monogamous, others are not. Gibbons form lifelong monogamous pairs and are the core unit of their communities. Among the rhesus, both sexes have many partners, and females mate freely both with males of their own troops and with those who roam alone. The mating patterns of African chimpanzees vary, as does the timing of intercourse, depending on the rank not only of the male but of the female as well. A female may choose one sexual partner and refuse others. Some females may engage in brief consortships, at times mating regularly with one particular partner. They have also been known to stop even in the middle of intercourse, simply pulling away from the male.

Feminists' research indicates as well that nonhuman primates, both male and female, can be both aggressive and cooperative. Orangutans typify the stereotypes of male aggressivity and female submissiveness since they are the only known species of nonhuman primates in which males have raped females. On the other hand, female chimpanzees, like males, sometimes commit infanticide. Among the Ethiopian gelada baboons, males fight with each other, but so do females, who compete to be socially closer to their harem leader and who edge each other out to secure a coveted morsel or to control a feeding site.

In fact, feminist-inspired research on apes and monkeys has revised ideas about primate aggressiveness altogether. Monkeys and apes cooperate as much as they squabble, compete, and kill. The community, for all but solitary species like the orangutan, is generally the unit of survival. Among chimpanzees, both males and females in the social group offer protection, nurturing, and education for the young, and the sharing of food, feelings, and companionship.

The same revisionist process is taking place in all scholarly disciplines. As feminists have begun to study women, they have uncovered a world either unknown or trivialized as unworthy of serious study. Feminists investigating the history of Western women—including women of color as well as white women—have documented the wide range of women's work, their artistic achievements of lasting merit, their community service and political activism, and their sexual and nonsexual intimacies with other women. Anthropologists have discovered cross-cultural variation not only in women's roles but in forms of patriarchy as well, revealing that, for example, women tend to have more power in cultures in which they contribute to economic production as well as domestic work.

Feminist psychologists have been reevaluating patriarchal stereotypes of gender. The femininity once caricatured as overly emotional and involved with others is now characterized as rich and complex, even in some respects healthier than the excessive differentiation encouraged in men, which often leads to emotional isolation and numbness. Furthermore, instead of the moral shallowness formerly attributed to women, feminist psychologists find many of them expressing an underground cultural morality. While men tend to articulate an absolutist morality of individual rights in which the central moral problem of adulthood is how to realize one's individual interests without interfering with those of others, women often voice a morality of responsibility in which the principal adult dilemma is how to live morally by being responsible to both oneself and others.

Finally, the field of feminist writing brings "the personal is political" theme into scholarship. Feminist biographers, for example, are inventing a new form in which the author engages with the subject as though in a dialogue of friendship. The relation of biographer to subject, indeed, of Subject to Subject, informs the biography. The exploration of the subject becomes a discovery of self, which in turn leads back to the subject, as well as to the revelation of women's experience and history altogether.

The feminist perspective is, however, no more "objective" than any other. Indeed, the feminist critique of the patriarchal bias of traditional science and scholarship dovetails with the debate about the nature of scientific knowledge that has been taking place in the course of the twentieth century. Social criticism of science, impelled in part by recent scientific breakthroughs and in part by the political radicalism of the 1960s, suggests so thoroughgoing an influence of culture on scientific theory and method as to cast doubt on traditional canons of truth. Science appears to be not the source of universal, value-free truth but the result of what scientists, living and working in particular epochs, say that science is. Furthermore, the revolutions in physical theory, notably those of relativity and quantum mechanics, suggest that no one theory, perhaps not even theory itself, is capable of completely and accurately representing reality. While the practical success of science indicates that there is some truth to scientific method and theory, the scientific claim for a one-to-one correspondence between theory and reality is no longer tenable. Other theories, as yet unknown or unrecognized, can reveal new truths and so change old ones, as well as alter our understanding of how and why the scientific enterprise itself works.

Feminist theory pushes this debate further with a specific critique not only of *what* scientists see but of *how* they see. It characterizes Western science by both its cultural and its gendered biases. Western science assumes that the scientist is an "I" coming to know an "it," that is, a detached, masculinized person knowing a feminized reality. This sharp distinction between self and other that typifies the traditional scientific mode of knowing the world not only suits the character style prescribed for men. It also fits into a culture of omnipotence in which the ideal human being is the self-as-individual, disconnected from others, and in which mastery of the world is the prime cultural goal and value. Traditional Western science thereby creates a kind of knowledge that, in its interest in the "I," the scientific self, disregards the interests of the other, the "thing." At the same time, its pretense to universal truth and value-free neutrality has been instrumental in the destruction of the earth, which is presently threatened by industrial pollution and potential nuclear holocaust.

Feminist scholarship, making use of its own discoveries about gender psychology, contrasts the traditionally scientific point of view to the one inherent in relatedness. Relatedness encourages a conviction that reality comes to be known by our engagement with it, not our removal from it. The observer is a separate person who connects actively and even, in imagination, empathically, with the subject matter. Such a relation of knower to known shows up in the work of the recent Nobel laureate in medicine, geneticist Barbara McClintock, which proceeded, as she described it, by her attempt to imagine herself as if she were inside the cells she was studying. Nor is she alone in demonstrating the importance of the nonrational, associative, even mystical processes to scientific research. Other, male scientists have occasionally reported their own nonrational approach to science. What the feminist critique suggests is that, although such processes may be common, their disfavor as second-class, feminized ways of knowing prevents their acknowledgment and absorption into the canons of scientific method.

The "objectivity" of orthodox science, based on the impersonal detachment between knower and known and claiming to generate universal truth, begins to appear not so much impossible as false. All science is a form of engagement. As so far practiced, it is an unintentionally masculinized mode of knowing the world, done as the self-as-individual might do it, valuing firm boundaries between self and other and devaluing the connections between them. Ignoring the interaction between knower and known, as well as the effect of the knower on the known, it consequently disregards the resultant indeterminacy of truth. Indeed, the epistemological revolution in twentieth-century physics makes this precise point, that the particular perspective of the observer necessarily changes, or may even create, the data.

Engaged feminist scholarship itself exemplifies the dialectical nature of how human beings come to know the world. Feminist research necessarily comes up with results that change the world of sex and gender as we know it. Coupled with the political force of affirmative action, feminist scholarship justifies and paves the way for alterations in private and public life. Informed by the insights of feminist psychological research, heterosexual and homosexual couples have begun to revise traditional breadwinning and nurturing roles, providing their children with alternative role models for mothering and fathering. Now that the history of women's participation in public as well as private life has been demonstrated, their presence in scholarly disciplines as well as in the arts has become more acceptable, even though they must still battle against sexist prejudices and behavior. In ideal theory, if not always in practice, then, the world of men and women looks different now than it did twenty years ago, in part because what we have learned about it has changed what we think it ought to be and how we sometimes behave in it. Therefore, when next we study it, what we learn will be different.

The feminist critique suggests that truth is not absolute but multiple, partial, and ambiguous. Indeed, the scientific insistence on omnipotence and absolute truth may have heretofore precluded our understanding of the indeterminacy inherent in human sexual arrangements. In the West, we turn to nonhuman primates in search of absolute answers about our own complex, variable, and therefore ambiguous sexuality, supposing that, even though nurture varies, nature holds eternal truths. What we find, however, is more ambiguity. Monkeys and apes, like human beings, live in the context of social institutions and patterned communication and can and must learn social rules in order to survive. Their behavior, while more fixed at birth than is the case with human beings, is nevertheless quite flexible. Indeed, the variability is so great that it provides evidence to prove almost any proposition about human nature. The primate heritage, then, offers no final answers, only an array of variation, choice, and change.

The inherently ambiguous nature of sex and gender emerges from the primate capacity to symbolize, to endow experience with meaning. This ability, rudimentary in nonhuman primates, develops into a qualitatively different phenomenon among human beings. To be sure, monkeys and apes exhibit signs of merriment and sadness and can shriek not only in adults' defense of territory but in youngsters' mock fighting. If the meaning of their sexual emotions were entirely dependent on reproductive biology, sexual intercourse would be restricted to estrus, they would neither masturbate nor have homosexual encounters, and females would be unable to exercise choice when approached by males for sex.

Among human beings, however, sexuality becomes essentially free of biological determinants. Human beings, in contrast to nonhuman primates, can weave an extraordinarily intricate net of cultural and psychological meaning that makes their sexuality into a multidimensional source of pleasure, pain, and confusion. The irrevocable severing of human sexuality from reproduction, brought about by the cessation of estrus, allows sex to be shaped by culture and informed by the twists and turns of psychological fantasy.

Sex is therefore a zone of freedom. But the price of freedom is ambiguity. The meaning that human beings can create out of their experience enables them to turn sex into a means of expression as well as a means of satisfaction. Sexual behavior can be a way of doing something with someone else, to someone else, or by oneself; it can be, as well, a form of communication, companionship, or withdrawal. Sex can take place for purposes of procreation or recreation, in love and in hate, out of tenderness and out of cruelty. Sex can become a personal and political play-ground and, sometimes, a battleground as well.

Kathy leans back in her chair. "I have a question. When human beings evolved and estrus stopped, that made a big change, didn't it?"

"I was thinking the same thing," chimes in Rosa. "Without estrus, human females are continuously available for sex, unlike even the most, shall we say, liberated chimpanzees."

We all laugh.

Mason, with characteristic West Indian gallantry, objects. "Ah, but excuse me, ladies. I do not follow. It has not been my experience that women are always sexually available. Indeed, it seems to me that, without hormonal imperatives, choice becomes more than possible. I would say that it becomes necessary."

I add, "As necessary as the cultural framing for it." I can always rely on Mason's perspicacity. "However, given that choice is necessary in human sexuality, don't you think it's odd that rape is so common in human life? It's found in every known culture. To be sure, it is not as frequent in other societies as it is in ours. But still, it's universal. Even with the social reforms that have given women more economic power, rape is an ever-present danger."

"So what's so bad about that?" asks Joe. "I'd rape someone if she was pretty." He looks at Dennis and laughs; a few other students, female as well as male, join him.

But Mason and a couple of other men are silent, a number of women exclaim loudly, and Kathy fairly leaps out of her seat. "Rape isn't about sex," she exclaims, "it's about violence. It has nothing to do with anyone being pretty, and grandmothers of eighty-three get raped, you male chauvinist pig."

Joe, outnumbered, looks down at his desk.

"Is it that simple? Aren't women sometimes provocative?" Leave it to Rosa to ask the hard questions.

"I suppose that must happen occasionally," I respond cautiously. "But to use that as the sole explanation is to blame the victim, to make women responsible for their own subordination. Let me say just a few words about this to close the class. You don't, by the way, have to worry about what I'm going to discuss for this exam, but it will be on the final."

Felice, who was starting to fold up her notebook, keeps it open and looks up attentively.

THE MYTH OF THE EVER-READY FEMALE

Rape occurs in every known culture. Among the !Kung San of the Kalahari Desert in Africa, it seems to be an infrequent act of individual passion. In other cultures, it is possibly a more common, socially structured fate. Among the Mundurucú of the Brazilian Amazon, the woman who walks alone outside the confines of her village is automatically thought to be on her way to an assignation and is therefore held to have made herself available for any male who observes her departure and wishes to take advantage of it. In still other cultures, like the Cheyenne of Wyoming, gang rape is an institutionalized punishment for women who indiscreetly cuckold their husbands. However, because cultural conventions vary so much and because rape, like sex, has been so little studied outside our own culture, it is difficult to say anything binding about its political meanings, much less about its personal significance in different cultures.

In our culture, rape is a crime in which the victim is frequently presumed to be at least a co-conspirator, if not at times the sole guilty party. It epitomizes women's status as Subject-as-Object. It is an act that presumes that men have both desire and choice and that women have, on the one hand, the same capacity as men to act on their desire and, on the other, neither desire nor the possibility of realizing it. Rape incorporates both erotic and aggressive wishes. And it represents patriarchy, for it is a nonreciprocal act of power: Since it can take place only if a man is aroused, its threat becomes a means by which men control women and by which women, in fear of it, come to control themselves.

Rape is as ambiguous as any act that involves the reproductive and sexual organs. Technically, it is the forcible penile penetration of a woman's orifices—vagina, mouth, anus. Its psychological and social meanings, causes, and effects are far more difficult to decipher. It has been described in terms of innate male aggressiveness and innate female submissiveness. Rape has also been explained by the fact of greater male musculature, ascribed to men's economic and political deprivation or to their fear of women's mysterious life-giving capacities, linked with women's sexual provocation, or interpreted as resulting from men's genetically or psychologically induced madness.

Although no sane person would approve of rape, sympathy for the victim is often very mixed. When a woman is raped and tells, she is often presumed guilty until proven innocent. Her word is in doubt because the question of consent arises. The first thought in the minds of the police and others is that she might have participated in the assault. They wonder whether or not she, like the woman who is street-hassled, "asked for it." If she is raped by a boyfriend or husband, it is thought that she might have, in some way, agreed to or provoked the assault. If she is raped by a stranger, it is thought that she may have put herself in a situation where such violence might happen. If she lacks bruises as evidence of her resistance, she is suspected of complicity. Nevertheless, should she injure or kill her assailant, she is liable to prosecution.

The suspicion that women participate in their own victimization by rape emerges from the ambiguous status that women occupy in our culture, the Subject-as-Object. This status is validated by the notion of "the ever-ready female." According to this unconscious cultural notion, women are ever-ready for sex; they are eternally receptive to male sexual initiative. Whenever men are ready with their erections, women's legs are spread invitingly. And all that needs to happen next is penetration and ejaculation, for sex, in this view, is simply about procreation. Pleasure has nothing to do with this activity; should males enjoy penetration and ejaculation, that is but a fortunate side effect. The clitoris and, by implication, women's eroticism, do not and need not exist at all.

The "ever-ready female" is a cultural myth given legitimacy by science. According to biological determinism, continuous female sexual "receptivity" is essential to human survival. Because human females do not go into estrus, there are no reliably visible or palpable signs that they are fertile. Because ovulation and sexual receptivity are not necessarily coincident, the birth of a new generation requires that intercourse be possible at any time. In order for this to obtain, women must be available for sexual intercourse all the time. They should, in fact, be ready whenever men are, since, although ejaculation is necessary for reproduction, it is only as predictable as the penile erection, which is about as predictable as female desire—of which the myth takes no account at all.

The myth of the ever-ready female is not science but a buttress for male desire. It portrays sex as an act in which one thing goes into something else, and depicts women as empty holes waiting for something to go into them whenever it wants. It is true that the vagina is a cavity that an erect penis is capable of penetrating. But, just as men are not erect penises, so women are not vaginas. And sex is not a matter of cylindrical objects entering receptive round holes. In the absence of estrus, human sexual activity requires the catalyst of desire, which is what makes penile and clitoral erections possible.

But desire requires form, which is in turn given by the interaction of culture and psychology. Even among nonhuman primates, nonestrus sex does not take place without what would be called consent among human beings. If nonhuman primates can sometimes choose when and with whom they will have sex, and if they can, at will, stop in the middle, then even more so can human females. For sex to take place among human beings, there must be not only desire but choice. Women are not continuously receptive or available. Sometimes they want sex, sometimes they don't, and, when they do, they choose either to act on their desire or to ignore it. Without women's choice, what looks like sex is really rape.

The myth of the ever-ready female, utilizing the ambiguity of sex to justify rape and thereby blame women for their own victimization, embodies the central contradiction for women in our culture. The yawning female hole is a double symbol, signifying both voracious desire and its frigid absence. In other words, women insatiably want "it" all the time, and, simultaneously, they do not want anything at all. And—or but—in a final twist, the hole severs male desire from male responsibility. Always desiring, women become all desire. They become, once again, the Subject-as-Object, the one in charge who is not in charge. Since women are in charge of desire, they are the ones to make choices about it. But since objects can neither take charge nor make choices, they can be raped. And when they are raped the responsibility for it can be laid at their feet.

Whatever its individual psychological motivations, rape is a political act rationalized by the myth of the ever-ready female. The culturally accepted possibility of rape provides men in general with a fantasy of potency that is comforting in the face of the disappointing limits to power in a culture demanding an impossible omnipotence. Although most men do not rape, some do, and not all of them are strangers. Just under half of all female college students raped were attacked by men they knew—first dates, casual dates, or romantic acquaintances. But to those men who have never raped in fact or fantasy, rape represents mastery in a society asking them to be the self-sufficient individual yet requiring them to be dependent on others for their well-being. Reciprocally, rape keeps women under control in a system in which their power is less than men's. Its threat to bodily integrity and self-respect not only serves to control women but gets them to control themselves. If women must always be in fear of rape, then they must always be on guard, wondering, when attacked, whether or not it was their faulty grasp on the leash of their own passions that caused someone else's desire to escape control.

Rape, key to maintaining women as the Subject-as-Object, thereby maintains social hierarchy altogether. It represents domination and subordination in the language of heterosexual violence. It embodies the powerful, masculinized "I" dominating the weak, feminized "it" that crops up in both street hassling and conventional Western science. Even the rape of men by men makes use of this symbolic linchpin of domination, which is the reason it can play a central and even ritualized role in establishing power relations among men, gay or straight, in prison. We do not yet know the significance of rape in every culture. Nor can we predict whether any given individual will commit a rape. But it is certain that, as long as hierarchy exists, there will be social institutions to buttress it. And as long as hierarchy is founded on patriarchy—and the two may be coextensive—rape will be one of those institutions.

The students are getting up, shuffling their papers. There is no need for me to say that the class is over.

"Remember," I shout, "the exam will be on Monday, right after the break. Have a good vacation."

Power and Sex
(11:00 A.M.)

*D*ennis stops at my desk while I'm putting my notes back into the folder. He presses my elbow lightly. "That was a good class."

My lower abdomen contracts against a pleasurable but still unwelcome quickening, and for a moment I feel as though I'm being street-hassled.

What is he doing? I ask myself in some anger. *He's giving me a new variety of apple for the teacher, I suppose.*

"How thoughtful of you to say so," I reply, raising one eyebrow and hoping that I do not appear as off-balance as I feel.

"This sudden praise wouldn't have anything to do with the exam, would it?" I smile lightly.

He grins suddenly, then as quickly sobers up. "Hey, you know I wouldn't do anything like that. I just really learned a lot from the lecture today. So have a nice vacation, Professor."

"You too, Dennis." I watch him as he scoots out.

This would be funny if it weren't so annoying. What's weird, though, and even pathetic, is that he seems to be unaware that this seductive ploy is likely to backfire. He's made me angry by trying to butter me up in the first place. And he's made me even angrier by presuming on me. When I get angry at students, I want to retaliate, which I can do very easily by grading harshly. But then I am inclined to bend over backward to be fair, which makes me even more prone to be severe in the matter of grades.

It's all a vicious cycle, really. They have to flatter you because you've got the power; and you in turn have to push them away, so they try even harder. Or else you reward them by giving them better grades than they may deserve and thereby teaching them that they were right to suck up to you in the first place.

I take the elevator this time and go straight to my office, where Sojourner Truth, the former slave who became an abolitionist and feminist, greets me from the poster on the front of my door. I unlock the door and go inside.

At my desk, I lean back in my chair and rub my fatigued eyes thinking with outrage, *He really went beyond the pale. Imagine, touching my arm like that.*

My conscience asks, *Now is this really such a big deal? One student tries to flatter your middle-aging self, and it wipes you out.*

To be sure, there were girls I knew who had played similar tricks. Lisa, a senior in my dorm during my first year at college, had devised what seemed to me an effective plan for gaining her history professor's favor. Lisa was a bohemian, and when she wasn't in blue jeans it was because she was in black leotards (except when she was in bed with her boyfriends, when she was naked). However, in anticipation of a term-paper conference for which she had done no preparation (having spent the semester practicing her Martha Graham dances and drinking beer), she put on a dress. "After all," she instructed me about her teacher, "he's a man."

I felt very ambivalent about Lisa's strategy. I was extremely impressed with her daring and hardheaded use of sexuality, but

I also believed that women shouldn't have to resort to such transparently manipulative schemes to succeed. I believed in honesty and accountability no matter what the cost.

Or, at least, I thought I did. But, as I think back, I remember one or two occasions when, much to my astonishment and against my will, I found myself crying in a professor's office over a paper I couldn't finish, and other moments when, in speaking to them and other authority figures, I would smile cutely and in other ways act like a little girl.

Maybe it would have been better to be like Lisa, aware that manipulation was possible and necessary. I bet she felt more in charge that way—and had a lot more fun besides.

WOMEN AND HIERARCHY

Women have sought equality in the public domain and have found instead that their battle against second-class citizenship continues. Many have wanted, and have achieved, the opportunity not only to earn a living but to have careers, to become powerful in public life. And many, believing that they were "as good as men," have longed for the chance to prove it. Yet whatever the degree of their success, they have often found, to their surprise, disappointment or anger, that their gender remains a factor in how others treat them and in how they treat themselves. Realizing that they are at the bottom of a hierarchy the top of which they cannot reach, they discover that the self-interest they pursue eludes them.

In seeking equality with men, women have tried to act as men are supposed to act in the business world. They work hard, tailoring their lives to the career plans they make and, sometimes, sacrificing personal life. They are hard-nosed and put self-interest above all other values. They strategize, taking clients out to power-lunches, where they make business deals. They compete, edging others out as they jockey for promotion. In professional meetings, they bluff, stand their ground, and win their points. And, like men, they dress for the part. They have modified the masculine sartorial code to make it their own, wearing "dress-for-success" suits of gray, burgundy, or black, feminizing them just a little but not too much with pretty ties, high heels, and matching briefcases.

Women who make this effort have succeeded to varying degrees. Women have become lawyers, stockbrokers, account executives, doctors, professors, engineers, corporate executives, and public officials. Some have achieved prominent places in the communications industry, anchoring television news programs, directing movies, writing books and columns. Some have started their own businesses. In many cases, they have power over other people; some have their own employees, others manage departments, still others have secretaries who type, file, make appointments, and shop for them. Many earn handsome salaries and travel extensively.

At the same time, however, women on career tracks have begun to suffer the stresses afflicting men in similar positions. All women who work for wages show signs of physical and emotional strain resembling those that men experience as a result of the objectification of the workplace. As women dedicate themselves to financial ambitions and/or professional achievement, they begin to display many of the symptoms of workaholism. They smoke and drink too much. They have mysterious physical ailments and feel emotionally depleted. Personal life may often become unknown, even frightening, territory, and as a result they turn all the more hungrily to their work. They act and feel as though they had no insides, no inner life at all.

Nor have they been entirely prepared for this venture. While men may anticipate the lack of emotional nurturing characteristic of public life, women may become distressed, if not disoriented and angry, because of it. Because the self-as-individual is an emotional style that can smother feeling, it can damp the longings for and expectations of care that relatedness kindles. Women, especially those middle- and upper-class women whose mothers did not do paid work outside the home, may find it difficult to grow the emotional calluses so commonly developed by men as part of their preparation for an adulthood lived largely in public.

Moreover, even though women have now shown that they can be as smart and successful as men are expected to be in the public world of work and power, their femininity has not become the neutral factor they hoped it would. Rather, it continues to be significant, even if only in subtle ways. Sometimes they are reminded of it by specifically work-related incidents, as when professional newswomen find that their panel on "Women in Broadcasting" is scheduled, at a broadcasters' convention, so that it will be heard not by other professionals but by the newsmen's wives. Women who are surgeons find in some hospitals that they have to scrub with the nurses, the doctors' scrub room being reserved for doctors, that is, men. And, in the academic world, there are still instances when the scholarly achievements of women scheduled for promotion are far more severely judged than those of male competitors or when research on women is considered to be inferior to that on other topics.

Even when women are not discriminated against in the work to which they are assigned, the conditions under which they must carry it out, or the criteria used to evaluate it, the subterranean belief remains that under their clothes they are, after all, only sexual beings, just like all the other women with whom they are categorized or closeted. It is as if their hard work and seriousness were held to be but garments that are donned and removed. This belief in women's essentially sexual nature is the reason that women must take as many pains with their everyday appearance as if they were dressing for a Saturday night date. It is also the reason that the sartorial dilemma is far more perplexing for women than for men. Men's mistakes in attire say nothing about their masculinity but are chalked up to ineptitude or, should they have otherwise proved themselves, to quirks of character.

Women's mistakes are, in contrast, volatile. While women are expected and often want to play up their sexuality on Saturday night, they must neutralize it during the week. Yet they are equally threatening if they appear to be sexually unavailable. Women must therefore tread a thin line between excessive and insufficient interest in men. If a woman errs in the first direction, she is assumed to be making a sexual invitation; some men may even take her up on it and, should she complain about sexual harassment, will argue that she had asked for it—just like the woman who is raped. On the other hand, if she adopts too masculine a style that includes no insignia of femininity at all, she will be considered to be a lesbian, secretly ridiculed, and subtly ostracized. Neither consequence is of much use to her career.

Femininity remains a hidden influence on women's progress in public life because, although there is a strong belief in our culture that every person has an equal opportunity to rise to the top, women are permanently at the bottom of a hierarchy. Like the other principal hierarchies in our society—class, race, religion, ethnicity, and sexual preference—the gender hierarchy distributes power and privilege not only unequally but relatively permanently. Some hierarchies permit more mobility than others. Although most people tend to stay in or near the class into which they were born, some manage to travel, in their lifetimes, from bottom to top of the class hierarchy or from top to bottom. Most people, at least in public, manage to get to and remain at the top of the sexual hierarchy; they are at least nominally heterosexual, whatever homosexual or other predilections appear in their fantasies or in the privacy of their personal lives. Many people have been known to change their religion in their efforts at upward mobility. And ethnicity can sometimes be disguised by alterations of name and accent.

In contrast, the hierarchy of gender, like that of race, permits very little mobility at all. Since sex, like skin color, is difficult to disguise, the stigma it confers moderates only slightly according to how much money or political power one acquires. To be sure, some women are better off than others, because sometimes hierarchies overlap, and gradations of power within them are created. Upper-class women, for example, are wealthier and therefore can satisfy their material desires more easily than other women. White women have "skin privilege" and therefore are less discriminated against in the workplace than nonwhite women. Heterosexual women have more sexual privilege than lesbians, who must usually keep their sexual preference hidden. And women who achieve positions of management have power over women who are their subordinates.

Yet, just as well-to-do black men and women can receive discriminatory treatment anywhere they go, so women of any color who secure public power continue to be insecure on the street, facing the same risks as any other woman who walks home alone at night. This permanent hierarchy is the reason that even a woman who runs for the vice-presidency will be patronized, rather than straightforwardly confronted, by her male competitors and will be badgered by the press and the public about her family's supposed faults.

Given that women are therefore permanent underlings, they must frequently resort to manipulation. Manipulation is one customary way that people in general, and those subordinate to others in particular, acquire, maintain, or increase their power. Manipulation proves effective because financial and political power do not always provide a sense of personal power. Those at the top of business or governmental hierarchies often have irrational soft spots; they may be insecure about the opinions of other people or highly vulnerable to sexual advances. Irrationality pervades the public domain even though it is officially banished from it, as well as from the masculine character demanded by it. Feelings such as pity, compassion, greed, lust, vanity, and arrogance, which motivate both those in power and those who want to replace them, are the chinks in the political armor. And manipulation takes advantage of them.

Yet, as necessary as it may be, manipulation can endanger women seeking power. Since anything women do is likely to be read for its hidden sexual meanings, they have to think very carefully about whether and how to use their sexuality. While a student who bares her legs in a conference with a male professor risks only the short-term consequences of either failing to influence him or, at worst, earning his contempt, a woman who uses her sexuality manipulatively on her job risks professional or financial disaster. Certainly there are women who fuck their way to positions of power, but, should their strategy become public knowledge, they are likely to lose the very positions they have gained; at best, their personal lives provide the raw material for public gossip. A safer, desexualized, and not uncommon strategy is to comport onself like a little girl, in effect, like a daughter, a ploy that has the advantage of sometimes being useful with women as well as with men. Charming smiles and tears judiciously shed in business meetings may win more points and arguments for women then the bullying power plays with which men often triumph.

Women's use of manipulation has not only conscious and rational motives. Since women are brought up in patriarchy, their sexual and little-girl ploys tend to be lodged in their unconscious and to show up in their behavior willy-nilly. For example, from conversations between their parents, girls can observe and absorb the way women work the gender hierarchy to their advantage. They see that men are often able to dominate conversations by constantly interrupting and that women tend to cede control by such habits as ending declarative statements with a questioning tone. But they also observe how women solve this problem. Sometimes women protest it. Sometimes they walk out on it. Or, with apparent docility or flirtatious grace, they can act the loser and thereby become the winner. Allowing the conversation to proceed normally, they may appear to give ground while waiting for the appropriate moments at which to make points that will further their goal, whether it be to win the argument or to get the man to do something they want him to do. From these lessons, girls learn similar strategies that as adults they can use to circumvent those with power over them. The power they thus exercise might not be first-class, but it gets them what they want.

The necessity to manipulate, the traditional mark of women's supposedly inferior abilities, turns out to be in fact a sign of the universal elusiveness of power in the public domain. Instead of leading to independence, power demands subordinations of its own. Success requires unrelentingly hard work that frequently becomes an addiction replacing the pleasure deferred. The corporate chief, male or female, is as much a creature of the profit margin as the secretary who must obey her superiors. Rich or poor—it is better to be rich. But, in work life, we are as manipulated by our goals as we are by our efforts to manipulate others to achieve them. In the process, self-realization gets lost and self-respect becomes contaminated.

I rummage through my briefcase looking for the handwritten midterm, which I take to the main office where Ginny, the departmental secretary, is reading something on her desk. Ted is bent over her shoulder looking at it too. "Is it clear?" Rugged and dark-haired, Ted is fifty-nine, and his six-foot two-inch frame displays no middle-aged flab.

Ginny nods, her newly set hair glinting under the fluorescent lights. Her rimless, purple-tinted, initialed glasses slide down her nose, and she pushes them up with her index finger.

"Good. Thanks so much. No rush. After the vacation will do."

"And how many copies will you need, Professor Jones?"

"Fifteen. Sorry, I should have told you."

"Hi, Ted," I greet him as he walks toward the mailboxes.

"How are you? I haven't seen you in a long time. Say, those are great-looking boots."

"Oh, thanks very much. I'm well. But you look tired."

"Nah, I just finished correcting the galleys of the new book at two in the morning, that's all. Not that that would tire you out, being just a little bit younger than me." He smiles as he takes his mail.

After Dennis, I'm not in the mood for flirtation. I decide to keep the conversation on a professional level. "I'm just finishing a draft of that paper on 'Sexism and Authority in the Classroom.' I'd love for you to have a look at it when you've got some free time." Ted was my adviser in graduate school.

"Is that still a problem?" He flips through his mail.

So I tell him about Dennis.

He looks at me directly. "Ah, come off it. He's just a kid. Anyway, sometimes I think you girls, sorry, women, hate men."

"Sometimes I, we, do." Annoyed at him, I pull my own mail out of the box.

He offers me a cigarette. I shake my head. His blue eyes, with their gorgeous weathered crow's-feet, literally twinkle at me over the match he has lit. "So, what else is new? You shouldn't take it so personally. Women hate men, men hate women, and still we love each other."

I smile and duck my head, falling for his charm as I always do and feeling like a little girl. Then, recouping, I repeat, "So, will you read my paper?" But I wonder, as I ask, why I want him to.

"Sure, great, give it to me whenever." He looks at his battered watch and picks up his mail. "Gotta go. I've gotta get the galleys back to my publisher today."

I walk over to Ginny's desk. "Hi, how are you?"

"Oh, good morning, dear. Okay, I guess." She smiles, her face pale. "My father felt very bad this morning. I called the doctor but had to wait two hours to find out whether I should bring him in."

"Emphysema again?"

"Yes. And I can't get him to stop smoking. At eighty-one. Well, what can you do?" She inserts the diskettes and turns the word processor on.

I feel as if I'm standing on one foot. "If it's not too much trouble, I wonder, could you type up this midterm exam for me and run off sixty copies, please?"

Ginny continues to bring up the program, staring at the screen. Then she flips through her steno pad. She carefully positions it so that she can read it. She marks the place with her index finger and then finally looks up. "Well, I don't know. I'll see. . . ."

As usual, I stonewall her. She's supposed to work for all of us, damn it.

"Well, I can't have it for you until after the vacation," she says finally.

"Of course. I don't need it until then. Thanks a lot."

As I walk back to my office again, I converse with myself, trying to dispel my confusion. Why doesn't she want to type for me? Is it because I'm a woman? Does Ted get his exams typed because he's a man? Because he holds the Alexis de Tocqueville Chair of Social Science? Because he twinkles? Perhaps I don't speak to her with sufficient authority. I'm too hesitant. But that's because I feel guilty when I ask her to do my typing. It's like having a maid. How can you give orders to another woman if you think all women should be equal?

Thinking that all women are equal has made difficulties for me before, only that time I was the subordinate. I nearly destroyed my first opportunity to do independent graduate research with a woman. Since I usually felt about two feet tall with my other professors, I desperately hoped that Julia would treat me like a grown-up. So, when I made the first appointment to see her, I also made the mistake of treating her like the friend I wanted instead of the superior she was. I casually rejected her suggestions for time and place; one seemed too early, another too late, a third inconveniently located. Finally, she seemed to give in and proposed a midmorning time at a very accessible location. Shortly into our meeting, however, she told me how thoughtless and immature she'd found my behavior. Mortified, I somehow mustered a defense, demanding in turn to know why she had gone along with behavior she had so heartily disliked. She answered with a stammer I had never heard before and have never heard since: "Well, I, I, uh, I wanted to help."

RELATEDNESS AND REVOLUTION

Just as women are assumed to be simply sexual beings underneath their dress-for-success suits, so their authority is thought to be but a cover for their fundamentally nurturing tendencies. Unlike men in positions of power, to whom authority is granted first and only questioned should reasons later arise, women's authority is in some doubt from the start. The doubt exists because, even while they are in pursuit of self-interest, women are seen, and see themselves, as selves-in-relation, as responsible for the satisfaction of others' wants and needs. Consequently, their authority is not usually taken for granted. An authority, representing the clearly bounded adult self, must stand aloofly above others. In contrast, women's responsibility for others' welfare injects a discomfiting intimacy into hierarchy. If one is as interested in the other's well-being as in one's own, one cannot remain cool and remote, much less manipulate other people to one's own satisfaction.

As with the use of their sexual wiles, sometimes the obligation to nurture is thrust upon women by others, and sometimes they take it on themselves. Women who teach, like women who work in other social-service professions, discover that students and clients will ask for, indeed expect, the sort of altruistic understanding of their situations they would never ask of men. Students may, for example, ignore rules of deference and behave familiarly: A woman who teaches may find herself physically intruded upon not only by a male student who takes advantage of his gender-privilege to invade her privacy but by a female student who, assuming that she is on an equal footing with her professor, puts her arm around her in comradeship or otherwise asks for friendly treatment.

And, intentionally or not, women often find themselves compliant with these demands because, feeling obligated to look after the needs of others, they feel guilty when they do not. They may even initiate the nurturing themselves, notwithstanding any disadvantage to their own best interests. Women researchers may offer advice and share information with colleagues who are, as well, their competitors. Women executives or professionals may be reluctant to add to the burdens of those who are supposed to work for them, such as secretaries, and who, reciprocally, expect their female bosses to nurture.

Pursued by relatedness as she pursues self-interest, a woman may never feel quite entitled to her authority. The existence of authority depends on dominance and subordination. Someone in a position of authority cannot occupy it unless there is someone in a lower status looking up, perhaps in respect, perhaps in fear, but certainly in obedience. Since power over others contradicts relatedness, the woman in a position of power may suffer an inner conflict that shows up in feeling fraudulent. She may feel that she does not belong where she is. But, since she is where she wants to be, she does not know where else to go.

In pursuit of a solution to this dilemma, she may look outside herself for confirmation that she belongs in the position of power she has achieved. Her sense of security may increase if she believes herself to be special. If there are no other women in her position, then it may be inferred that she is no ordinary woman. As a token woman, she seems to be more like a man, more of a self-as-individual and less of a self-in-relation than other women. Honored by the men who allow her into their club, she is therefore uniquely entitled to her power. Or she may feel more legitimate if she has the same perquisites as men in her position, such as secretarial help, an expense account, a corner office.

However, for the same reasons that she wants to be a token, her female secretary may be unwilling to recognize her authority. A female secretary may not only expect her female boss to be nurturing but may feel demeaned by having to work for a woman. Like the domestic servant whose status rises with that of her employer, so women, like men, take their prestige from their superiors. Under these circumstances, many people will find it better to work for a man than for a woman.

The pervasive, personal uneasiness often experienced by women who seek power is the symptom of a political pathology. Women's discomfort emerges from and represents a fundamental social and moral conflict between the egalitarian ideals of our culture and the realities of "the state." The state, the political structure of our society, is so fundamental to our way of life as to define it. Power within the state is premised on a scarcity of power, the bulk of which belongs to a top-heavy government operating in the interests of the society's wealthiest classes and protected by a robotlike bureaucracy. Power within the state has two primary, complementary, and sometimes interchangeable sources: wealth and the power of political decision making. A secondary but occasionally interchangeable source is "privilege," the socially endowed ability, based on the perceived right to define one's self, to command respect from others; in its extreme, privilege takes the form of celebrity.

In our culture, some people have much power and therefore great sway over how the society is run while others have little or no influence over the running of society and therefore over the course of their lives. Power, unlike kinship, is not awarded equally at birth. Some inherit it. Others acquire it by work, their wits, luck, or ruthlessness. Many never have access to power at all, for want of social position, inheritance, will, or ability. And, since power within the state is structured pyramidically, only those few people near the top are truly powerful at any given time.

In the context of the state, individualizing and relatedness become contradictory ways of being. Since individualizing takes place in a public world of scarce power and permanent hierarchy, the self can be realized only at the other's expense. To be "as good as men" in this context, to be the Subject in such a world, is to objectify others. Individualizing therefore necessarily entails not only self-interest, self-sufficiency, and singularity but selfishness, greed, and the wish to dominate. And these values, however contradictory they might seem, typify public adult life.

Relatedness, in contrast, occurs in the domestic place that is supposed to provide a refuge from the impersonal scrappings inflicted by the public domain. Its delivery of personalized care for the particular desires of particular people seems, as if in deliberate opposition to the public domain, to offer the true self-realization that people want, need, and seek. Indeed, relatedness appears to champion the idea that everyone, having equal worth, ought to have an equal share of power. Its insistence that the satisfaction of one person's wants and needs is contingent on others' satisfaction becomes an argument for generosity and altruism.

The antipathy between public individualizing and private relatedness can amplify women's feelings of fraudulence. Women who are at ease with the values contained in relatedness may feel like poseurs when they seek public power. They may feel constrained to treat those subordinate to them as equals, especially other women. Teachers who are reluctant to be unfair may allow students to impose on them. Identifying with another woman lower in the hierarchy, an executive may go out of her way to help an assistant to climb the management ladder, even at the cost of her own power or self-esteem. These wishes to ensure the satisfaction of others' desires can therefore interfere with women's own individualizing interests.

Yet, in a public world in which power is scarce and inequality abundant, relatedness is revolutionary. Functioning as a critique of hierarchy and greed, it is potentially subversive of the normal, objectifying order. No matter what the individual differences between self and other, relatedness asks that the other's needs and wants be regarded at least on a par with those of the self. Indeed, it makes those very differences cardinal. Its focus on the particularity of individual desires is the direct opposite of objectification. It criticizes the social rules that allow people to become the means to others' ends, to become the desire-less objects of others' desire. Relatedness expresses an underground cultural fantasy. It places a demand on public, political life, asking that people no longer be exploited as though they were objects. It articulates the wish that each of us could be the full subject that our culture promises, and says that this wish can be realized only by recognizing one's connectedness and responsibility to others.

The gender hierarchy masks the cracks in our cultural foundation. It maintains the contradiction between the equality of relatedness and the hierarchy of public life. Patriarchy, by splitting relatedness, the domestic domain, and women, on the one hand, from individualizing, the public sphere, and men, on the other, pretends that the state is fundamentally sound and is, indeed, as good for people as it is for business. Because egalitarian ideals have been hidden away in the domestic domain and made second-class by being associated with women, the drive for power carried on in public life can continue undisturbed, while relatedness becomes even more explicitly undesirable.

The equal distribution of power and privilege and a fundamentally egalitarian, nonsexist structure of personal relations are mutually contingent. The problem will not be solved simply by reforms. Only part of the solution is to allow women to step into the career treadmill. Women have now, and before now, proved themselves quite capable of adopting and hanging on to the style of the self-as-individual even when sexism tries to dislodge them. It is only another part of the solution for men to trade places with women and engage in the personalized, particularistic activities of the domestic domain that create and call on relatedness. Trading places assumes that the "places" remain completely distinct and absolutely different. It means that the structure of power remains the same. It means that everyone, including women, can continue to seek equality in a culture based on hierarchy, a contradiction from which there is no escape except self-deception or total revolution.

The entire social structure must be taken apart and put back together again. The qualities of individualizing and relatedness have to be not only freed from gender but detached from the hitherto and only apparently separate domains of home and work. Relatedness must enter the public world, and individualizing, the private sphere. If social conditions were such that both the self-as-individual and the self-in-relation could be realized in both domains, then both these qualities could truly be available for everyone without the risk of losing personal or political power. If the responsibility for relatedness were shared by all, if each person could not but feel that the other's desires were of equal importance to those of the self, then everyone's needs and wants would receive equal time, and individualizing could not mutate into objectification. If each person had an equal chance to succeed to a position of authority, then the hierarchy inherent in authority would be only temporary, as is that of parent over child. Under these circumstances token women—on whom the structure of power depends to prove that equality is available to all—would disappear, as would the longing to be one. Women would not have to deny their kinship with other women, nor men with other men.

The evil of public life is not news. But since feminism began knocking at the corporate doors and since those doors have begun to open, more women than ever before have begun to realize the extent of the evil. As more and more women enter public life and the harder they work, the more they begin to experience the alienation that has led men to hate their work and themselves, to become alcoholics and suffer heart attacks, and to bemoan the betrayal of their ideals in the books they write and the movies they make. As women's way continues to be hard to make, the glitter of the public domain begins to tarnish. Those who went to work for love are discovering that, unbeknownst to them, they really did it for the money. Having idealized the public world, they have become privy to the knowledge, held by working-class women and men of all classes, that you work, finally, to get paid. All else is gravy.

Some women, having made this discovery, are leaving the field, permitted by husbands' paychecks to return to home and children. Others, who cannot afford or do not wish to depart, have two solutions. One is simply to work even harder, ignoring or perhaps continuing to blame themselves for their difficulties. Women in corporate hierarchies tend to choose this solution. They have a great investment in denying their disillusionment. On the one hand, having worked very hard, they do not wish to imagine that their personal drive could fail to realize its goals. On the other, they often wish to deny that their gender could be a handicap because, like most women who came of age before feminism revalued femininity, they are still so influenced by the patriarchal derogation of women that they feel the second-class citizenship accorded all women means that they personally are second-class human beings. By denying the persistence of sexism and therefore of institutionalized disrespect, they hope to ensure their own self-respect.

The second solution for those women who stay in the workforce is to protest. Many women continue to do this, especially at the lower reaches of corporate hierarchies and in blue- and pink-collar jobs. Although feminism has been until now largely a middle-class movement, it now also includes more working-class women or young women of color, who, entering the workforce for the first time and at the bottom, have their eye on the top of the ladder but clearly see the obstacles in their way. Because they came of age after feminism's reappraisal of women's character and personality styles, pride in their gender comes more easily. They are consequently less motivated to deny that gender is important to them and more motivated to complain when it begets discrimination.

But, as this new protest continues and spreads, women will be criticizing the evils of public life from a different vantage point than men. Their critique will emerge from the traditionally second-class, but newly validated, domestic place of relatedness to which they have been encultured. Their plaint will be, as it has been, that freedom requires not only political power but personal power. People need both the material things by which to live and the ability to give meaning to their lives. They will argue that the meaning of their lives depends on their relations to each other as well as on themselves. Since relatedness is as fundamentally human as individualizing, people must be free to pursue their self-interest in such a way that the interests of others, too, are satisfied. Only when this mutuality is possible for everyone can individual freedom obtain. Only when people have no grounds to objectify each other will they no longer objectify themselves.

When this happens, the mutual regard that men and women feel for each other beneath the antagonism created by the gender hierarchy will not be as rarely or as hestitantly offered, or disguised by nervous flirtation, as it is now.

Once again in my office, I gaze out the window at the parking lot. Somehow, I ruminate wearily, I wasn't prepared for all this. This wasn't what I thought work would be like. Not that I had had any very specific idea of it. All I knew was that my mother was lonely, bored by being a housewife and mother, and eager to get a job as soon as her kids were old enough to give themselves breakfast. By contrast, I guess, the unknown world to which she wished to escape and into which my father disappeared every morning seemed like the key to freedom, to a place where you could be . . . I don't know . . . whatever you wanted. I don't think I bought a bill of goods, but. . . .

Enough. I decide I'm too tired from last night to keep my office hour. I put on my coat, say good-bye to Ginny, Ted, and the other faculty members who have come in, and stop in the bathroom to check on my period. Then I trot over to the bursar's office to pick up my paycheck and walk to an off-campus coffee shop near the subway to sit and space out before I have to catch the train uptown on my way, first, to my analyst and, later, to my patients. As I walk, I look for buds on the trees.

I stare out the window at the clogged traffic. Nikos, the counterman, gives me my usual cup of coffee. Both tense and exhausted, I blow on it, watching the steam, wishing I had a cigarette so that I could be calmed by the arabesques of smoke. I think about a former student of mine, smart as a whip and now a teller at my bank, where I see her every time I deposit my paycheck. I chatted with her one quiet day, learning how much she had accomplished in getting this job, coming, as she does, from a Hispanic family on welfare. She has high hopes for promotion. I imagine she'll beat the odds. She inspires me.

I smile and take out my wallet to pay, but Nikos waves the money away. "Today I treat you, lady."

"Oh no, you can't. I won't accept it," I say, moved and grateful.

"It is to celebrate your smile, because you looked so unhappy when you came in," Nikos answers, clearing the dishes. "Sometime you treat me." Looking down at his work, he swabs the counter, then looks up and winks in a friendly manner.

I stop the tears that always attend unexpected kindness. *"Efcharisto,"* I say in the Greek that he has taught me. "Thanks." I leave a large tip both for the coffee and for the warmth that melts the splinter of ice in my heart.

I wend my way through a traffic jam to catch the subway to my analyst's office.

Dependency and Empathy,
or Autonomy's Better Half

(2:30 P.M.)

*D*elayed by traffic in the taxi that I hailed on leaving my analyst's office, I reach my own at the very minute when my session with Lorraine should be starting. By the time the elevator stops at my floor, I am five minutes late. I nod to Lorraine sitting in the waiting room of the suite I share with two other therapists and tell her to follow me into my office, which is decorated in earth tones.

I hang my coat in the closet, put down my briefcase, and sit down in my armchair, which is angled slightly toward the one in which Lorraine, her hair in a fashionably asymmetrical coif, has already seated herself. I put on my glasses to review my schedule, then remove them and place them on my side table along with my appointment book.

Lorraine takes a container of yogurt out of a paper bag, as she usually does, her lunch hour being the only time she can afford to take off from her job as a stockbroker. "The worst thing just happened. I have to work late next Thursday to entertain an out-of-town client. But that's the night of Bobby's school play. What am I going to do? Maybe I should ask my mother to go to the play, but I know she'll guilt-trip me, and I feel guilty enough already. Maybe I should ask Gillian, but a friend isn't the same as a mother."

She eats a spoonful of yogurt. "Oh, maybe I could take my client out for a drink. Or lunch. Or maybe he'll be in town on Friday. Or I could ask Bill, except that he's suddenly become completely rigid about seeing Bobby only on weekends. Well, something will work out. It always does.

"So I guess it seems pretty stupid to be thinking about having another child. But, as I was saying last week, I've always wanted two kids, and it's now or never. I'm thirty-three and I don't know when I'm going to meet someone I want to do it with. The problem is how to do it. Gillian said that her friend in Boston had artificial insemination and got pregnant the first time. On the other hand, I think it would be better if the kid had a real father available. Except I can't think of anyone I know whom I'd want to ask. I suppose I could just forget my diaphragm one night and not tell Larry. He doesn't want kids anyway. Besides, our relationship is about to go on the rocks."

She crosses her legs, clad in black-tinted stockings. "Of course, I have a lot of other things to do first. I'll have to figure out how to tell the people in my department, not to mention my boss. I don't think they're very accustomed to single mothers. But, if I keep getting the sort of raises they've been giving me and if Bill continues to pay Bobby's child support, I'll certainly have enough money.

"Then there's my apartment to think about. In the beginning, of course, the baby would sleep in my room and then move into Bobby's room, though it's hard to ask a five-year-old—no, he'd be seven or eight by then—to share his room with a toddler. So I might have to find a larger apartment. Of course, if I keep getting raises, I'll be able to hire a housekeeper. But I don't think

I could also afford an apartment in Manhattan. So I'll have to look elsewhere. Maybe I'll move to Brooklyn."

"You seem to have returned to the questions of money and housing that concerned you last week," I note.

She shakes her head decisively. "Oh no, I've also been thinking about the best way to take care of her. Whoops, wasn't that a Freudian slip or something?" She laughs. "But I really want to have a girl. Anyway, I don't want to just take two weeks off and go back to work the way I did with Bobby. I want to be able to work half-time for at least eighteen months, so I don't miss seeing her grow up. But I don't know if I can swing that with my job. Maybe I should try to find a company that provides flex-time."

She eats some more yogurt and then continues. "Well, anyway, if I have a girl, I'm definitely going to be different from my mother. I'm never going to worry about whether my daughter gets married or not."

Finishing her yogurt, she lights a cigarette, then says, "I've got to stop smoking and get my body in shape if I'm going to do this. I'm going to start swimming again. Also, I just heard about a terrific exercise class for pregnant women."

I point out, "We've come back to the brass tacks of having a baby. I wonder why."

She frowns. "Well, how can I have a baby if I don't figure out the brass tacks, as you call them?"

I respond, "Certainly, those are important issues. But I think they're also obscuring other, emotional concerns of yours."

She puts out her cigarette. "You mean my guilt. Well, I know a new baby will be hard for Bobby. He's been used to being an only child. That's what my mother was saying when I told her on the phone that I was thinking about doing this. I guess I was trying to test the waters. Her reaction to the whole thing was completely predictable. She freaked out. She didn't say anything at first. You know that wounded silence of hers. I couldn't stand it. Then she said, in a very clipped tone of voice, that she thought I shouldn't have gotten divorced and that I was being irresponsible. So I lost it."

She speaks more loudly now. "I said that if I were five years younger I would wait, but that it's almost too late now. I don't want to wait until I'm over thirty-five, when I'll have to have an amniocentesis. I know the amnio isn't all that risky, but the possibility of a Downs baby goes way up after thirty-five. And, if a baby has been in you for five months, you are not going to want to abort it, and, if it's a Downs, then I'll want to. I just don't want to have to face that conflict.

"So I told her all that, and she said that I should either wait until I meet the right man or try to patch things up with Bill. Can you imagine me doing that? Then she asked me how come I didn't think of all that before. So I told her that I had thought about it, but that I had been waiting and, anyway, maybe I didn't want to get married again. And, I said, besides, a lot of women are choosing to be single mothers these days, so there's a lot of network support for me. So she said what she always says when she's trying to get me to do something I don't want to do, that I'm the most important thing in her life. Well, how can that be true if she's being as unsupportive as she has ever been?"

Thinking of other occasions when Lorraine has informed her mother of decisions about which her mother might disapprove, I say, "I wonder why you were testing the waters."

SINGLE-MOTHERHOOD

Women's identity has, in Western tradition, depended on their relationships to others, principally to children and men. In reaction to this denial of women's independence, many second-wave feminists decided not to have children. Some also rejected marriage and the family. Some chose to become homosexual. Yet, in the late 1970s and early 1980s, many of these same women were changing their minds. In particular, they were starting to have children. Some did so by benefit of marriage. Others, in lesbian couples or on their own, persuaded men friends to donate sperm, were artificially inseminated, or, if they could not conceive, adopted infants or young children. One reason for the timing of this shift in attitudes and behavior was the biological clock. At the end of the 1970s, many active feminists were approaching forty. Nearing the last of their reproductive years, they realized that if they waited too much longer they would lose their chance to bear children at all.

But, had all other aspects of pregnancy and childrearing remained the same, it is unlikely that so many minds would have changed. New technology and changes in the political and social climate made child bearing and childrearing seem less threatening to women's independent identity. The advances in reproductive technology, the legalization of abortion, and progress in the women's health movement permitted women to feel more in charge of their own bodies. The willingness of some firms to provide maternity and paternity leaves and, in fewer cases, flextime, allowed many women to hope that they could combine motherhood and livelihood. The feminist critique of the nuclear family, in which women did all the child care, persuaded many men that child care was not only a responsibility but a pleasure. Many women therefore felt that they could try to have children in nuclear families without losing their identities as their own mothers had done.

At the same time, feminism, coupled with the countercultural ferment of the 1960s, had generated alternative social institutions that reassured many middle-class women, usually but not always feminists, that they could have children on their own. As men became less central to women's identity, women felt able to live alone without automatically being dismissed as old maids. Nor were divorcees any longer stigmatized as wicked or sexually dangerous. Even homosexuality among women gained limited social recognition. Furthermore, women's friendship and support of one another had become desirable and respectable, no longer the booby prize for failing to catch a man. In some parts of our society, women's networks began to serve many of the support functions usually served by the family alone. There developed as well groups for single mothers—and single fathers—in which common problems could be shared and solved. With these changes in women's lives, single-motherhood, too, has become both more feasible and acceptable.

However, single-motherhood is not a unique invention. Rather, it has for many years been a commonplace, though not usually a choice, in poor black and Hispanic communities. Single women in these subcultures have borne and reared children for a myriad of intersecting cultural and psychological reasons. Poverty and social hierarchy have put severe stresses on black and Hispanic family life but have had different, even opposing influences on men and women. Incomes made low and often unpredictable by racial discrimination hinder men from living up to the values of responsible husband and father that are as crucial to minority subcultures as they are to the dominant culture.

Nor is the subjugation and emasculation of minority men, which tends to leave minority women in charge of family and children, a recent phenomenon. Women's centrality to the family and their moral strength in holding families together have been part of black history since the days of slavery. They often became single mothers, either because their men were sold away from them or because they were impregnated by their white masters.

Present political and economic circumstances continue to make single-motherhood a likely possibility in lower-class Hispanic and black communities. Women facing ill-paid, dead-end jobs and battling the lowered self-esteem induced by racism may quite reasonably find motherhood to be one of the more certain sources of satisfaction. Lack of information about reproduction and contraception may further create conditions in which young women become pregnant, while lack of money may prevent them from getting abortions—either of which may occur among poor white women as well. Economic dependence on men may urge them to use pregnancy as a means of hooking a man—like middle-class women of another era. Finally, governmental regulations for those mothers receiving welfare indirectly reinforce single-motherhood and undermine families by prohibiting funds for dependent children if the mother is intermittently living with the father or even any adult male with whom she might be having a sexual relationship. At the same time, the government systematically avoids developing effective plans to find the fathers and provide them with work that would enable them to carry out their responsibilities. Under these political and economic conditions, then, single-motherhood is an acceptable alternative even though the nuclear family is the preferred way to rear children in these communities.

Generations of coping with poverty and discrimination have created social institutions that support single mothers. And now, with the increase in middle-class single mothers, new support variations are being produced. Extended networks of kin, and friends who become like kin, serve as family for children and for mothers. Children regularly visit grandparents for lengthy periods of time and are sometimes adopted, briefly or permanently, by other relatives. The women webbing these networks together help each other out not only with the actual activities of child care but with advice, comfort, clothes, money, food, and shelter in emergencies.

Although the institution of single-motherhood seems to be more a voluntary decision for white, middle-class women, their choice may be less free than it appears. As men's incomes no longer rise as high and as fast as they once did and as the economic insecurity of all families increases, some white, middle-class men may also find marriage and fatherhood less reliable sources of personal and social esteem than they once were. Furthermore, women's demands for the right to their careers and for men's parenting responsibility mean that men can no longer achieve career success on women's backs. At the same time, these men need no longer fear that they will be regarded as homosexual if they are not family men, because cultural images such as that of the *"Playboy* man" have been making single, male adulthood more socially acceptable for the past two or three decades.

Consequently, in the white middle class—and perhaps in the black middle class as well—women may find themselves with a far smaller pool of men from which to select husbands willing to father children. Therefore, however much middle-class single-motherhood reflects the increase in women's self-esteem and feminism's effect on our institutions for childrearing, it is also connected to fundamental changes in the structure of the nuclear family itself, changes that place women as much in social and psychological charge of children as they have always been, perhaps even more so.

As I listen to Lorraine speak in one way or another about her great attachment to her mother and her struggle to let go, or to pull free, I recall an incident during my own session two hours earlier.

Lying down in my analyst's white-walled office furnished in soft black leather and oiled teak, I relax, free of the morning's annoyances. I examine the drawing of the naked woman on the wall in front of me above the foot of the couch, which I have deliberately not seen for eight years. I wonder, Does he look at it? What does he see? Who was the model? Did she make her living posing for artists? Was she the artist's mistress? Was the artist a woman? Does he compare her with me?

"You know," I say to him, "when I was thirteen, my mom began to take art lessons. Once I posed for her and her friends. I wore a one-piece bathing suit and sat with my arms holding my knees to my breasts. Mom kept drawing a picture of a child. In each successive sketch the child got progressively older, but none of them looked like me. We all thought it was pretty funny."

I am silent a moment, then go on. "I know this is about her difficulty in letting go of me and mine in relinquishing her. I think I hung out with her too much. And she hung on to me too much. Except that, when I was thirteen, she began, sort of suddenly, to worry about my career, as well as her own. She would tell me that I needed to be independent and always able to take care of myself. And now that I was in high school along with my brother, she didn't have so much to do and so she was trying to figure out something to do with her time."

He speaks very gently. "The moment of letting go is a very painful one, and it is made particularly poignant when you feel as close as you did to your mother. But there is also something exciting about leaving."

"But what was strange was that she was so cool," I continue. "You know, it almost feels as though she never hugged me. I know she did, but I have no memory of her doing it." I feel upset and lonesome.

He responds, "You feel that she pushed you toward establishing your own separate life, but, by not hugging you, it's as if she withheld her blessing on your independence."

"I don't need anyone to hug me," I say coldly. But I am very aware of the defensiveness in my tone. "How come you have that damn picture up there anyway? It's a sexist cliché." How relieved I am to have something to be legitimately angry about.

WOMEN AND THEIR DAUGHTERS

Whether or not a woman makes a living, the first thing that people still want to know about, after they have inspected her body and her clothing, is how she fares domestically. The next question invariably is, Does she have children? Inquiries like these stem from the still-popular biologically determinist belief that women's reproductive anatomy is linked to "maternal instincts."

This belief persists despite research on monkeys that indicates the absence of such instincts in nonhuman primates and therefore suggests their absence in human beings. Experiments were performed in which infant rhesus monkeys were reared without live mothers and fed only by nipples protruding from dummies. The infants so reared grew up to be asocial and emotionally disturbed, a finding that supported one of the hypotheses of the study, namely, that a live, nurturing figure, a "mother"—and the study assumed that "mothers" must always be female—had to be in constant, early attendance for the well-being of offspring.

However, this experiment had another unexpected and, given the capacity of data on nonhuman primates to prove opposite hypotheses, at least equally plausible result, one that suggests that "maternal instincts" are learned behaviors, not instinctual at all. The female infants reared in isolation grew up not only socially inept but ignorant of how to have sexual intercourse or, when inseminated artificially, of how to care for their young. Brought up alone, they had matured without the opportunity to learn from anyone else. By inference, then, if female monkeys learn to mother, so do female human beings.

In the course of their maternal education, women in our culture learn that motherhood is defined by infancy. According to both the infant and the culture, which takes the side of the infant in the woman-and-child fusion, the mother is not a separate person. The mother is a "woman-and-child."

In this symbiotic, maternal state, the "self" drops out of the "self-in-relation," and the mother becomes only "in-relation." She is supposed to vibrate like a tuning fork to the wants and needs of her child. If her child needs her, she is supposed to be there. If her child needs her not to be there, she is supposed to make herself scarce. Nor is she to have any particular needs and wants. The Subject-as-Object, she lacks active desire; the child wants, and the mother wants-to-be-wanted. A mother is expected to give without ever desiring anything in return but evidence of her child's development, and much of the time seems to do so. She is to put herself on hold. Her occupation, her chores and headaches and friends and dreams, her own neediness and longings that someone might take care of her, her desire to be alone—these bases of her separateness have no place in the infantile-cum-cultural conception of motherhood.

This version of mothering, in which women prefer to be "in-relation," finds its way into women's psychology in general. Because "woman" is equated with "in-relation" and "in-relation" is equated with "mother," socialization for femininity tends automatically to train girls to be mothers at the same time as it inclines them toward relatedness. Childlessness, or even the thought of not having children, can therefore feel to a woman as disorienting as though her gender identity itself had disappeared.

At the same time as the desire to mother is thus instilled, women come to want and need to be connected to other people. It may feel agreeable to be always in others' company, emotionally or physically. It may seem quite natural to have around oneself others whose needs require attention. It may come to be central to self-esteem to be immersed in activities having to do with the satisfaction of others' wants and needs.

However, the unconscious underpinnings of this cultural definition of femininity can transform women's maternal wanting-to-be-wanted into a personal need-to-be-needed. Women's comfort with being "in-relation" takes psychological root because it connects to unconscious memories of infantile dependency, which may infuse maternal selflessness with a feeling that merging is imperative. Infants are at the start utterly dependent on their mothers, and they indeed experience their mothers as part of them. But the neediness of the merged infant that endures in the adult unconscious may make women's inclination to be connected to others an almost addictive dependence on being in others' presence, on being needed by them, and on being able to give them satisfaction.

Living out this sort of adult dependency with one's children can become seductive. If independence is something to be feared, then a mother may find it hard to let go of motherhood. She may hang on to her children, or have another child when the older ones seem to be growing up and away, or encourage her children to hang on to her. As long as children are needy, her neediness can go unremarked, as can any discomfort with aloneness that she may feel.

Although mothers sometimes make sons continue to depend on them long after they should have entered separate adulthood, they experience a special sort of entangling with daughters. While a son, being male, evokes otherness, a daughter is like a double. Not only is she the same gender, but the fact that she is a child may remind her mother of her own childhood and her relationship to her own mother.

A mother is therefore likely to treat her daughter in terms of her own self-image. She may worry about her daughter's life and body as if they were her own. She may give abundantly, even too much, either because she feels that in childhood she did not get enough love herself or because she got a lot of it. Or, hating the tendency to merge that she discerns in herself, she may despise it in her daughter and therefore be quite astringent with her, rarely showing any physical affection in an effort to discourage it. She may even be cool because she, like everyone else, regards women as second-class, in which category she places her daughter as well as herself.

Whatever the style of the mother-daughter relationship, mothers are often on daughters' minds. Women may take their mothers with them everywhere they go, finding themselves in involuntary mental conversation with them about everything that happens to them. They may love, as well as hate, the daily phone calls on which some mothers insist. They may feel guilty about impulses to do things of which their mothers disapprove or may in fact feel impelled to do whatever is contrary to their mothers' desires.

Such constant emotional contact between mothers and daughters makes them resemble each other and contributes to women's identification with motherhood itself. The mother-daughter identification across personal boundaries permitted by sameness of gender cultivates in daughters the very propensity to merge on which mothering and relatedness call. Daughters, then, are likely to merge with their mothers in the same the way that their mothers merged with their own mothers. And, thus, women who are mothered by women often want to become mothers themselves.

At the same time, daughters may feel reluctant to answer the maternal calling because of the sacrifice of self it exacts. They may admire this sacrifice in their mothers, yet not wish it for themselves. They may be grateful that they can share their decision making with mothers and sisters and women friends, but the dependency to which maternal selflessness makes them prone can unsettle them. They may find themselves longing for the psychological aloneness that is supposed to come with adulthood. For, even though it frightens them, it is a state of being that they, being "self" as well as "in-relation," are entirely capable of and, indeed, on which they must draw in order to create the selflessness that is held to be natural to them.

Lorraine speaks pensively now, sometimes looking out the plant-framed window, sometimes looking down at her fingernails, picking at the nubbly upholstery on the arm of her chair. "When my mother called the other night, she said that she and my father were thinking of retiring and moving to Florida." She smiles brightly, removes a cigarette from her pack, then replaces it.

I ask, "What did you think about that?"

"Oh, I think it's great." She stares, continuing to smile.

"You seem a little ill at ease," I remark.

She seems confused. "Maybe it's silly, because I never see them, but I'll kind of miss them."

She looks away from me, out the window again, then down at the shaggy flokati rug. "I get so angry at her, but I know she isn't really unsupportive. She's been as good to me as she can be. Sometimes she goes out of her way to come into the city to treat me on my lunch hour. Even two weeks ago, she surprised me by buying me a blouse I had talked about. That's why it was so awful to fight with her when I was a teenager. I hated myself, but I couldn't help it. I was surly, slammed doors, and came home late. Now that I think of it, in the seventies, I hated her for being just a housewife and mother. I wanted her to be a feminist like me, even though she was just an ordinary woman." She begins to cry. "How could I say that about her?"

Reminded of similar feelings about my own mother, I simply say, "It hurts to love whom others devalue, and to devalue those we love."

She continues to cry. "I feel so terrible when she's unhappy. She works too hard. Ever since they've been married, it's been the same. My father goes to the store six days a week, seven A.M. to seven P.M., he comes home exhausted, and his clothes stink of benzine. When I was four, I asked him why he couldn't clean his own clothes. It became a standing joke.

"But my mother had both the house and the store. She had to help him out, especially when he was so depressed the year that he almost lost the business, before the chain store bought him out. He was so unhappy that it was almost like we didn't have a father then. So, until Jenny and I were old enough to take care of ourselves, mother would take us along with her and we'd watch the television under the counter. But still she had to get home to make dinner, and then, as she was saying the other day on the phone, even though she took orders from him at the store, he was like another kid to take care of, coming home and sitting right down at the table, waiting for his food with his napkin tucked in his shirt collar. And then her own mother was sick a lot."

I am mulling over her recurrent guilt about her mother's un-happiness and about her concern for how much work her mother had to do. "You are very absorbed in your mother's problems."

"You're right," she says with some surprise, as if a new thought had dawned on her. "And, you know, she doesn't even under-stand that. On the phone, she started complaining that I don't visit them enough and she doesn't understand why I don't un-derstand her even though I have a child of my own now. But I do understand her, and it makes me feel so bad that she thinks I don't."

I say quietly, "It occurs to me that you may have been dis-tressed about my having been late today. I wonder if you feel that you can't burden me with a complaint about my lateness because I, like your mother, have so much work to do."

"Well, I was pretty upset while I was waiting. But I'm sure you couldn't help it." She takes a tissue, wipes her eyes, sniffs, smiles again.

EMPATHY, AUTONOMY, AND THE GIFT OF PSYCHOLOGICAL LIFE

Were childhood simply a matter of dependency, motherhood might be a straightforward job. But since psychological growth takes a subtle, sometimes backtracking route from dependence to independence, mothering is a complicated skill that is as dif-ficult to carry out as it is to learn. Unlike the machinist's mastery required to design and cut out a well-shaped piece of metal, mothering must be actively and flexibly responsive to a contin-ually evolving and shifting material—a growing child, whose in-terests are ultimately different from hers and sometimes in conflict with them as well. The child's evolution alternates between mo-ments of dependence and moments of independence, and the mother must fit herself in with these fluctuations, even though they may be contrary to her own.

The heart of maternal nurturing is empathy, the capacity to put oneself in another's place. Empathy requires an ease with both dependence and independence, connectedness and sepa-rateness, merging and aloneness. Rooted in the understanding that human experience alternates between dependence and in-dependence, it demands the capacities for both connection to and separation from others. It is a process, one moment of which is the merging of self and other, another moment of which is the absolute and sometimes lonely differentiation between them. It therefore entails patience.

In order to be empathetic, mothers must use their own separateness as well as their propensity to merge. A woman brings to her newborn her intelligence, thoughtfulness, and emotions, using them in the act of empathic imagination. In nurturing her baby, she draws on all her past history: her knowledge about pregnancy, mothering, and children gained from her own mother and from her culture; her feelings about herself, her own childhood, her pregnancy, her other children, and women in general; her sense of values; and her notions of the meaning of life.

Mothers make great use of this store of experience particularly at the inchoate start of an infant's life, when the clues to the baby's wants and needs are new, ambiguous, and therefore difficult to decipher. The neonate can do nothing, depending absolutely on the presence of another person for physical and emotional survival. The mother, therefore, must do everything. At this stage of the game, she really is in service to her infant. Even should she not feel as symbiotic as cultural ideals insist, she must use whatever she knows and whatever she can intuit, lest her baby die or fail to thrive; any other compelling interests that she may have are secondary.

As absolute dependence quickly recedes during the first year of life and the child's strivings toward autonomy emerge and multiply, the mother must begin to walk the fine line between encouraging independence and not discouraging dependence, a line that will be hers to follow until the child reaches maturity. Even in the first weeks after birth, babies show their separateness, actively taking in what they receive, building a relationship with their mother and others. These impulses toward independence require her notice and approbation, so that in the future they may become the kernels of adult self-containment.

As time passes and the child's input increases, the mother's work becomes both simpler and more complicated. The same capacities that allow the child to become more independent require more thought, insight, and negotiation on the part of the mother. During the second year of life, when walking and talking begin and gender identity sets in, the mother has the frustrating task of allowing her child to pull away and hang on at the same time.

While she has to make room for the child's independent strides, she must continue to anticipate resurgent needs for nurturing. Sometimes she must let her toddling child fall down, sometimes she must not. When her child begins to speak, the mother must modify her own intentions to incorporate the independent desires of this newly emerging self. When her child goes off to school or visits friends, she must provide the frame, being there in person or spirit at the beginning and end of the day or visit. And just as the toddler who is learning to walk needs someone there to prevent a fall and to gaze with admiration at the accomplishment, so children and adolescents need parents to provide a home that can be returned to for physical and emotional sustenance until such time as they can establish their own homes as independent adults.

Mothering is a contradictory enterprise because, although it formally asks for selflessness, dependence, and merging, it also requires empathy, which in turn entails self-possession, independence, and the capacity to be alone. Considerable reflection, observation, and introspection are necessary in deciding when to allow a child to proceed alone toward separateness, when to provide a guiding hand, and when to insist that a child is still too young to make independent decisions. Thinking about another's well-being while suppressing one's own immediate interests calls for a great effort of will. Without the self-possession that facilitates her thought and will, the dependency that a mother may feel with greater or lesser intensity would run amok, creating daughters and sons who could never leave home at all.

This enormously complicated work is worthy of worship, so worthy, indeed, that the threat of its absence can beget hatred. Somewhere inside us is a permanent hallelujah chorus in mother's honor that is too good to give up. Mother is our first love object, our first passion. We all, female as well as male, want to marry her. She is sexy and she is powerful. She puts her hands where she likes, inside, outside, around, between. She is wondrous, omnipotent, knowing magically what we want and able therefore to give or withhold it. When she takes herself away from us—when she is late with the bottle or a diaper change or a hug because she was on the telephone or writing her book or washing another child's face or making love—it is a mortal insult, a wound preserved in the unconscious and thereby made immortal. And our hatred for her is equally undying.

However, the mother's separate interests, as painful as they are to infants and children, turn out to be the gift of psychological life. Her interests may be those of intimacy or those of work. There may be a man in her life, either the father of her children or a lover. Or her lover may be a woman. She may have friends, male and female. She may have a job to go to or a portrait to paint or a cooking class to attend. What is significant in this context is not that a man interrupts the relationship with the child, nor even so much that anyone new comes into the relationship, but that the mother turns away to something of her own. She has another relationship or activity from which the child is excluded. Without them, she would have nothing to live for but her children, through whom she would in consequence live, making them extensions of her. Her other life marks her differentness and autonomy and therefore guarantees that of her children.

Contrary, then, to the hypothesis that the experiment with rhesus monkeys was designed to demonstrate, the child's well-being depends not on a mother who is there all the time but on one who can come and go as she pleases. To the extent that she is there with her infant because she is fulfilling a social requirement or a psychological compulsion, to that extent will she continue to reproduce in her daughters, and sons, the merging that is meant to characterize her life. To the extent that she is there with her infant because this is one of the various activities that she chooses to do at any given moment or in her life altogether, to that extent will she rear children who come to be truly self-contained and self-possessed adults.

As my own session continues, I go on with a memory. "Once, when I was eight, my father and little brother were going to take a shower together. 'Me too,' I yelled. I wanted to see my father's genitals. I distinctly remember that. My mother said, 'No, no, dear, daughters don't take showers with their fathers.' It's hard to describe my reaction. But it was something like, 'This is news to me. Since when have the rules changed? I know what I want. They know too. Do they know that I know that they know what I know?' "

"Perhaps she thought it was time for you to recognize your own separateness. You couldn't stay a little girl forever."

"I think she was jealous." Uneasily, I feel both hatred and contempt for her right now.

"It's certainly possible. But I have a hunch that today you're talking about the pleasures and difficulties relating to being alone as an adult."

"Don't you have a wife somewhere?" I retorted snappily, yet even to my ear I again sound defensive, as though his comment had challenged me.

"Could it be that you are angry I am both different from and unavailable to you, that, like your mother, I have my own preferences, such as drawings of nudes, and, like your father, I belong to another woman?"

KNOWING WHAT YOU NEED

The adoration that mothers receive is one of motherhood's chief attractions and compensations. There are few personal powers equal to that of a woman over a tiny infant with whom she identifies, whose life depends on her will, whose well-being comes to seem the most important thing in the world, and who thereby fills her with an unquestionable sense of her own value. Furthermore, the physical and emotional sway that she has over her baby and the sacrifices she makes yield her a certain public power as well. Indeed, the cultural reverence for motherhood reflects the infantile adoration of mother remembered in the adult unconscious.

Yet mother worship can mutate into misogyny. While people may admire the woman with a newborn infant much as they might a statue of the Madonna and Child, they look with a little less rapture at the mother yelling at her squalling, snotty-faced three-year-old who, suddenly going limp, demands to be carried even though, or because, mother's hands are weighed down by shopping bags. Not only cultural reverence but the child's adoration are less in evidence as independence proceeds along its complicated route. Where once the infant blindly worshiped in intimate merger, the child comes gradually, and often with confusingly complicated feelings, to see mothers, and other people, from the distance of an increasingly differentiated selfhood. Furthermore, children learn, as they grow older, that adults are not supposed to be like mothers. An adult is supposed to be a Subject, not a

Subject-as-Object. In time, then, mothers may receive from their children a wide and not always pleasant range of behavior. They may be cordially liked as well as devotedly loved, benignly neglected as well as unrelentingly hated, and often treated with irritated contempt while accorded reverence only on Mother's Day.

Yet, although the intricacies of maternal empathy have no place in the neat dichotomy between independence and dependence mandated for adulthood by cultural values, they are in fact central to the formation and continuance of adult life. Some psychoanalytic theories, like popular cultural beliefs, hold that the struggle to achieve maturity is a tug-of-war between a feared and longed-for dependency, on the one hand, and an admired autonomy, on the other. But adulthood in fact results from a diplomatic negotiation between the two. The dependent infant progresses toward separateness on the basis of the mother's ability to intuit its desires, one of which is that she reflect its developing autonomy with a glowing message that transmutes into the child's self-esteem. As the child first toddles, then later reconnoiters the perimeters and surroundings of the parental home, this glow must take up residence in the child's mind in the form of an image of a receptive caretaker, a home that can always be returned to. Then, somewhere in the misty borderland between adolescence and adulthood, this image of one person empathically nurturing another allows the actual parents and home of birth to fade into the home made later for oneself and, perhaps, for others.

Finally, although our culture insists that the psychological umbilical cord dry up and blow away, it endures, transformed, in each adult. In maturity one can become a friend, lover, parent, worker, or colleague only because one has early on taken in from one's caretaker a vision not only of a singular self—which indeed comes later—but of a self-in-relation. As life goes on, the cord frays, gets repaired, thins out, until, later on perhaps, it is re-plaited as roles reverse, grown child sometimes nurturing aging parent.

Independence, dependence, and empathy together constitute the psychological basis for all social life. In the absence of self-containment, the dependence that all adults continue to feel brings about the loss of self. But a purely independent adulthood without acknowledgment of dependence turns into isolation. "Life is with people," goes the proverb of the Eastern European Jewish *stetl*, or ghetto. People live their separate lives in connection—close, conflicted, attenuated—with other people. They do this out of desire, out of need and want. If not at home, then at work, if not at work, then at play, they want to be with others and they need the care and response that others provide.

Independence and dependence are contradictory only in a culture that excludes empathy from public life. Human life proceeds on the basis of mature dependency, but our culture invalidates the one image that exists for it, namely, the empathy that is fundamental to maternal nurturing. Empathy abrogates the dichotomy between independence and dependence on which adulthood in our culture is founded. Empathy is the root and balm of adult life. But insofar as it is eliminated from the values of adulthood by being hidden in the private sphere with mothers and children and despised because it smacks of dependency, empathy leaves adults vulnerable to isolation and helplessness.

Mothering is worshiped and denigrated unlike anything else in our culture, except, perhaps, money. At the same time as misogyny hides in the closet of domestic life, mothering is honored as the shrine of the family. It represents both utopia and nightmare. It contains both a vision of altruism that critiques the greed of public life and an apparition of selfhood dissolving into infantile symbiosis. Culturally ordained as women's biological imperative and therefore as the responsibility of individual women, motherhood becomes an almost irresistible prize, yet simultaneously a nearly unbearable burden that, as such, harms both women and the children they raise.

The work of mothering could be differently organized, for every person is capable of relatedness and empathy. It is true that in the ideals of every known culture, a "mother" is a woman. But not all cultures rigidly insist that the biological mother be the actual mother. In some cultures, including subcultures within our own society, other people in addition to the birth mother contribute to the work of mothering. Among European aristocrats, hired nannies and governesses, like the wet nurses of the past, take over the bulk of child care. In peasant societies, the extended family, as well as adoptive mothers, have played major roles in nurturing the young. In our culture, networks of kin and friends, traditionally part of motherhood in poor, black communities and presently becoming part of it in white middle-class communities, have shared some of the work of mothering.

Furthermore, the traditional nuclear family is becoming a decreasingly important part of the scene in which children grow up. In some cases, this process has lightened women's maternal labors. The increased rate of divorce, as well as its heightened social acceptability, have created rather complicated extended-family relationships. Children of divorced parents sometimes relate to four parental figures, the mother as well as her husband or lover, the father as well as his wife or lover, not to mention various stepsiblings as well as their own full siblings. Occasionally, such "new extended families" have been able to transcend the bickering and recrimination that have traditionally accompanied divorce. Fathers participate in childrearing equally with mothers, and the parents of each nuclear unit negotiate amicably with one another about child-care arrangements. Mothering is beginning to be a job not only of women, as is demonstrated by the increased participation of married fathers and the single heterosexual men, single homosexual men, and male homosexual couples who have adopted children.

However, these unusual developments are restricted to a very small segment of the middle class. In the remainder of our society, mothering remains the lone, female mother's work. Indeed, it may be becoming increasingly so. If present trends continue, over 50 percent of all children born will spend at least part of their time growing up in single-parent, usually single-mother, families. Should there be, at any given time, two parents, they are less and less likely to be the same as those who conceived the child or were there at the birth.

The burdens of mothering are particularly heavy for divorced, working mothers. The double day is hard enough for married mothers. Divorced women have not only to cope with the anxiety of juggling work and children, they must often negotiate with ex-husbands about visiting rights and child-support payments. Furthermore, if their paid work is a career that commands as much dedication as children require, their lives may be liberally laced with guilt. Every decision in favor of work seems to deprive children; every choice to be with their children, to threaten their careers. And despite the greater frequency and social toleration of divorce, divorced mothers with careers still face social condemnation, as though their careers were but self-indulgent vanities carried out at the expense of children.

The continuing weight of maternal responsibility on women means that motherhood is still not a genuine choice for them. It also increases women's tendency both to cling to and resent their children. Neither choice nor a less tangled motherhood will be possible until our society has been entirely revolutionized. Were mothering an activity that men as well as women could and would choose, then it would be an authentic choice. But this could not occur unless empathy were as central to the cultural conception of independent adulthood as autonomy. Were this the case, then autonomy as well as dependency would be the prerogatives of all adults, and women would no longer lose themselves in their children, and children in their mothers.

For now, autonomy can not be fully realized in our culture, which secretly expects women to be independent while overtly cultivating their dependence, openly requires men to be independent while making their dependence a source of shame, and makes all adults dependent on the decisions made by the remote forces of hierarchy. But to the extent that self-containment is approachable, it comes with the acknowledgment of dependency that empathy makes possible. For independence means not the absence of dependency but the ability to know what you need.

Lorraine sits up in her chair with a start. "I just remembered a dream I had last night. I was standing in front of the beach cottage we used to rent for one week every summer. It was warm and sunny, with a delicious breeze. I was wearing my mother's long summer nightgown, but I reached into the pocket and found a pair of granny glasses. And then I saw farther down the beach that very high waves, so big you could surf on them, were beginning to crash on the shore. A beautiful darkness passed by, the waves poured around my feet, then rolled on along the beach. As the sky started to get lighter, I looked up and saw glowing planets, inside of which strange and lovely geometric forms were dissolving into one another."

I glance at the clock on the side table. Although the session is officially over, I want to make up for my delay. I think a little uneasily about my next patient, who is always punctual. "What comes to mind about this dream?"

She smiles brilliantly. "Oh, we loved that house. Somehow when I think of it, it's always sunny. My mother and father didn't fight, and we all felt close. They couldn't afford more than a week off, but they got so much out of it." She pulls another tissue out of the box and dries her eyes. "But why was I wearing my mother's nightgown?"

I ask, "What do you think?"

She shrugs. "Well, I guess this relates to what we were talking about before, that she doesn't want me to be on my own and have a baby the way I want. And she cried the first time I told her I was going to therapy. But in the dream I find the granny glasses in her pocket." She points to mine resting on my appointment book. "Does that mean it's her fault that I'm in therapy? Or that she's giving me permission to go?"

"Perhaps you are hovering on the edge of being on your own, while still looking back to her. The waves and darkness and planets suggest, on the one hand, the turmoil of creating your own life. But they also intimate the beauty and power that can come from the sunny goodness of her love."

She frowns again. "Yes, but where is my father in all this?"

I reply, "I think we'll have to take that up another day, because our time is up now."

She stands up, sighs, and then smiles. "Oh well, have a nice weekend."

"Thank you. I'll see you next Friday." I am pleased by the session, yet sorry that, as always, the closure is never complete. I recall my own disappointment when I left my analyst's office an hour and a half ago.

Still, I am relieved that there is only one more hour till my workday ends and my vacation from teaching starts. I feel another cramp and go to check on my period while the next patient enters the office.

Normal Envy

(5:15 P.M.)

Just as I leave my neighborhood drugstore, where I have stopped to buy the box of tampons now tucked away in my briefcase, I spot Phil, walking hand in hand with a woman across the street. After two years, he looks as good as ever, which was always almost too good to be true. And every time I try to describe him, I feel as though I'm writing a Harlequin romance: golden hair, chocolate eyes, a nose usually referred to as "chiseled," the great bone structure of a model, a delicate but full mouth ready to promise you anything. The woman matches him. She is slim, with straight, ash-blond, shoulder-length hair, and her clothes,

113

style, and manner are perfectly synchronized with the most current fashion. Together, they look as if they have just stepped out of an ad in *Gentleman's Quarterly*.

Phil stops her, pointing to one of the trendy, new bars that have begun to glitz up my once rather sober residential neighborhood. They scrutinize the neon-lighted façade for a moment and then look across the street at a second one. As they turn to enter the first, Phil sees me, stops, and waves. There seems to be no way to ignore his greeting. Somewhat reluctantly, I cross the street.

As I approach them, I return Phil's smile and find myself breathing more shallowly. Saying, "Hello, what a surprise to see you here," I touch his shoulder with my left hand. We each manage to offer a cheek for the ritual friendship kiss without accidentally allowing lips to brush.

Casually finger-combing his now shorter, fashionably trimmed hair to one side with his free hand, a charming habit of his that I instantly remember, he introduces the woman to me. "We," he explains to her, "are really old friends."

Joanna and I shift our briefcases and shake hands.

"Nice to meet you," she says, smiling, then looks at him, tucking her hair behind one pearl-studded ear.

"Likewise," I say, fascinated as always by hair that stays tucked in.

And now the very awkward moment. Phil and I look at each other. "So," we say simultaneously, then laugh.

"S-," he laughs again, "no, you first."

"So, what I was going to say was, so, what's been doing? What are you doing in this neighborhood?"

"Well, Joanna's secretary is leaving, she's about to give birth, so they all took the afternoon off and had a party for her. And since Jay, Joanna, that is, was ready to leave early, I thought I'd take a break too, didn't I, Jay? And we decided to explore your neighborhood. A lot of changes here."

"Oh, do you work together?" I pull my lapels closer. As sundown nears, the air is suddenly much cooler.

"Not exactly. I'm in public relations," says Joanna.

"And I was consulting for a corporation that Jay's firm represented. That's how we met." He winks at her. Her lips fold in a demure smile.

"What consulting?"

"Oh, yeah, I guess you don't know. That's what I've been doing since I last saw you. Consulting on ecology projects. I was advising on an environmentally sound waste-disposal system, and Jay was conferencing with them on how best to impact the public. Next month, I'm taking off for Paris and then going on to Hong Kong." He rubs his hands together and grins. "A lot of businesses doing a lot of ecology these days. Makes for interesting travel. Not bad money either. And I'm angling now so Jay can come along as a special PR consultant. Right, hon?"

Joanna smiles again, looks away, shifts her briefcase back to her right hand and her weight from one to the other high heel.

Spreading out his hands, looking from one to the other of us, Phil says, "Look, why don't you join us for a drink?"

"Oh, I really can't, I've got to get to the laundry, feed the cat, you know, the usual."

"Come on, just a quick one. Okay with you, babe?"

Joanna, scanning the street, nods. "Fine."

I'm not sure I want to have a drink with either of them. On hearing Phil talk about money and around-the-world travel and his girlfriend accompanying him, I begin to find my life very boring. And Joanna's clean blond-and-blue beauty makes me feel a little rough around the edges.

Come on, says the Club Med voice. *Lighten up. It's all over—it's five o'clock, the spring break is here, soon there'll be forsythia. Besides, who's waiting for you at home?*

The cat.

I look at my watch, "Well, good, okay, thanks."

"That's my girl." Turning around, he steers Joanna to the door, then pulls it open and lets us precede him, resting his hand ever so briefly and lightly on my back. Joanna stops and waits for him.

I feel as if I'm walking into a grade B movie. "Let's take a booth in the back." Ahead of them, I pass the bar, which is already packed with people trying to rev themselves up, or calm themselves down, during this eagerly awaited slack tide between day and night, work and play.

"I'll be right back," I say, dropping my coat over the back of the seat in the booth. I hurry to the bathroom for a quick period check.

PENIS ENVY AND BREAST ENVY

A woman, upon meeting an ex-lover with his new love, is likely to have a rather complex set of feelings. Even if she is glad to be rid of him, she will, not uncommonly, size the other woman up—and vice versa. If she judges herself to be better-looking, she may feel smug. If she considers the other woman to be more attractive, she may doubt her own value, feeling a sad, wistful longing for a beauty that is not hers or perhaps the motivation to improve her appearance. Alternatively, she might feel contemptuous of the other woman for being a slave to fashion. Or she might find some pretext on which to fault her and thereby be angry with or sorry for her.

She, like the other woman, may be jealous as well. Each of them envies the other's intimacy with the man, seeing the other as having a different but exclusive claim on him. The first lover is jealous because she feels excluded from the immediate intimacy between them, while the second lover is jealous because the first lover's claim is prior and therefore oddly primary. If only for a moment, each seems to have something better, the first envying the second for the past, the second envying the first for the present.

Envy, then, is the dominant emotion in this situation. Envy is usually thought of as an emotion destructive to others and diminishing to the self, as a hate-filled wish to deprive another of something particularly desirable. But envy has another side. It is also the desire simply to have for oneself the admired object or quality. For example, for the infant, what is admirable and enviable about mother's breast is not only the milk, but what the breast embodies—mother's loving, life-giving power, which the infant would like to possess for itself. To the adult, some of the infant's envious behavior, such as biting the nipple as a way of incorporating it, seems destructive. But this aggressive lunge for power is not, properly speaking, hostile, because it emerges before the infant can distinguish between good and evil. Envy becomes destructive only when there is not enough of the desired thing to go around, an eventuality that may be especially frequent in our society, where the possession of goods is a hallmark of prestige, but the means to acquire them, money, is scarce.

Women's mutual envy is frequently attributed to their differing power to attract men. When a woman attracts a man, she becomes enviable to other women because her possession of him makes her somehow special. It suggests that she has succeeded in compensating for the social inadequacies of being a woman. In our culture, even if not in all women's conscious minds, getting a man remains the public seal of women's power and success. When a woman gets a man, she acquires a legitimacy that she lacks on her own. Once a second-class citizen, she now has for herself a first-class citizen whose access to authority—over her if no one else—and to more money than she can usually earn protects and elevates her. The Subject-as-Object, she has gained through him the full subjectivity necessary for the completion of hers.

But, to the unconscious, the woman with a man has gained not only political power. Through him, she appears to have been able to compensate for her lack of personal power as well, just as her mother did before her. In the unconscious, just as "woman" means "mother," so "man" represents "father." A woman with a man has acquired father, and father is the route not only to worldly power but to that which the unconscious regards as the origin of all power—the bounteous "breast" that nourishes life. "Father" is the one who possesses what the infant dominating the adult unconscious desires, "mother."

In other words, in the circular logic of the unconscious, the man, the possession of whom makes another woman envious, is himself enviable because, as father, he reciprocally possesses her, that is, mother. Father gets what the child in all of us wants. He has reunited with the omnipotent, protective, nurturing mother, the all-good mother who was in symbiosis with the infant without an independent life of her own. He therefore seems to have a magical power that the infant wishes to possess too.

Father begins to acquire this magical power in the unconscious at the same time as mother is losing hers in real life. Although mother initially incarnates milk and honey, she is not always good. Sometimes, because she is late, absent, in error, or simply living her own life, she is bad. It is nearly impossible for the infant, who cannot yet tolerate ambivalence, to reconcile this all-bad mother with the all-good breast. One early way out of this dilemma is conveniently provided by the structure of the nuclear family, which is the ideal if not the reality of domestic life in our culture. The child may divide goodness and badness between mother and father. While the actual mother comes to be equated with the all-bad mother of fantasy, the imaginary all-good mother, whose loss would destroy the basic sense of security necessary for living, goes underground, resurfacing in the father. In other words, as selfhood crystallizes in the painful perception of mother's separateness, father takes on all the wonder and goodness once attributed entirely to mother.

As the child matures, patriarchy soon endows father with magic and power of his own. In contrast to the fusion with mother that now becomes tarnished with childishness and femininity, the independence toward which development proceeds glows with both adulthood and masculinity. As the child strides toward autonomy, mother worship fades, and father and his work take center stage. Father stands outside the rejected merger between mother and child, bearing no taint of its stickiness and disappointments. His work is important not only because of its association with money but because of the real or imagined power that it affords him. And, finally, father's absences from home tend to cloak him in mystery and importance, while mother's presence renders her familiar, known, and commonplace.

By means of this reversal, misogyny sets in. Mother and therefore all women come to seem deficient; father and all men appear supremely admirable. Just as mother represents all women, father comes to stand for all men. Through the figure of mother, women symbolize not only the awesome, contradictory forces of life and death but domestic ordinariness. In contrast, father represents the shining, unambiguous difference between self and other, not the ambivalent fusion between them. He signifies the separation and independence to which children aspire and which some girls have a difficult time achieving. Standing for all the excitement of the outside world of work, power, and self-realization, father becomes the figure that both boys and girls want to emulate. This emerging inequality between mother and father transmits to the child the culture's message of men's first-class citizenship and women's second-class citizenship. Since gender identity is consolidating at this time, boys tend to absorb an unambiguous sense of pride with their masculine selves, while girls are likely to regard their femininity with doubt and ambivalence.

Because of the way that language reflects social reality, fathers take this admirable place even in families in which fathers are absent or mothers work for wages. The multiple but fused meanings contained in the words *mother* or *father*, brought into play with their every utterance, undercoat our understanding of particular mothers and fathers no matter what they are actually like. "Mother" represents "woman," "self-in-relation," "merging," and "childhood." "Father" connotes "man," "self-as-individual," "autonomy," and "adulthood." Since the word *mother* evokes the word *father* just as *day* evokes *night*, then even in father's absence "father" will be a glamorous role model. And, even when a woman works the double day, she will in all likelihood find her children insisting that only fathers, and not mothers, work for a living.

Just as we all want to marry our mothers, so we all want to *be* our fathers. This is the meaning of penis envy. All children have penis envy, even boys. The girl, and the woman into whom she matures, may sometimes express a wish for a penis, but the boy, and the man he grows up to be, often enough wants a bigger one, one more like father's than his own tiny thing. What children envy, however, is not the actual penis, the biological organ through which men urinate and ejaculate. They envy the symbolic penis, the "phallus." They desire to possess what the phallus represents—male privilege, comprising both the right to the exhilarating power and autonomy reputed of the public domain and the right to marry mother and acquire omnipotence, which the child imagines will provide total security and well-being.

According to the rules of patriarchy, however, only men are permitted to possess the phallus and therefore male privilege. Men are defined by what they have, the penis, and women by what they lack, the absence of a penis. On the basis of this definition, men are entitled to privilege, and women are not. Men's entitlement confers on them not only public power but personal power, not only first-class citizenship in public life but a special place in sexual politics.

While the possession of this privilege minimizes men's penis envy, women's lack of privilege maximizes theirs. Although women as well as men want to return to mother, only men manage to do so. Men, when they marry or live with or even simply have intercourse with women, are, in the reasoning of the unconscious, marrying, living with, or fucking their mothers. Women, or at least heterosexual women, must make do with second-best; the only way that they can realize this unconscious fantasy of repossessing their mothers is either by marrying men and thus coming into possession of their phallus or by becoming mothers themselves.

The inevitable loss that girls thus experience haunts them in adult life. Like men, women themselves lack the breast and long to attract it. When a woman envies another woman's beauty, she sees in her not only the capacity to win a man but the breast on which life once fed. Indeed, the core meaning of feminine attractiveness is the limitless love, strength, and nurturing attributed to the perfectly good mother. Therefore, when a woman, ineffably yearning for a beauty that is not her own, doubts herself, her doubt reflects her sense of the absent and seemingly lost maternal love that is her birthright. And her competitiveness, contempt, and anger proceed as much from her own felt failure as from the success of other, more beautiful women.

Women's mutual envy, then, is not only about men. It is about women as well. The popular notion that women dress more to please one another than to please men is correct. Women want one another's approbation because they want what men want, the protective omnipotence that mother once provided and of which only she is thought to be capable. Women, like men, want mother to desire them as much as they desire her.

But the only way to get the breast is to get the phallus. The only way to become the object of mother's desire is to have something mother desires, to be that which mother herself lacks and longs for—the phallus. The wish to have—or be—the phallus is fundamental to the psychology of patriarchy. Since women do not have the phallus, the only way they can become the object of mother's desire is to get a man and merge with him. Thus, through the circular logic of the unconscious and patriarchy is heterosexuality perpetuated in women and men.

I return to the booth and slide in, opposite Phil and Joanna, at which point, as though on cue, Joanna gets up. "Would you order me a white wine, darling? I'll be right back." She disappears in the direction of the ladies' room.

"I'll have a bourbon and water," I tell the waitress, who is outfitted in a resurrected miniskirt and fishnet stockings.

"Two," Phil signals, "and a white. Well, that hasn't changed. So, what's with you? How've you been?"

"Teaching, shrinking, writing. Same old stuff."

"Seeing anyone?"

It would be bad luck to tell him about my (my?) painter at this early point. "Not really. Nobody special."

Phil leans forward and almost whispers, "You meet anybody as good with you as we were together? Remember the last night?" He sucks his breath in through those lips, which are now rounded in a tiny O.

As he speaks, the barroom din recedes, and it is as if once again we were in our own little world. I laugh, and a small warmth travels from the bottom of my heart to my crotch, hands, legs, and cheeks, while I remember another night in the middle of our passionate affair: Standing, drink in hand, leaning against the wall, Phil said, teasingly, lovingly, "When we get home, I want to fuck you. I'm going to put it in you, and go in and out, in and out, real slow, for a long time." He moved his hips slightly. "That's how I'll fuck you," he said softly. "And when I'm done, you'll look a lot better. It'll perk things up here"—he lightly touched my breasts—"and make things smaller here"—patted my waist—"and smooth things out here"—and caressed my hips. An ancient ache of apprehension about my physical imperfections cramped my thoughts, and all I could do was laugh. That I wished that he were taller and looser I would never tell him, knowing how sensitive he was about his slight stature. Instead, I usually consciously fed his vanity by telling him how lean and well-proportioned he was, how beautiful his classic features were, how graceful his genitals were. But, just as his body awed me, his insecurity about it made me slightly contemptuous.

Our lovemaking was wonderful that night—as always. We did it in missionary position—as always. He did all the work—as always. That night, he was hurt that I was not as grateful as I usually was.

Phil and I didn't do much else besides eat, drink, and have sex. Only rarely did we go out to movies, dinner, friends' houses. We preferred to drown ourselves in sensual oblivion, locked in his apartment or mine. You could even say that, just between the two of us, we created our own little family. Together, we were father and daughter, mother and son. Like a father, he ran the show, and, like a daughter, I sat back and admired what he did. Like a son, he showed off. And, like a mother, I was the mirror that reflected his hedonistic sexual expertise; the breast that rewarded him before, during, and after; the body on which he fell asleep. His occasional cruelties seemed a small price to pay for the sexual and emotional magic he created. Perhaps they were even part of it.

ASSERTION, AGGRESSION, AND HETEROSEXUALITY

Sometimes otherwise assertive women find themselves attached to men who hurt them. They may benefit greatly from their romance, affair, or marriage. They may get immense sexual pleasure or give and receive intense love. They may learn a lot from a lover, even be mentored by him. But, to their dismay, they may be hurt repeatedly while simultaneously feeling, at least for a time, unable or unwilling to call on their assertiveness to alter or end the relationship and thereby protect themselves. Even if nowhere else, some women can feel as defenseless in their intimate relations with men as others feel in their encounters with the public world.

Defined by what they lack, women are also trained to minimize whatever self-assertion they have, whether at home or at work. The psychological basis for independence and autonomy, assertiveness belongs to a continuum that bridges activity, assertion, lust, anger, hostility, aggression, and violence. Beginning in infancy's spontaneous, active expressiveness, it embodies the thrust of self upon the world: the neonate's noisy truck-stop suckling; the crawling baby's rush toward the lamp cord hanging from the table; the toddler's purposeful removal of books from the shelf; the little boy who plays with his penis as he urinates; and the little girl who inserts her finger into her vagina, smells it, and, then, graciously offers it for her father's delectation.

Since assertion in little boys shows up in a lot of penis play, it is often called phallic. But "phallicity" is in fact less about penises than about a particular, strutting variety of self-assertion. Phallic sex—sex that is mostly about penis-in-vagina and orgasm—has to do with the insertion not so much of cock into cunt, although certainly that, as of self into the world. In other words, phallicity is about self-assertion on whatever there is to receive or can be made to receive, involving little if any attention to the desire or integrity of the other.

The assertion of self, even phallicity, is an essential moment in any social or creative act. It affirms that, although selves exist in relation to others, the self also stands alone. A protection against regressive longings for merger, self-assertion expresses personal uniqueness. Declaring the difference and separateness of each individual from every other, it underlies the sense of self-possession, of the ownership of self, essential to adult life in the public domain. Self-possession states and affirms the personal entitlement to do with one's own body what one wishes. It thereby permits not only the pleasures of competitive sport but those of sex, including sex for love and sex just for the sake of lust alone. It also expresses the claim to do the best for one's self that one can, to protect body and mind from harm.

Although assertiveness appears in all children as they invade the world with lusty curiosity and greedy pleasure, it, along with the rest of the continuum, is encouraged much more in boys than in girls. Adults tolerate activity, assertiveness, anger, and violence more easily in boys than in girls. By responding to boys when they are active and physically separate, parents reward their sons' desire to explore the world by inserting themselves into it. By responding to girls when they cling close by, parents discourage their daughters' physical assertion and emphasize the desirability of their self-restraint.

From their relationships with their fathers, girls often learn to downplay their assertiveness with men in particular. Embodying the rightful Subject, the first-class citizen, fathers are meant to teach their children how to assume the authority of an autonomous person voyaging out toward self-realization. Because fathers are, according to the conventional division of labor, familiar with the rules, regulations, dangers, and adventures of the public world, they are expected to provide a road map to them. They can illustrate the principles by which that world is negotiated— how one chooses one's goals, how one selects measures for the achievement of them, how one decides when and how to protect oneself, how one determines whether and how much one can avoid hurting others in the process, and how one evaluates how much damage to self and others is tolerable.

Often enough, fathers teach the skills of first-class citizenship less to daughters than to sons. Daughters, like sons, adore their fathers for their mystery and glamour, their representation of autonomy, phallicity, and power. They want to benefit from the same lessons as their brothers, and some are lucky enough to do so. In general, however, fathers, adoring their daughters not only because they are their children but because as females they contain the germ of maternal nurturing, play to daughters' capacity for receptivity and empathy. In consequence, daughters, wishing to be as assertive as their fathers, empathically play the part requested and make themselves the objects of their fathers assertion instead.

Fathers often tease daughters when they are babies and young girls, flirting with them and poking at their bodies, while daughters frequently respond with an excited, if sometimes frightened, delight that is rewarded by and rewards father's pleasure. Later, when puberty makes direct physicality inappropriate, a father's behavior may take the form of a sexually anxious joking or a marked, possibly awkward, withdrawal. Although this behavior can genuinely confuse and discomfort his daughter, it can also please her because she knows that his intent is primarily a loving one, and she often lets him know of her pleasure through her understanding or uncomplaining tolerance of his treatment of her. When, as occasionally happens, a father's assertiveness slips into the extreme of aggression in the form of cruel words, physical violence, or sexual abuse, his daughter all too often will keep silent out of shame or fear or loyalty to one or both parents.

This daughterly experience of carving out an inner, psychological space for father and, by analogy, for men in general, is central to the process by which women become the Subject-as-Object waiting to be completed by a full Subject. Daughters learn to hold themselves back for men, who thrust themselves forward. They do not, however, lose the assertive part of themselves that they withhold. Rather, they store it in men. Embodying wanting-to-be-wanted, women project into men their own wanting, assertiveness, self-possession, self-protectiveness. Under these circumstances, the only way to retrieve this lost part of the self is through an important connection to a man with whose active desire they can identify. Therefore, women's wish to reappropriate their own desire is a major dynamic in the psychology of heterosexuality.

The merging of selves in erotic passion is chief among the heterosexual connections that permit women to repossess their desire. Although women sometimes get little pleasure from sex because their active desire is alienated from them, occasionally they can enjoy it immensely by using this alienation to their own advantage. Sometimes, self-assertion is so discouraged in women that they do not feel entitled to sexual pleasure at all. In these circumstances, not even masturbation will be enjoyable. Or women may lose touch with their own lust because they feel obligated to subordinate their desire to the other person's. These problems, separately or combined, can not only make orgasm difficult to attain but seriously limit sensual gratification itself. Finally, with men who do not wish or know how to please women, women lacking a sense of their entitlement to erotic pleasure are likely to have very unsatisfying and demoralizing sexual experiences.

On the other hand, given her own sexual entitlement, a woman can get pleasure by overtly or subtly letting men "run the fuck." Given the right partner, that is, someone who is at least not uninterested in pleasing her, she may get what she wants in a seemingly passive way. She may, for example, allow him to choose the sexual position. She may permit him to set the pace. She may keep silent about the sort of caresses that she likes or train herself to like the ones he prefers to give her. Or she may routinely make sure that he initiates their sexual encounters.

Whichever tactic she chooses, she indirectly puts the man in charge, thereby consenting to his possession of the phallus, in effect doing all she can to ensure his erections, pleasure, and sexual assertiveness, with which she can then identify and thereby reappropriate her own active desire. She, as the Subject-as-Object wanting-to-be-wanted-by-the-one-who-wants, lets him be the desiring Subject, with whom she then unconsciously merges. The more that a sexual relationship affords her this unconscious recouping, the stronger will be her attachment to it and the more likely she will be to ignore or minimize any hurtful actions that her lover might take against her.

In turn, he may be reassured by this seemingly self-effacing strategy. If she is too lusty, she may seem to be too masculine and therefore to be competing with him, instead of hollowing out a space in which he may remerge with mother. If she is too assertive, she may rouse in him unconscious doubts as to his ability to get what he wants, which in this case is mother's power to give or take life and therefore his own personal power. His hopes for omnipotence dashed, he may become impotent.

And, although she has satisfactions other than penetration, such as clitoral orgasm, he does not. Without an erection, he may feel pleasantly sensual but misses out on the climactic ecstasy that accompanies ejaculation. His impotence triply deprives her as well. She loses the erotic sensation of his penis sliding in and out of her vagina. She forfeits her pleasure in being able to make him happy. And, finally, she lacks that most certain sign of his active desire, his erection, which is, in turn, the unquestionable sign of hers. As his erection disappears, so, too, does the palpable symbol of her own projected assertiveness.

Women's capacity to hold back is reassuring to them as well. It relieves them of shame, self-hatred, and guilt. If they are not assertive, they conform to the feminine stereotype and maintain gender identity. They may also thereby ignore in themselves the very maternal power that they, like men, adore, envy, and hate. In addition, their passivity lessens the guilt that they may feel for having used that power to get a man, thereby, unconsciously, to have stolen father from mother and to have separated from her as well.

In sum, then, the pretense to passivity is a game that cannot be won. Women's self-restraint leaves them unprotected. Intended to reassure, it nevertheless reveals the strength it conceals, for it is an act of will. Meant to create pleasure, it nevertheless causes fear. The power behind it is what can frighten men, causing them to be cruel to women, if not by physically attacking them, then by disparaging the very physical qualities that stir in them hopes for the realization of their own security. Without this self-restraint, women are defenseless against such attacks. Yet the additional self-hate generated by their passivity makes the abuse seem all the more deserved.

Still, the rewards for walking the line between too little and too much assertion are great. By association with a man, by identification with him, by merging with him in marriage and taking his name, a woman gets to possess, even if at a remove, a man's political and personal power. She benefits from his wealth, his first-class citizenship, his assertiveness, even his cruelty that he exercises on others besides her in the interest of making a living. And she gets the unconscious benefits of his phallus as well. Repossessing thereby the active desire that she has projected into him, she can feel complete. His phallus even compensates for the virtue that becomes, in the context of patriarchy, a liability: her capacity to represent the power of life and death itself.

Remembering—how could I not?—that Phil had always had several relationships going and enjoyed the jealousy of his women for one another, I realize, with a wry inner smile, how much he is enjoying this moment as he rises to allow Joanna to slide her straight and narrow hips and thighs across their side of the booth.

"Ah, here we all are. I like your skirt," Phil says to the waitress as she sets the drinks in front of us.

"No, I get the bourbon, thank you." I take my glass.

Joanna lifts her glass. "Happy spring."

I return her toast and sip, then say, "So, Phil, what sort of ecology are you into?"

Setting his glass down, he replies, "All sorts. I've worked mainly on the usual industrial problems—air and water pollution, like that. But lately I've been having preliminary talks with the fellows at the nuclear power plant on the Island."

"Nuclear ecology?" I exclaim in shock. "Phil, there's no such thing. You ought to know better than that." I look at Joanna. "Why, I first got to know him in an antinuke group."

As Phil blushes slightly, Joanna intervenes, explaining earnestly, "Oh, I share your concern, I really do, but look at it this way. Nuclear power's got its faults, but since it's inevitable we may as well make the best of it."

"Well, I disagree completely, but maybe this isn't the time to argue." Then, wanting to defuse this awkward situation, I change the subject. "You look like you're in terrific shape, Joanna. So do you, Phil."

She smiles. "Oh, thanks, thanks very much. I've just taken up jogging. We jog together weekends. Do you run?"

"No," I answer, feeling that I ought to. "I find it hard on my feet, and, besides, I get bored."

"Oh, you should get a walkman. It makes all the difference."

"Oh, yes, I see a lot of joggers with walkpersons." The joke, I realize as soon as I make it, is a dud. Wrong company.

"You know," Joanna says, looking at Phil, then at me, "I think people make too big a deal about things. I mean, why can't you just say 'walkman'? That's the name of the product. 'Walkperson' sounds clumsy. I can see why they named it 'walkman.' It sounds like a cute, spacey little robot, like R2D2. I like it."

She takes a sip of her wine. "Anyway, I get tired of people complaining all the time. Like women who say they can't get ahead at work because they're women. Well, of course, if you're too pushy and aggressive, you're not going to get anywhere, but if you deliver, really do the job, they forget you're a woman and you can get where you want to go eventually." She glances at a man passing by.

"You know," Phil leans forward, resting on his elbows and fiddling with the ashtray, looking down and then up at me as he continues, "I think Jay's right. There's been too much emphasis on how women are the victims of society. There's got to be more going out and getting what you want."

"Really." Her tone conciliatory, Joanna leans against the seat, her hands on either side of the base of her wineglass.

"All this talk about what society does to you saps your self-confidence. You have to be able to depend on yourself. You have to go for it."

"I couldn't agree more," I answer, shaking the melting ice cubes in my glass and watching the amber pale. "But that doesn't mean that society plays no role."

"Well, no, of course not," she says.

"Jay is a real go-getter. Two raises in one year. And she's only twenty-seven." He chucks her under the chin.

I subtract. Oh dear. 1957. Born in 1957. So, let's see, when she was seventeen, and I was twenty-seven, abortions had become legal. Contraceptives were available, equal pay was legislated if not always enforced, marijuana was a fact of everyday life, the war in Vietnam was over, the so-called sexual revolution was in full swing, and the "me" generation taking over. Feminism, like abortion, contraception, drugs, the Vietnam War, and free love must seem to her to be issues from the age of dinosaurs.

"Damn, I forgot, I told Stuart I'd call his publisher about the press conference." Joanna leans forward to rise from her seat.

"Forget about it now, hon, it's six o'clock. It's Friday, for God's sake. He must have gone home."

"No, you know how people hang around at the end of the day. Nobody ever wants to go home right away. I'll try him at the office."

As Joanna weaves her way through the mob at the bar in search of a telephone, Phil comments, "Jay is almost a workaholic. Still, she's careful. She takes work home, but she takes weekends off. She goes to the health club three times a week. And she's learning New American cuisine."

THE PHALLUS AND THE STATE

The glamour in which patriarchy enfolds fathers is usually completely at odds with their own daily lives. Most men do not occupy the pinnacle of any hierarchy outside the home, being in fact juvenilized if not feminized by those few men, and even fewer women, who do. No man or woman who goes to work, pays taxes, and reads the newspaper can feel as omnipotently wonderful as mother may once have seemed or as father may appear.

Work may be exciting or it may be drudgery. But it is located in a public world that is as antithetical to autonomy as it is insistent upon it. This is not to say that there are no good people in it but simply that it is often a mean place. In the end, then, the public world is not a place where someone looks out for the other guy. Rather, one has to look out for oneself. The public world calls for individualizing and assertiveness, not relatedness and empathy. But since objectification routinely turns assertion into aggression and since everyone, including men, at times remains a frightened child yearning for tender nurturing, anyone can be bruised in such a world.

Under these circumstances, the best defense is a good pretense. We adopt a pose like that of the cowboy hero. We wear a poker face, which works like mirrored sunglasses, mimicking the social gaze so as to deny it access to the vulnerable self inside. We act as though we were never scared. We create a self that sheaths the interior soft places with an intimidating exterior that projects toughness and meanness and creates a tolerance for pain and loneliness. This impassive mask enables men to kill themselves with work. It permits women as well as men to treat themselves like pieces of wood, and with determination and pride, jog themselves black-and-blue, if not to death. It allows them, finally, to look on others as if they, too, were either invulnerable or dead.

However, the cowboy's cultivated insensitivity to the delicacy of self, and of the tendrils between selves, leaves men raw. Men usually work with other people as members of a team, from which they are expected to depart cleanly at the end of the day or the job. They are therefore often subject to the same relational conflicts as women. Teamwork calls for relatedness, even as it demands individualizing. When people work in a connected, intimate way, they necessarily become emotionally vulnerable to one another. But the cowboy mask, as a personal style well suited to public life, tends to prohibit men from acknowledging and understanding their vulnerabilities. In the absence of emotional self-awareness, the ragged emotions stirred up in the course of the workday can therefore feel as jagged as a fresh wound, which is the reason that men can be found drinking in the saloon at five o'clock, imbibing three martinis at lunch, or frequenting liquor stores at any hour of the day.

Nevertheless, many women in public life find that the cowboy pose protects them in the same way that it protects men—it prevents them from being scared. The cowboy mask conceals a big secret about life that adults keep from children because they are afraid of it: We never stop being scared. The neediness of infancy survives in all of us, and we are all perpetually frightened by the economic and political uncertainties of twentieth-century life. The trick to becoming an adult is to ignore the fear, to go on and do what you have to no matter how afraid you are.

This is a trick that fathers are supposed to teach their children but tend to pass on to sons, not daughters. Instead, daughters learn that fearfulness means failure. Their lesson is that nervousness and anxiety are signs of danger, not, as they may sometimes be, the result of eager anticipation such as precedes an interview, a performance, or a triathlon. Women are thereby trained to infer from fright that they should stop whatever it is they were about to do or else they will get hurt or fail; indeed, they may learn to equate pain with failure. And should they get hurt or fail, they are likely to conclude that they should not have tried at all.

The self-protection afforded by the cowboy posture is, then, another reason that women may envy men. As imposture, it allows one to act as though the normal fears of adulthood did not exist and to numb oneself to others' pain as well as one's own. The capacities to hurt oneself and to hurt others at minimal cost to oneself are not necessarily laudable. However, given the power structure that informs our society, and given that women's socialization tends to make them unfamiliar with their assertiveness and aggressivity, women's imitation of the tough, mean, impassive cowboy can serve them well. It helps to know how to be aggressive and how not to feel bad when others are aggressive in return or from the start.

Nevertheless, as a solution to the problems faced by conventional femininity in adult, public life, the cowboy mask is sorely incomplete. As second-class citizens, women lack the buffer that heterosexuality offers to men. When, after work, men go home or out on a date, they can expect that their wounds will be bandaged. They can anticipate either tenderness or admiration from their women or, failing that, at least the softness of their flesh. They can, as well, dominate them, physically if not emotionally, in principle if not in practice, and thereby compensate for feelings of inadequacy churned up during the day. In contrast, most women can no longer get by on the deal they cut in the past, when, not earning their own money, they exchanged their public assertiveness for the protection and care provided by their husbands' income and authority. The job confronting them now is to get that empathy where they can—from the men whom they train to provide it or who, in rare cases, know how to give it already, from women friends, from their children, and from themselves.

Women, untrained for and unentitled to assertiveness and aggression, are poorly equipped to negotiate public life in the state. Autonomous self-assertion is absolutely essential in a society that increasingly isolates people from one another by emphasizing the self-as-individual at the cost of the self-in-relation. But aggression is required as well. In the state, where winning and losing sourly signify moral worth, self-assertion curdles into aggression. Unless one can comfortably utilize one's own hostility and destructiveness, public life can be quite hazardous.

However, assertiveness and aggression have traditionally been male property. The cultural hallmarks of masculinity, they are symbolized by the phallus. Representing as well masculine privilege in a culture of hierarchy, the phallus comes also to signify that culture itself, the state. Other symbols of culture—of the human necessity for social life—are possible, such as bosomy and hippy female figurines of Stone Age cultures in Germany and other parts of Europe, or the animals in whom reside the inseminating clan spirits of the Trobriand Islanders, or the female jaguars worshiped by the Olmecs who lived in Mexico in 1200 B.C. But when the actual configuration of power is male over female, rich man over poor man, and state over citizen, only the phallus will do.

In our culture, therefore, we all have penis envy. We all want the phallus, because it promises to deliver us control over personal fate. But our longing is not merely fantastic. Some people really do have the sort of power that can determine the rest of our lives. Some of them are in power because they control the money and jobs the rest of us need. And others have ultimate power because, holding the keys to the halls of state, they have their fingers on the nuclear buttons that can destroy human life itself. As long as their destructive power exists, the rest of us will legitimately continue to envy it, and hostility and hatred will define our culture.

"So, what are you doing this weekend?" Phil asks me.

I hesitate. "Well, I'm meeting William later."

"Hey, I didn't know you were into leather."

"Well, you know me," I say as brazenly as I can, "I always want to try new things. Anyway, I was supposed to go to the Spring Equinox party last year, but I missed it, so I promised him I'd go this year."

"Yeah, I could see you doing a little bondage. Yeah. Remember—?"

I cut him off. "So, are you and Joanna serious?"

"Women always want to get married." He waves. Joanna sits down. "Oh, hi, babe, was he there?" Phil finishes his bourbon.

"No, but I left a message on his machine at home. What was that you were saying about marriage?" She reaches for her wine.

Phil puts his arm around her shoulders. "There's still a basic difference between men and women. No matter how liberated the woman, she still wants to get married. Men don't. It's probably biological. Right, Jay?"

Suddenly white wine is puddling amoebalike all over the table, around the glasses, the ashtray, the plastic-coated menu card, and the fringed wine list. Joanna's glass falls off the table and shatters. Fortunately, the waitress is passing by. She mops and sweeps up and brings another glass of wine.

"You okay, hon?" Phil asks solicitously. "I remember the first time Jay made dinner for me, didn't you drop the salad bowl or something?"

Pink suffuses Joanna's cheeks. "How come you keep bringing that up?"

"Just joking. Can't you take a joke, Jay?" He tightens his hold on her shoulders. "Ah, come on, babe, you know I really didn't mean it."

"He's just jealous." Dimpling adorably, she has rallied. "My cooking is better than his."

Phil kisses her cheek. "Ain't she great?"

I feel envious of and sorry for Joanna, annoyed with and jealous of Phil. Maybe he really wants her. Maybe she really wants him. Maybe it will work. Maybe they deserve each other. Who knows? I feel old and leathery and battle-scarred and vulnerable. I also feel a strong cramp. I want to go home.

"Well, I'd better be on my way. Nice to meet you, Joanna. And it was wonderful to see you again, Phil."

"Yes, a pleasure," she says.

"Really," Phil agrees, looking at my hips as I rise to leave. "You look great, by the way. Let's have lunch some time, and, oh, have a real good time tonight."

Women Alone

(6:45 P.M.)

*E*ntering my apartment with my mail in hand, I walk into a silence that proclaims what is absent—no kids, no husband, no lover, no family.

Oh well. At least, in the embrace of my little home, I can temporarily shut everything else out. I can shut the door on Phil and Joanna, my analyst, Lorraine, Ted, Ginny, Dennis, Andrea, the people in the subway car, and—

Ohmigod, did Daniel leave a note? Where is it? I look down at the hall table filled with everything but. I was sure he would.

Perhaps it's in the bedroom. I drop my briefcase and the mail on the hall table and rush inside. He's made the bed, leaving a few lumps, which I automatically straighten out. But no note. Why not? Is this part of the usual masculine pattern? Is he pulling away because we've gotten close? But he's never been the sort who says, "I'll call you," and then doesn't.

I check the answering machine. Two hang-ups. (Who? Him? A shy patient? One of my friends who hates machines?) Damn. Well, if my desire to talk to Daniel overwhelms me, I can always call him to ask about the key. Except that I have to wait until he gets back from Colorado.

The cat wanders in from the closet, where he has been sleeping all day, and rubs my ankles, purring in anticipation of dinner.

"Yes, yes," I say, "but first things first, my dear."

I go into the bathroom, carrying the tampons, and, just before I sit down on the toilet, I see, with my normal combination of relief and vexation, that blood has finally overflowed the diaphragm, staining my panties.

Jeans and panties around my ankles, I squat, stick my thumb into my vagina, hook it on the edge of the diaphragm, and tug. The flexible rim contracts and expands pleasurably as I pull it out. The dome brims with a red viscous fluid so oddly dark that it could never be mistaken for the blood from a wound. After twenty-four years of menstruating, it still shocks and awes me to see so much of it in one place.

I turn on the cold water in the sink and hold the diaphragm under the torrent, watching the diluted blood surge up and over the rim, then streak down the drain, leaving some fleshlike bits amidst the swirl.

Something else spirals away too, doesn't it? I look up into the medicine cabinet mirror.

You know, dear, you're going to have to decide soon, says my mother. *It's getting late.*

Thinking of Lorraine and feeling very alone, I soap and rinse the diaphragm, then leave the stained panties to soak in cold water as she told me to do the first day of my period.

I pat the diaphragm dry with the special towel reserved for this purpose and sprinkle it with cornstarch. I'd better test it for holes soon, and I hope I don't need a new one—my gynecologist is always booked up weeks in advance. And, even when you finally get an appointment with her, chances are you'll end up sitting and waiting in her crowded office.

WOMEN'S SECOND BIRTH OF SELF

Menstruation is a central, organizing factor in formulating feminine subjectivity in our culture. It is to some extent a second birth of self. The changes of puberty, sharply discontinuous with earlier growth, bring into being a new body that disrupts existing body image and therefore self-image. The regular periodicity of menstruation provides one marker by which this disrupted experience of self can be reordered. Moreover, menarche, or first menses, represents the commencement of sovereign adulthood. It therefore affords a very private pleasure and pride in the body, heightening a sense of hoped-for autonomy. In principle, first menses is the moment when a woman's body begins to become her personal property and she can do with it what she pleases.

Yet the whispers in which menarche is announced, even in families otherwise pleased by it, suggest not only a delicate respect for the young woman's privacy but a kind of secret shame. Sometimes, the shamefulness is bluntly summarized in euphemisms like "the curse." These negative evaluations, learned early on at home, herald the cultural devaluation of femininity. Although fertility, which is signaled by menstruation, is culturally valued, the cyclical hormonal changes necessary to it are thought to handicap women for participation in public life. Even though erroneous, this negative estimation of women's ability seeps into their identity.

Menstruation is therefore a very mixed experience, sending messages of both power and weakness that excite, but also generate anxiety. This uneasy mixture is the reason that women have many different attitudes toward their menstrual cycle. Some women think and talk about it a lot, others never do so at all. Some women actually like the cramps that periods bring, while others hate them. Some become depressed at menopause, others cheerful. And some feel both the pleasant and the unpleasant emotions at once. Menstruation therefore surrounds adult femininity with an aura of ambivalence that informs and describes women's attitudes about themselves altogether.

As the gateway to adulthood, menstruation symbolizes the moment when a girl looks out upon the world and sees it divided into two portions having separate but not equal attributes:

Independence	Dependence
Activity	Passivity
Assertion	Receptivity
Aggression	Selflessness
Autonomy	Empathy
Desire	Need
Adulthood	Childhood
Masculinity	Femininity
First-class status	Second-class status

In this absolutely ambivalent moment, a young woman must feel simultaneously hopeful and disappointed. Contemplating a halved world that offers wonderful possibilities to some people but not to others, she will want the best, yet will have to recognize that her portion is judged inferior. She will also sense, perhaps with confusion, that not all of the qualities deemed first-class are good and that some of those listed as second-class are, otherwise viewed, in fact valuable. Menstruation therefore confronts her with the necessity of developing her own opinions about how she will handle the divided and unequal set of human possibilities offered her by her culture.

Menarche is a moment of profound aloneness. It is the embarkation on a long-awaited, very problematic journey involving many nearly impossible choices and gigantic efforts to create and preserve self-esteem. From this point on, girls begin to pick their way carefully among the sexual contradictions that simultaneously affirm and deny women's social power and self-respect. Although some girls begin to do so sooner than menarche and others later, the self-reflective awareness that dawns at puberty focuses and accelerates this process of selection. Young lesbians may find this moment of self-awareness infused with an additional measure of self-consciousness, in contrast to girls whose heterosexual preference smoothly matches social convention. But whatever their sexuality, girls, like boys, begin, with the onset of adolescence, to shape themselves in their own image, and part of doing so is deciding how they will relate to the gender hierarchy.

In other words, girls have to decide whether and how they will be women. Although gender is not exactly a matter of personal choice, it can nonetheless be psychologically accepted or rejected.

One comes to terms not only with one's reproductive anatomy and its consequences but also with the cultural meanings and values with which they are imbued. Women's acceptance of their gender requires them to be at ease with ambivalence. It means to assume femininity with pride all the while acknowledging the social dishonor it entails. It requires one to learn to behave as though autonomous, all the while remembering that one is defined in relation to others. In effect, it is to realize that one is Subject-as-Object and then to use one's subjectivity to soften the blows to self-esteem delivered by objectification, losing as little self-respect as possible in the process.

The acceptance of femininity, mixed as it is, begins a process in which young women reach personal decisions about the sort of women they will be. With varying degrees of certainty and success, they begin to determine how to comport themselves in private and public. As part of this process, they sort out heterosexual and homosexual feelings and explore, in act or fantasy, the variety of their sexual desire. As they mature, they choose whether to be sexy or not and how to respond to the attentions of the boys and men, and girls and women they know, as well as of strangers. Over time, they resolve the matter of adornment, deciding how important physical appearance is to them and creating a personal style that reflects or rebels against fashion, yet also expresses personal values. They come to learn how to manage the responsibilities of relatedness, including, should the matter arise, housekeeping and childrearing. Gradually, they survey the public world and find their own place in it.

In whatever ways a girl's personality develops before puberty, menarche is the moment when the truth comes home to her, consciously or unconsciously, that she is responsible for herself. She is alone in the world as a separate human being, even though she is defined by and in relation to others. Like all adults in our culture, she has the freedom and sometimes lonely obligation to create herself.

But since women are supposed to do what they want even though they are not supposed to want, they have to fight this battle with one hand tied behind their back. Yet they fight it anyway, because they are subjects as well as objects. Like others stigmatized by the biology of race or physical handicap, women invariably assert their right to first-class citizenship in the face of all cultural denials of it. They, like men, make decisions about how they will live, making mistakes but also passing through the Scylla and Charybdis of adulthood with a heroism of their own.

In the bedroom I put on the chenille bathrobe that I've managed to preserve from my early adolescence.

I return to the hall and stand at the table sorting my mail—copies of my tax returns with my accountant's bill, an application to renew my expired passport, a fund-raising appeal from an activist reproductive-rights group, an advertisement for a new book on psychoanalysis and literature, an offer to take out a new credit card, the preliminary program of August's annual sociology convention, to be held this year in Mexico City, and *The New York Review of Books*.

I skim through the convention program until I see, with relief, that my presentation has been scheduled for an afternoon session. As I read the titles of the other papers, I am conscious of mixed feelings. I used to love the erotic euphoria permeating the nonstop gossip, parties, flirtations, and even the academic babble of conventions. However, the older I get, the lonelier I feel in those vast, impersonal hotels, and the more conventions resemble the business trips that they are. Still, a tax-deductible vacation in Mexico is nothing to sneeze at, especially if you include a trip to the Yucatan as part of it. I'd better renew the passport soon.

Carrying my spectacles and *The New York Review of Books* with me, I go into the kitchen to give the cat his milk and Super Supper. Then I spot the sticky champagne glasses and cigarette-filled ashtray on the kitchen counter. Disgusting. I remember my mother's ritual morning sweep of the kitchen and living room, despite her constant complaints about being a housewife. I wish I were as neat as she. Or maybe I wish I had someone to neaten things for me.

Since you don't, maybe you should do the dishes yourself, suggests my conscience.

In a minute, I say.

I sit at the kitchen table and flip through *The New York Review of Books,* noting one or two articles to which I will return when more alert. Then I turn to the back pages to peruse the personal ads. As usual, there are at least twice as many women as men who advertise. Everyone seems so lonely. Two ads, one from a man and one from a woman, match quite nicely. Will they write to each other? What would it be like to put in an ad? I'm glad

I've never felt the need to. The anticipatory shame and anxiety would be a hundred times worse than what you feel on a blind date. Or would they? Is it really so different from looking to meet someone at a party? I get a pencil and a sheet of paper from my desk, then return to the kitchen table, where I doodle for a bit, then write the words, "Attractive, divorced, psychothera . . ." and stop because I feel so self-conscious.

Then, yielding to impulse, I open the spinet bequeathed me by my grandmother because my father was her favorite son and because we used to play four-handed pieces, she on the left and I on the right. I leaf through the books that are out, then take from the bench Hérold's *Zampa* overture, one of the first pieces she agreed to play with me after she judged me sufficiently skilled. I run through the first allegro and then skip to the end of the last repeat to finish off the final triumphant bars, my favorite part.

THE EVOLUTION OF THE FAMILY

The emergence of the woman alone is inextricable from the evolution of the family. Although there have always been some women who lived alone, women now have far more freedom to live by themselves if they choose. In the past, women have led autonomous lives on the margins of mainstream society, as eccentric spinsters and widows of independent wealth, artists and lesbians in bohemian communities, courtesans and prostitutes serving men of all classes, and "witches" inhabiting the outskirts of peasant villages. But economic and political changes now offer this autonomy to all women. No longer dependent on the legitimacy granted by a husband's name, credit rating, and even reputation, women need not marry to take a public place. Jobs, the entitlement to own property, and the vote give them an opportunity to try their luck in the public arena.

Women can have not only relative economic security without husbands but sexual satisfaction as well. A liberalized sexual atmosphere permits women to have sex at will, albeit with some remaining risk to their reputation and physical safety. And they can do so without having children. The availability of fairly reliable contraception, backed up by legal abortion, means that heterosexual intercourse does not necessarily result in reproduction, which in turn means that women need not live their lives as unwilling mothers.

However, even though some women opt to live alone, most take enormous pleasure in sharing their lives with others. Those who work for a living suffer the same hardships as men in the public domain and long for some intimacy to relieve their stress and alienation. Furthermore, they, like women who neither want nor need to earn money, are pushed and pulled by their psychological and cultural connection to relatedness. The equation of "woman" with "mother," and "mother" with "self-in-relation," the tangling of selves between mother and daughter, the training toward empathy and away from autonomy—all these forces dispose women to being with other people in general and being in families in particular.

In addition, women, like men, are attracted to family life not only by gender training but by memories of childhood. In going forward to create their own lives, adults keep looking back to the security and love found in their youth. The chief, sometimes unconscious, memory pulling adults toward the family is that of the reliability and solidity provided by the parents' protective love and care. Even among those adults who had miserable childhoods, there are many whose hopes of creating satisfying family lives probably originated, at least in part, in some early experience of goodness. Moreover, the models of adulthood with which most children grow up are of men and women who live together as kin.

Sometimes these wishful or real memories of childhood happiness coat "the family" in a romantic haze. Interweaving with the frequently difficult experiences of adult life, these memories incline adults to see families solely as sources of strength, higher purpose, and pure love. Mother's apparent selflessness makes the home into a refuge from marketplace greed. Paternal reliability makes it a reservoir of trust and loyalty, countering the ordinary betrayals of public life. For the adult wage earner, the tenderness once received in mother's embrace underlies the anticipation of the day's end. For the full-time housewife, the personal power to satisfy her family can compensate for her second-class political power. At the same time, wage earners and housewives are unconsciously impelled to live up to or compensate for the past. Some create families in order to reciprocate whatever goodness they received as children. Others wish to prove to themselves that even though their own families were not the most loving, they can nevertheless create, against great odds, a perfect family for and by themselves.

Like society itself, individuals romanticize the family. In our culture, we speak of "the Family" as if only one kind ever existed—the monogamous nuclear family of man-the-breadwinner and woman-the-full-time-housewife with their dependent children and no one else. But this small family unit, free of other immediately compelling social ties, is in fact quite limited in time and space. In most cultures, the extended family predominates, embedding the nuclear family economically and politically in a web of kin.

Even in those preindustrial cultures, like the !Kung San of Africa, in which the nuclear family is a temporarily viable economic unit, it is nevertheless not the same family that our culture idealizes. The high frequency of divorce among the !Kung San means that, at any one time, one or another family will be breaking up or reconstituting. But stability and continuity are provided for adults and children by the larger, kinship-based community in which all individuals are equal members. Adults' overall dependency on this community, their rights and obligations to share food and work, means that the !Kung San nuclear family—not to mention the individual—is not at all "independent" in the sense of the isolation expected of it in our culture.

The Western family has, however, been undergoing continuous evolution in response to wider political and economic change. The nuclear family emerged as our main domestic unit from the extended family only during the last century. As industrialization removed economic production from peasant and artisan homes to centralized factories during the nineteenth century, the three-generation, multifamily extended households shrank to the two-generation nuclear family. At the same time, the public and the private domains split apart, with the latter, organized by the nuclear family and run by women, coming to serve as a receptacle into which workers tumbled at the end of the day for food, companionship, and sleep.

Concurrently with the family's dismantling, patriarchal power decreased and women's access to public power increased. The status of most men diminished as the corporation rose to economic predominance and the economic autonomy of the extended family household declined. While many men had once been heads of peasant and artisan households that owned their own land or hired themselves out collectively to wealthier landowners, now they sold their labor as lone individuals to the owners of factories or other businesses to whom they became subordinate. This loss of public power began to qualify their personal power at home and in their own minds. Patriarchal authority lessened also because, at the same time, the expansion of the money economy occasionally drew women, especially in working-class families, into the marketplace, giving them the beginnings of independent economic power.

In the twentieth century, the extended family fell apart as the ties between generations and the bonds of inheritance—the latter always more important for the upper classes—no longer made economic sense. During the middle part of this century, many people came to live in the idealized, "Ozzie and Harriet" nuclear family. However, the bonds between men and women having been loosened at the same time as the ties between generations, those between husband and wife began to unravel as well. As households came to require two incomes, women began to work for wages regularly. As the welfare state began to aid impoverished mothers of dependent children, much of women's economic dependency on men disappeared. As this dependency eroded, so too did part of the nuclear family's groundwork. When single-motherhood therefore becomes, as it has, merely difficult rather than impossible, and living alone even more feasible, then the nuclear family loses much of its rationale.

Furthermore, the nuclear family no longer provides many of its emotional benefits as its political and personal burdens multiply. The double day requires husbands and wives to have enormous and self-renewing stores of emotional energy and goodwill in order to make their own lives and those of their children as comfortable, if not as happy, as they can. But, having the obligations of traditional gender roles while lacking the rewards of either, the married couple may be prone to find fault with each other rather than with their situation.

Additionally, for all the freedom from patriarchal authority and interfering mothers-in-law created by the disappearance of the extended family, the nuclear family can also be a very lonely place. Husband and wife, now each other's only immediate family, stagger under the weighty responsibility of alleviating their sense of lonely togetherness. Women, either stressed by the double day or feeling demeaned by being "only a housewife," chafe at the family's bit. Men, feeling bruised and sometimes powerless in public life, come home expecting care and hoping for power but sometimes find yet another wearisome battle.

The very small proportion of nuclear families with the luxury to approximate the old ideal of division of labor do so by getting outside help. Well-to-do families manage to maintain the illusion of the nuclear family by relying on the same method that families of equivalent class status used during the nineteenth century: They employ servants who wash and cook and clean and watch children, who help out with all of the many tasks that the full-time middle-class housewife of the mid-twentieth century was once supposed to do for love rather than money but was frequently worn down by trying to accomplish.

As the extended family gave way to the nuclear family, so the nuclear family is now unfolding into a variety of domestic units. Nuclear families persist but have changed so much as to be no longer what they are supposed to be. Some, founded on "open marriage" or constituted as much by divorce and remarriage as by an original wedding, are frequently not monogamous, nor even heterosexual. Single-parent families, set in a network of kin or friends, are found not only in the working class, as was the case in nineteenth-century cities, but in the middle class as well.

Nor do households always consist of families. Urban, Western culture has a long-standing tradition of single people living alone for longer or shorter periods of time. The anonymity and services of city life allowed the formation of homosexual, artistic, and intellectual communities. These communities have always included singles, among whom there were more men than women, of course. However, single adulthood is no longer restricted to these avant-garde or renegade communities. Now the households of the separated, widowed, or divorced person and those of roommates or cohabiting lovers make up the fastest-growing kind of household in our society.

Single adulthood has become a mainstream possibility because new social institutions have developed that furnish some of the material and emotional supports that families traditionally offer. The service economy, of which fast-food restaurants are emblematic, performs many of the functions once carried out by full-time housewives and mothers. Men and women who can buy good take-away meals are far more free to live singly than those dependent on others to cook them decent food. Apartment complexes built for and rented exclusively to singles serve as communities providing social gatherings, organized recreation, and all the pleasures and drawbacks of small-town life. These communities tend, however, to be a rest stop on the way to marriage, as evidenced by the fact that those over thirty who remain unmarried feel somewhat out of their element and often move elsewhere.

However, other institutions serving the single life exist even in the absence of community. Friends and groups of friends can provide intimacy, comfort, and shared history as they age together. Friendships are particularly important for divorced women over thirty, who are less likely to remarry than their male peers. Neighbors, therapy groups, and organizations founded on specialized interests also provide varied sources of security and companionship. Personal ads in the newspapers and on television offer a limited but occasionally effective route of communication for singles wanting love, marriage, or sex. Singles' bars, health clubs, and dating services, as well as workshops on topics ranging from stock-market investments to shower singing, allow increasingly isolated single individuals to meet one another. None of these arrangements, however, helps those who are perhaps in most dire need, the widows who, their children grown and gone, make up the largest portion of single adults. Nor does any fully assuage the frequent loneliness of the single life.

Nevertheless, younger men and women can choose among these evolving forms for companionship, intimacy, and sexuality. They can live in families or they can live alone, even though a woman alone is still more of an oddity than a bachelor. Just as men, once duty-bound to support the well-being and reputation of their families, have become free to pursue their personal self-interest in an increasingly individualized society, so, too, have women, even though society and psychology incline them not to. Just as men have been losing the economic protection afforded by large kinship groups and therefore becoming ever more vulnerable to an impersonal and anomic society, so, too, have women. Women, like men, have therefore begun to acquire the uncertain but real freedom of the lone voyager. Like men, the greater their opportunity for independence, the more they choose to take it. Women share with men the heritage of individuality that has been emerging out of the social mosaic of family and class since the time of Homer. And they therefore have to decide what to do with this ambiguous prize.

I pull my old expired passport out of the filing cabinet; write checks for the tax returns, my accountant, and the passport renewal; sign the tax returns and fill out the renewal form; and put all the papers and checks in their proper envelopes, which I then seal and stamp.

Then, feeling sufficiently unwound, I lie down for a fifteen-minute rest before doing the dishes. On the couch, I drift into reverie, recalling a Saturday evening with Daniel, one that followed the early rush of all-night lovemaking, endless talk about music and movies, arguments about the cost of psychoanalysis and the insularity of the art world, comparisons of hometowns and families and travel.

On the spur of the moment, we decided to go to a movie but arrived to find that the showing had been sold out. He called a friend from a telephone booth but reached only an answering machine. So we strolled around Washington Square, where we bumped into an old acquaintance of his. They talked shop for a bit. Feeling a little excluded, I turned slightly aside while I waited. When we walked on, I linked my arm in his, pleased to be with him even though the evening was a little boring, even though I also felt a little tied down and locked away from all the people who passed us seemingly free of obligations.

Back at his loft, we read Sunday's *New York Times* in an easy silence that was warmly familiar even though I had never before shared it with him. I made tea, mistakenly brewing it a little longer than he liked. But when I offered to throw it out and start over, he looked at me over his half-glasses, shook his head, and blew me a kiss, saying that it tasted fine. I watched him as he read and drank, liking his body because it was slightly thickened and substantial, lean but no longer a boy's. In a little while, he got up and washed the pot and cups, and then we went to bed.

The phone rings, interrupting the memory. I leap up.

"Zena, hi . . . oh, I'm seeing William. . . . When? . . . Okay, I'll see. I hope he's home. I'll call you right back."

I dial. "William, listen, Zena just called. She's going to San Francisco on an assignment tomorrow and she's nervous. So I said I'd have dinner with her, that is, if you don't mind my changing our plans. Could I meet you a little later than we planned? . . . Thanks. Sorry I had to. . . . I'll see you at your apartment at eleven. Bye."

I call Zena back and agree to meet at a downtown restaurant.

I lie down again. The cat suddenly comes in for a landing at my feet, the front paws touching down a split second after the hind ones. Licking his chops, he picks his way along my side and nestles in the curve of my waist. It's too bad I can't curl up around him in the same way. We doze off together.

THE HETEROSEXUAL WOMAN ALONE

The evolution of the family, coinciding with the rise of the twentieth-century state, exacerbates both the yearning for intimacy and the vulnerability felt by adults seeking it. As the family has evolved, individuals have become socially alone in a historically unprecedented way. Previously, family and extended kinship networks, and sometimes the communities based on and incorporating them as well, served as shock absorbers against the rough power of the state.

The ability of kinship to cushion the shocks of everyday life has dwindled slowly but enormously. As the extended family contracted into the nuclear family, the protective weaving of kin and community wore thin. With the prevalence of the two-income family, the abundant, rejuvenating nurturing provided by the full-time housewife becomes a luxury affordable only by those who can hire domestic help. Now almost no institution exists to buffer the individual from the state, which has become the individual's silent, all-encompassing, and abandoning partner. At the same time as families, kin-based communities, religious institutions, and, occasionally, private enterprises were ceasing to supply the safety net required by individuals, governmental institutions were emerging to take over and fill in the gap.

Today the government provides certain essential services without which industrial society could not exist. It establishes and regulates systems of education, health care, and social welfare. It creates and maintains systems of transportation. Government interdigitates economic enterprises through rules of exchange formulated by its legislature and judiciary, as well as by the money that it prints and endows with value. Through its power to regulate weapons, its standing army and police force, and its right of imprisonment, it maintains social control and keeps conflict, an ever-present possibility given existing, substantial inequities, from breaking out into violence.

The government accomplishes its tasks through a centralized, rambling, convoluted, and impersonal bureaucracy. Unlike the kinship, community, and religious organizations that once carried out many of these activities, the bureaucracy is anonymous. While the elders of a community, or the religious leaders who led their flocks, or even the lords who ruled serfs were often linked by personal as well as political ties to those whom they represented or governed and were thereby known to them, the bureaucracy is as approachable and humanly susceptible as a robot. Masked in red tape, it converts services vitally important to individual lives into products as neutral and lifeless as commodities bought and sold in the marketplace.

The faceless bureaucracy thereby transforms the individual, who is equally connected to and separate from others, into a solitary, isolated creature. It cuts people off from the social context of their lives and glues them to its record books. Even though its census identifies households by their heads—in which category it has only recently deigned to include women—it nonetheless keeps tabs on each and every person. Life begins with a birth certificate. As it proceeds, documents accumulate into personal biographies inscribed in public ledgers—school records, working papers, social security numbers, driver's licenses, income tax returns, documentation for unemployment compensation and welfare receipts, passports, prison records, marriage licenses, divorce papers, and death certificates. This bureaucratic control is seemingly invisible during the ordinary course of events, at least for middle-class people, but it frames every individual life as surely as a cage.

By thus underwriting the cult of individualism, the state synthesizes the elements of twentieth-century individuality. It creates in mind and culture an image of a person who can look like a loner, never feel lonesome, be merged in dependency with the unapproachable state itself, and never cry need. Ideals of heroic autonomy to the contrary notwithstanding, this combination of masculinized and feminized qualities is what life in the state really requires. One should be comfortable with loneliness, while at the same time capable of loyalty to remote, often callous, and usually faithless institutions like the corporation for which one works or the bureaucracy meant to fulfill the fundamental organizational requirements of twentieth-century living.

Yet people, born into mother-infant symbiosis and living their lives with others, do feel lonely. They feel especially so when they become dependent on institutions that dominate them in the name of taking care of them. By thus stirring up dependency feelings, the state in fact guarantees that people will turn to each other for protection and solace. The irrevocable impersonality of the bureaucracy arouses longings to be known and incites a resistance to being treated as a number or category. The isolation felt on making one's single-minded way through the public world energizes its opposite, the hoped-for merging of selves that allows one to know another's thought before it is voiced, to enter another's private places as if they were one's own, to recognize another's smell. The state's overwhelming dominance provokes a desire for simple equality, for the possibility of looking another in the eye without fear or shame. After the anomie of a day's work, intimacy feels like a privilege and a luxury, even though it is a necessity. And both women and men long for it.

Despite the mistrust generated by patriarchy, many women turn toward men, and men toward women, for the realization of their yearnings. Propelled both by gender training and the excitement of difference, they seek to find recognition, renewal, and hope in heterosexual intimacy. And they often find it in the differences between them, differences whose origins, like those of any character trait, are psychologically and culturally determined and therefore determinable, but whose cumulative effect is as irreducible as individual personality. These culturally shaped differences tend to make men's and women's solutions to problems of adult life complementary. Moreover, the protection that men traditionally offered women and the nurturing that women gave men sometimes still surface in spite of the antagonism inherent in their unequal citizenships. Nor, finally, is their capacity to care for each other based solely on the conditioning of gender. Having absorbed the contrast between male and female in the course of coming to be adult men and women, their psyches contain images of both Self and Other. Each can therefore empathize across boundaries of gender to the other's wants and needs.

Nevertheless, both men and women can be quite vulnerable as they seek intimacy. Stimulated by public loneliness, the wish for intimacy also originates in and reawakens infancy's needy pining for maternal love. Since adults are supposed to want but not need, those who desire intimacy may sometimes feel ashamed in searching for it. They may feel diminished and weakened by what seems to be abject need. Moreover, intimacy once gained can be lost, putting one at the risk of the abandonment and terror experienced by needy infants upon being left alone. Since most people therefore tend to feel clumsy about their desire for intimacy, they often express it awkwardly.

Women, finding their longings for intimacy both less and more threatening than men do, have their work cut out for them. On the one hand, women's socialization for relatedness makes them good at creating and maintaining intimacy. They can switch with relative ease from the distance that existed prior to the beginning of a relationship to the merging allowable once it has begun. But this familiarity with intimacy disposes them to push sooner and harder than men for the closure of cohabitation or marriage. Furthermore, women's lack of practice at autonomy can make men's separateness difficult to tolerate, thus weakening the basis for the mutuality they seek. In order, then, to compensate for their own tendency to slide into merger, as well as men's temptation to pull away from connectedness as intimacy deepens, women have to bind their longings tightly, letting them out only enough to reveal a polite but never a voracious hunger.

On the other hand, even though women long for intimacy more consciously than men, they are inclined to be emotionally polygamous, while men tend toward emotional monogamy. A woman usually has another confidante in addition to her man. Since unconscious identification with her mother underlies her adult relatedness and since she grows up expecting men to provide little more than a semblance of maternal nurturing, she will often turn for support to other women, to mothers, sisters, and friends, and even, often unfortunately, to children.

In contrast, a man, unconsciously expecting mother's bounteous breast to be exclusively his, is likely to imagine that he has found it in the woman he loves and, whether or not he is or intends to be sexually monogamous, will have few or no other relationships of such emotional intensity. He will be inclined, then, to be jealous of her other intimacies, including those with their children. Given that a woman and her man, although in the same relationship, experience and construct it differently, and given that she is in charge of the emotional housekeeping, she must juggle her time between her man and her other intimates in such a way as to lessen the threat that they pose to him and to maximize his feeling that his possession of her is secure.

In addition to these complex negotiations that women carry out in order to preserve the intimacy between them and their men, they must also transcend the lie at the heart of heterosexuality. Feeling weakened and diminished by public life, women and men alike seek equality in their relationship with each other. Yet perhaps the saddest aspect of their heterosexual longing is their pretense that they are equal. For everyday purposes, they must pretend that their relationship is not contaminated by the hierarchy of gender. Although this necessary, mutual self-deception puts intimacy just out of reach for both of them, it leaves women the more aggrieved party. A man and a woman are likely to have different feelings as they look each other in the eye. Although guilt, and even shame, may gnaw at his love, he also senses the satisfaction of having more personal and political power than she.

However, not only shame but feelings of inferiority, helplessness, fear, and anger can undermine her love. Sometimes she keeps quiet about these mixed feelings, sometimes her rage at them explodes, and sometimes together she and her man can work out domestic and other arrangements that mitigate the political corrosion of their personal lives. Whatever their collective and individual solutions, they find that their intimacy is always ambivalent and partial. They are held together by a bittersweet appreciation that for them, as for all adults, intimacy is not of whole cloth but a patchwork sewn from intervals of authentic recognition, horrid periods of distance, and sweet moments of merging.

Emerging into adulthood and out of the family, the woman who is alone enters the public world with few guidelines other than the twentieth-century cult of individualism. A travesty of individuality, this cult creates modern loneliness because it isolates the individual from all others. Yet it will not do to romanticize the families and communities of the past. For all the warm protection and companionship they offered, their stifling moral obligations constrained the individualized search for personal uniqueness, subtly binding people to the personally framed hierarchies between lord and serf, landowner and tenant, as well.

Not only are these restrictive comforts gone forever, broken down by economic change and the invasive power of the state. The state's provision of social services permits far more individual variation and personal choice in life-style than have obtained in any hitherto existing polity. It is on this basis, after all, that women have the enhanced, although still limited, freedom to make decisions about how they will live. Finally, the loneliness of life in our culture energizes its opposite as well, a utopian, perhaps one-day-realizable fantasy of a mutual, egalitarian, empathic, nurturing, and self-renewing relation between adults.

A phone call wakes me out of a disoriented but happy dream in which I bring our new baby home to the loft I share with Daniel, my mother and father glowing blissfully in the background. I jump up, dislodging the cat, who somehow ends up underfoot as I race to the phone. I trip. Wrong number.

Time to clean up and get dressed. With a Sarah Vaughan cassette in the tape deck as accompaniment, I tie an apron over the robe, push up my sleeves, and wash the dishes with housewifely efficiency. All the while, I am thinking about a heavenly primeval lake in Vermont where I once spent a weekend and imagining with a smile that in June I will take Daniel there and will prepare a picnic for him of pâté and Brie and bread and fruit and red wine.

It's bad luck to have such fantasies, cautions my grandmother, *especially when the young man hasn't left you a note. Take things as they come, just have a good time.*

Grandma, he's forty-five years old, he's not young, and anyway I feel so anxious, I can't have a good time. Why are things so hard?

If things weren't hard, how would we know when they were good? she answers, with what I have always taken to be peasant wisdom, homely and probably true but irritating nonetheless.

Time to get dressed. I put the jeans on again, add a black satin blouse, and change earrings—my mother's rhinestone sparklers for evening, of course. In the bathroom, I fluff my hair, add some mascara and blusher. Then, turning to the full-length mirror for a once-over, I give myself the sideways test. Neck craned and eyes slanting down and back, I can see that I look just fine.

My ass may be big, but my stomach is flat. Even with my period.

I remember to get some money, turn on the answering machine and hall light, take the envelopes to mail, and pat the cat good-bye. I grab my coat, leaving in time to meet Zena at eight.

Women Together

*T*oward the end of every season, there is always a day when temperature or atmosphere announces the season to come. A hot summer noon in mid-May, a late August afternoon lit by pink-gold sunlight, a cold October morning that brings winter's chill, or a March evening, like this one, whose soft, warm air promises spring.

I walk downtown through streets deserted on winter evenings, now thronged with strollers who create rush-hour traffic conditions at all hours in warm weather. People amble two by two, in groups, and singly on this final upward swing of the day and the week.

I push through revolving doors into a very pretty restaurant that, like the doors, glows with highly polished dark wood and brass trim. The foliage is restrained to one or two leafy palms, and diffused light emanates from hidden places overhead. The tables, spaced well apart, are covered by white tablecloths, and on each there is a tiny candle and a small bouquet of fresh flowers.

The captain, who wears a tuxedo, poises her gold pen over the reservation book as I announce my name.

She then leads me through the wood-paneled bar into the rear dining room, where Zena is already seated at a table that affords a good view of both the bar and the spotlighted back garden, which is open for dining in summer. She is staring out the window, twisting a piece of her curly bronze hair. She turns as we approach, her amber eyes glowing.

"Honey! Hi, hi, hi!" She stands and flings her arms wide.

"You look lovely, sweetheart. Mmmmh." We hug, kiss on the lips. I feast on her smile.

"So do you, really great," she says, pushing me to arm's length.

"That's what Phil said. I think it means I lost weight."

"Don't be silly," Zena chides me, pulling me to her once again.

A waiter, his slender form tubed in black pants, white dress shirt, and tuxedo vest, steps up as we settle into our seats. "Hello. My name's Clive. I'm your waiter for tonight. Can I get you ladies a drink before dinner?"

We order.

"When did you see Phil?"

"This afternoon. I bumped into him with a new girlfriend, and we had cocktails. He was the same as ever. I couldn't help remembering the times he was so mean to me. But let's not talk about that, it's such a bore. Tell me about your trip instead."

"Well, I'm doing a story for the September issue of *Enterprising Woman* on an all-woman auto-repair shop in Berkeley and the woman who started it."

"Do they accept male customers?"

Zena nods vigorously. "Sure, of course, that's the point. And they're wildly successful. But I'm so nervous about doing the story I want to start smoking again. I have to read three auto-repair manuals to do my interviews, and you know what I'm like around cars."

"Yes, sweetheart," I soothe, recalling Zena's hysteria when my car broke down on our way home from Woodstock one snowy Sunday, "but you won't have to drive a car to do the interview. All you have to do is what you're good at, finding the story even in a situation that you know nothing about and writing it up in an authoritative and lively way. Don't worry. You'll do a great job. Like you always do. Maybe you'll even solve your driving phobia. And think how wonderful the weather will be out there this time of year. So let's celebrate." I take out my reading glasses and pick up the menu.

"Oh, god, I don't want to eat a thing. You know how fabulous the food is in San Francisco. I'll gain back all the weight I've lost." Zena runs her hand through her abundant hair. "While I'm in California, I'm going to squeeze in a visit to my folks." She leans back and pats her slightly bulging potbelly. "I thought I'd be able to get rid of this thing before I saw my ma."

"Oh, you're always so concerned about that. You look gorgeous. Don't worry." As I look down at the menu, I sneak a look at my own tummy, rounded only a bit even though I'm sitting down. I feel pleased and guilty. After all, Zena is the woman who, when she travels in tropical climes, eats fruits and vegetables with the skin on, hoping for a case of not-too-dangerous dysentery that would cause an effortless loss of fifteen pounds. Or so she claims.

"Well, I guess I'll never lose it. It runs in the family. Ma's got one and so does her ma. My pa was always going on about it. When I was in my teens, he would say, 'When you're thirty, you're going to be fat and beautiful.' God." She picks up the menu.

"Well, he was half right. You were never fat."

"A little plump, maybe." Zena's bubbly laugh makes me feel happy and slightly giddy, as it always does.

Clive sets down our drinks, tells us the specials of the day, and departs.

As I'm about to reach for my glass to toast her, Zena says, "Well, anyway, I'm getting more and more assignments these days, so I can't complain. I'm so glad that I went free-lance. It's much better than those boring jobs where you're stuck to somebody's else's schedule." She picks up her glass.

Feeling slightly stung, I say, holding mine in midair, "Like my boring jobs, right, sweetheart?"

Her eyes widen in surprise. "Oh, no, you know how important

I think your work is. I just meant—you know what I meant—I was just talking about myself."

As you often do, I think to myself, saying out loud as I raise my glass, "Apology accepted."

After toasting Zena's trip, we study the elegantly cramped purple script on the menu, evaluating the merits of various dishes and sauces. Clive returns, and we order our food and wine.

WOMEN AS FRIENDS

The conventional view of friendship between women is that it is a waste of time. Women together buzz and chatter about nothing at all, or about foolishness like clothes or hair or makeup, or they engage in spiteful gossip across clotheslines and kitchen tables. Sometimes this is true.

But, at its best, friendship between women creates a precious intimacy that permits complete trust and the freedom to tell all, to talk about everything, past and present experience and feelings jumbled together in a stream of consciousness that surges between narrow banks of domestic and public life. Sensuality swathes them in good feeling. When they compliment each other's appearance, when they shop for clothes together, when they discuss makeup and exercise and even ideas, their admiration is practically tactile, both balm and stimulant to the self.

Intimacy between women acts like a tonic, strengthening the spirit and sense of self while also serving as an antidote to the wounds of daily life. Two women in close communication across a table, on the telephone, in the office john, or sitting in a park playground can pour out and examine their anxieties, injuries, triumphs, and failures, and plot courses of action. Their communion serves to repair past and present damage by repeating the process of self-formation in a small but restorative way. They are able again and again to cross the boundaries between self and other, reexperiencing the empathic reflection of self in other by which selfhood comes into being in the mother-child symbiosis. Unlike that asymmetrical and hierarchical fusion, however, women's intimacy is reciprocal and equal, at least in principle. Each woman, schooled in nurturing, can mother the other in turn and then let her go her own way, being neither as realistically dependent as a child on a mother nor as obligated as a mother to a child.

Yet shadows darken the bright room of women's friendship. Sometimes there are power balances. One friend may set the topics of conversation, establish new directions of dress or activity, sway opinions. The other may eke out nurturing from the first and pay back in deference. To their discomfort, even otherwise loving best friends may find themselves in competition over almost anything. Monitoring each other, they calibrate cleavages, dress sizes, husbands' salaries, friendships made, calories consumed. They are made uneasy, as well as proud, by the other's successes in love or work. They feel secretly relieved that they do not suffer from the real or imagined physical defects about which they reassure the other. And, finally, friends are often unnerved not only by power imbalances and competitiveness but by any sign of differentiation and separateness. Divergent opinions emerging in soul-sharing conversation can seem as chilly as sudden emotional distance, impelling friends to rustle up a topic on which they can agree so that difference can be denied and merger maintained.

Although women compete, for everyone competes when power is scarce, a dense storm of feelings accompanies their competition, threatening the very differentiation they help each other to achieve. Women are as aggressive when they compete, as triumphant on winning or annoyed on losing, as anyone else. Like men, they have at stake money, success, and honor. But they also feel guilt, shame, even fright, because when they vie with one another it is as if they were competing against their mothers. Women's intimate friendships resurrect not only the process of self-formation but also, and as unconsciously, the rivalry between mother and daughter for father. A triangle breaches their intimate twosome. In it, mother has exclusive rights to father, father represents power and authority—in other words, he has the phallus—and the daughter is not only excluded from their intimacy but feels lessened by and jealous of it.

The daughter's jealousy combines envy and rage. At the same time as she covets her mother's intimacy with father because it is a ticket to first-class citizenship, she is furious that her mother has betrayed her for a man. In revenge, she may want to steal father from mother. Insofar as she cannot do so, she feels helpless, even attributing her failure to the missing phallus that her all-powerful mother might have given her but did not, and therefore is all the more angry with her. At the same time, she dreads retribution for these incestuous fantasies. Her apprehension may be intensified by the threat that her increasing sexual maturity poses to her aging mother. Since this hated and angry mother is the same omnipotent woman whose power over life and death awed the adoring daughter in infancy, her retaliation is terrifying.

For women who are intimate, then, competitive feelings become quite dangerous, albeit always resurgent. The original rivalry between women, which, given the context of the normative nuclear family, is over father, evokes the dangers encountered when the mother-child symbiosis cracks. As competition for father becomes tantamount to losing mother, it comes to be equated with difference and separateness and is tinged with a sense of helpless fright and rage. The guilt over aggression toward mother blends with the primal terror of her loss to create an injunction not only on competition but on individuation itself. In this light, intellectual disagreements arising in conversation can appear as contrary to intimacy as mother-daughter competitiveness is to the mother-daughter fusion. The end of the conversation can be unsettling, both because of separation anxiety and because of fears of mother's retaliation for a separation experienced as a competitive attack.

The closer women are, the more their intimacy invokes the fusion and competition between mother and daughter, and the more contradictory it becomes. Given the heterosexual nuclear family, the moment freeing the daughter to individuate from the symbiosis is the same moment when the mother is turning toward a man for intimacy. The differentiation toward which women support one another is therefore undermined by an impulse to minimize their differences in order to assuage mother's hatred and preserve her love. Although women probably remain at least unconsciously competitive with men for the attention of other women, they will tend to be more overtly and consciously competitive with each other for men. And this early heterosexual competition becomes an unconscious model for later forms of competition among them.

Yet, for all these contradictions, women's friendships, filled with love, tenderness, and nurturing as well as fear, aggression, and guilt, are central to their lives, as has always been true in Western history. Only in the twentieth century have they been demeaned as puerile or sexually suspect. However, the second-wave feminist notion of the "woman-identified woman," recognizing social contempt for women's emotional and sexual intimacy as a patriarchal tactic, restored the honor to women's friendships, a useful and timely reappraisal for women remodeling their traditional roles. Today, then, in contrast to twenty-five years ago, women can embrace one another's support with open pleasure. And they can and do go with each other to bars and restaurants on Friday night after work without giving a second thought to the shame that once covered them for being without men.

Clive sets the dishes down, saying, "Be careful, ladies. These plates are very hot."

I'm ravenous. Unfortunately, my dish of elegantly sautéed vegetables and tofu, carved and arranged with as careful a sense of color and design as a scattering of emeralds, rubies, and diamonds in Tiffany's window, doesn't look entirely satisfying. Maybe I'll get chocolate mousse for dessert. With a main course like this, I deserve it.

With a main course like this, anguishes my mother, *you'll have beri-beri in no time.*

"Is that going to be enough?" asks Zena, as she disjoints her orange-sauced duck with surgical care.

"Oh, sure, it's marvelous," I answer. "I'll have room left for dessert. How's your duck?"

"Great, really great," she says after she swallows. "Listen, I just had an idea. When I'm in San Francisco, I think I'll check out one of the new lesbian sex clubs. Do you think I should?"

Feeling a little alarmed, I put my fork down and ask, "What will Pamela say?"

Zena takes a sip of wine. "Oh, I don't care. We're fighting again. Anyway, we haven't been sleeping together recently."

I feel distressed. "Oh, no, what a shame. What's the matter?"

Zena sighs. "I haven't the vaguest idea. Maybe it would be easier if our occupations were different or our professional worlds didn't overlap. Or maybe we need couples counseling. I'll think about that after I get back." She cuts a piece of duck, then looks at me and winks. "Or maybe I'll have a fling with Renée when I'm out there."

I finish chewing and wipe my mouth, feeling jealous, as I never do about Pamela but always about Zena's lovers.

She giggles. "Listen, did I ever tell you about the first time Renée and I made love?"

"No." My heart thuds, once, hard, and then flutters rapidly.

What do you expect with dykes for friends? asks my father from behind his newspaper.

Language, dear, language, reproves my mother, looking up from her knitting.

Zena puts down her knife and fork, looks around, leans forward across the table, and lowers her voice. She looks intently at me and begins. "I was lying on top and kissing her and getting really wet. And then she spread her legs slightly so mine just naturally slid down between them. The next thing I knew, I was humping her. I was digging into her crotch with my own, and she was moving up and down with me. The wetter I got, the more I wanted to *do* something with my clitoris. It was almost as if I had a penis and wanted to stick it in. Of course, as soon as *that* popped into my mind, I couldn't go on. When we looked at each other, we smiled self-consciously and then just went down on each other."

She laughs merrily again. "So what do you think? It's almost a cliché, isn't it? That's what straight people usually say, that all we want is penises. Well, fuck them, right? Anyway, it wasn't like that. It was something else, but only lesbians can really understand it."

I want to share in her wonderment and amusement, but all I feel is cold. And hot. As she talks, I stare at the candle, recalling, as if it happened to someone else in another life, the first time that Zena and I made love during our very brief fling: *Her tongue slid along the soft involuted folds of her labia. Her tongue slid along the soft involuted folds of her labia. She licked her clitoris, she licked her clitoris. They came together, not knowing who was who.*

Ever since we made up after a quarrel in which I said I was basically straight and she angrily criticized me for "dabbling" in homosexuality, Zena has always told me about her sexual adventures, and I don't seem to be able to stop her. I'm not interested in sleeping with her now. But sometimes I still want to keep her for myself. Which is why I'd rather know about what goes on in her life than be excluded.

Feeling uncomfortable and alienated, I reach for some bread, slap butter on it like a mason mortaring a brick, and try a lighthearted response. "Maybe you should get a dildo."

"I've just been thinking about that." She heaps an orange section and some sauce onto a forkful of rice. "Or were you being sarcastic, dear friend?"

Suddenly the lustiness that I love and admire in her seems disgusting. "No, of course not. It sounds like it was great fun."

"As I look back on it, it really was." Then Zena lays down her cutlery and stares at me. "Hey, are you jealous?"

I look down at my plate. "Yeah, I guess so."

The crooked worry line between her eyebrows deepens. "Oh, honey, you know you'll always be the only best friend I'll ever have." She reaches over and holds my hand for a moment.

She wins me over every time, even if she really is trying to make me jealous.

WOMEN AS LOVERS

Homosexual behavior is as much part of human sexual inclination as heterosexuality. Found in most cultures, it is sanctified in some, despised in others, and given no more than a passing thought in still others. In Western culture, it has evolved from sexual practice into sexual subculture. Its documented history reaches back to ancient Greece, when Plato praised pederasty as the highest form of love for free men and Sappho wrote lyrically of sex between women. In the twelfth century, a male homosexual subculture, embryonic in European cities, was regarded in the countryside as a peculiar though not legally actionable form of lewdness. By the eighteenth century, however, homosexuality flourished in London in a matrix of public meeting places such as bars, cafés, and brothels frequented by men from all walks of life. A lesbian subculture coexisted but, less visible because of women's lesser financial and social independence, was carried on in salons and informal networks. Then, as in the nineteenth and twentieth centuries, these European homosexual communities were peopled with avant-garde intellectuals and artists. They also had their counterparts in urban, underground communities in the United States, communities that are surviving aboveground today.

Present-day homosexual subculture was created in part by laws passed at the turn of the twentieth century that defined as criminal homosexual acts that had previously been as unregulated as any sexual activity. In the course of turning homosexuality into a crime, this legislation established homosexuality as a recognizable social and personal, albeit ignominious, identity. The "homosexual" became a new category of social being, about which not only laws but medical and other theories grew the way superstition does, like a cancer. During the twentieth century, homosexual people could therefore become scapegoats, as when they were politically persecuted in Nazi Germany or by the postwar McCarthy witch-hunt in the United States.

Presently, homosexual preference is a more viable alternative life-style than it has ever been before in Western culture. As the single life becomes more acceptable and procreation more a personal choice than a social imperative, individual sexual desire is loosened from its ties to heterosexuality and the family. The gay liberation movement, given impetus by the women's liberation movement, created a new public image of homosexual pride with which individual gay people could identify in order to "come out of the closet," where they had been banished by heterosexual prejudice. Gay activism succeeded in repealing many sodomy laws, partially eliminating antigay discrimination in federal employment, gaining civil-rights protection for gays in some cities, and eliminating homosexuality as an official psychiatric category of mental illness. As Broadway plays respectful of homosexuality played to full houses, as formerly underground gay communities became political constituencies, and as overtly gay people ran for political office, homosexual men and women increased in self-confidence and population. Many old-timers came out of the closet, while many young, nominally heterosexual people discovered their homosexual preference for the first time.

Still, homosexual preference remains not only culturally secondary but culturally inferior. Like those in other minority groups, homosexuals still live in two cultures. Like dark-skinned men and women in a white world and heterosexual women of any color in the world of men, gay men and women travel back and forth between the dominant culture and their own, outsiders in one, insiders in the other. Expecting to be greeted by the straight world with prejudice, ignorance, even violence, or at best, discomfort, homosexual people take self-protective measures to maintain their reputations and their jobs. Chief among these is "passing," that is, not disclosing one's sexual preference and dressing in ways currently appropriate for one's gender. The hostile surrounding environment also engenders a wariness and even a cynicism that are sometimes taken as unnecessary defensiveness but are normal in any outcast group.

Although socially marginal, homosexuality is symbolically central to our culture. It represents tabooed sexual longings felt by most people but often experienced only unconsciously because they are deemed dangerous or morally reprehensible. Signifying the possibility of sex without procreation, homosexuality defies the two-millennia-old Judaeo-Christian binding of sex to reproduction. It breaks the hold of penis-in-vagina intercourse on our sexual imagination. Homosexuality, in challenging the dominant, heterosexual model for personal and social maturity, reveals it to be a compulsory, not natural, set of rules for behavior, deviation from which is punishable socially, legally, and physically. Homosexuality is therefore a powerful critique of sexuality and gender, striking deep at our cultural foundations.

The traditional wedding of procreation to femininity makes the archetypal lesbian stereotype, "the dyke," key to the homosexual critique. The stereotypically male homosexual pursuit of sex for the sake of lust alone is but an extension of the individualizing lone male voyager of Western tradition. But the "dyke" departs radically from the "true woman." According to stereotype, "the dyke" represents the woman who has defiantly appropriated the style and behavior traditionally assigned to men. Depicted as hard, tough, mean, and even violent, "the dyke" is thought to renounce the altruism, empathy, and caring associated with motherhood. No mother she, "the dyke" is single-mindedly engaged not in relatedness but in the self-interested enjoyment of lust and sexual conquest permitted for men and forbidden to women.

Although this stereotype superficially seems to reject femininity, it in fact epitomizes all of women's dormant, distorted possibility. Turned inside out, this negative depiction of a woman with a phallus represents the many positive qualities that women might have but are denied by the social construction of their beings. As symbolic figure, "the dyke" is the woman who wants. She is not the Subject-as-Object, waiting to be wanted. She is the Subject who both possesses her self and takes what she wants, who engages in and wants sex for itself and not for procreation. Neither virgin nor Madonna, she refuses to provide perfect empathy or to lose herself in relatedness. She is the female self-as-individual who can be assertive, angry, and aggressive. In her sexuality, she confronts, seemingly fearlessly, the engulfing mother symbolized by the female body. The emotional autonomy of "the dyke" is so secure that she, unlike heterosexual men and women, need not depend on the difference of her lover's gender to ensure her own separateness. In a culture that asks women to be dependent and passive, "the dyke" is an inevitable symbol of liberation.

But lesbian personal life is, of course, rather more complicated than this caricature. In certain cardinal ways, lesbian intimacy differs absolutely from heterosexual intimacy. For one thing, it lacks the barriers of Otherness that make heterosexuality an obstacle course. This clean slate—which, to heterosexual feminists coming out during the last twenty years, felt like, and sometimes was, the opening of freedom's gate—specifies lesbian hopes for authenticity. Although such euphoric hopes for clarity of desire and understanding bloom at the start of any love affair, the similarities between women intensify them. Shared gender identity coupled with physical and stylistic likeness amplifies the unconscious mother-child fusion that resurges in all sexual passion.

Futhermore, women's knowledge of their own geography of desire familiarizes them with each other's. By eliminating the explanation that so often awkwardly interrupts heterosexual intercourse, their sexual intimacy seems magically to gratify the infantile wish to be known without speaking. In particular, women understand the erotic primacy of the clitoris, secretly considered by many men, even in these supposedly liberated days, a nuisance to be tolerated on the way to the ultimate goal of penis-in-vagina orgasm. Women's empathic concern with the other's desires resembles the wished-for omniscience of maternal love. Finally, since homosexuality lacks built-in gender roles, lesbians may find room in their intimacy to discover preferences in sexual behavior and personal style prohibited by the constraints of traditional gender roles.

However, this oceanic bliss frequently threatens to drown the self. The re-created mother-daughter fusion, but a respite for women who are just friends, is for lesbians woven into the fabric of domestic life. The physical and emotional similarities between lovers can seem so overwhelming as to erase a sense of a separate self altogether. Furthermore, as between friends, any sign of difference may cause almost intolerable envy and anxiety, leading to overemphasized or manufactured similarities of thought, opinion, or style. Ostensibly encouraging individual growth and self-realization, lesbians' sexual and nonsexual merging in turn can create a new barrier to their personal autonomy and differentiation.

Lesbians sometimes resort to three problematic strategies, all of them known to heterosexual people as well, to solve the problems of intimacy. One solution is to sacrifice sex. Women who are lovers sometimes choose to remain separate sexually in order to continue to merge nonsexually. A second solution is to fight. Discord and acrimony may make each party feel wronged, but a wronged self is better than no self at all. And a third solution is to adopt roles that create a sense of differentness. Lacking prescribed roles, lesbian couples—and, probably, gay male couples as well—create others. In response to merging, some will accentuate or even manufacture differences of opinion, attitude, or style in order to fashion distinct personas. Others, however, may found their union on versions of the heterosexual model. In some couples, one partner is the "butch," who wears men's clothing or facsimiles of it and takes a dominant sexual position, while the other, the "femme," wears dresses and makeup and is more nurturing and receptive in role and demeanor. No more self-conscious than traditional gender roles, "butch-femme" roles are usually deeply felt expressions of self and sexual desire that can as well serve to mark personal difference.

To the outsider, "butch-femme" roles, muted sexuality, and fighting constitute another lesbian stereotype. But outsiders who gaze at the forbidden may find that they are in fact looking in a mirror. Heterosexual women and their partners also rush to fusion as they seek the infantile oneness that informs everyone's first experience of pleasure and security. Unwittingly, they, like their lesbian compeers, re-create patterns in their intimate communication and behavior that reduce each other's sense of separateness, difference, and autonomy. And, as among lesbians, once merger seems secure, selfhood threatens to disappear, panic sets in, and the difficulties of intimacy begin.

Heterosexual couples therefore do what lesbians do in order to make intimacy work. They stop having sex, they fight, and they play roles. Heterosexual people differ primarily in that their roles are ready-made. The traditional gender roles that underlie gender identity and sexual preference not only divide the family's labor. They also inform and, if necessary, reinforce the sense of self as well, which is one psychological explanation for the tenacity with which heterosexual men and women often cling to their roles, even when they no longer find them satisfying.

We all have trouble with intimacy. As the union of two separate selves who can care for and be cared for by each other, intimacy depends on the capacity to modulate between separation and merging. But no model of adulthood exists yet in our culture to teach us this trick. Nor are our conventional solutions completely satisfactory. In homosexuality as in heterosexuality, when a moribund sex life, continual fighting, or rigid roles become staple, the union either limps along in pain or comes to a complete halt. Each successful intimacy is, therefore, a sort of experiment. Nevertheless, just as the differences between lesbian and heterosexual intimacy must not be erased, so their difficulties must not be equated. That lesbians are public outcasts may strain their personal lives, albeit strengthened by having to fight oppression, all the more.

Still, homophobia is harmful to all women, whether straight or gay. As the symbol of the "woman-identified woman," "the dyke" represents not only women's emotional and sexual intimacy but women's self-love. However, by symbolizing the outcast as well, "the dyke" also alienates women's own personal power from them. This contradictory symbolism thereby denatures women's physicality. It coarsens and degenders their robust lust, obscuring their sexual desire and making some afraid to masturbate, others to have sex with a woman, still others to sleep with a man. And, as well, it makes them regard the calculatedly polished demeanor of, for example, women politicians as "hard" and unfeminine.

The point is not that women have to have sex with each other to be strong. But the public ridicule of women who love each other puts beyond comfortable reach all the power signified by "the dyke," all the love represented by the "woman-identified woman," and therefore the self-regard available to autonomous women. One cannot be self-possessed unless one is in possession of all of one's possibility, but self-possession is unlikely if the qualities that permit it are made to seem not only inappropriate but repulsive. Recoiling from part of their own possibility, women recoil from each other, thereby being deprived of the empathy and care underlying adult strength that women are trained to provide and of the solidarity generated when women group together to contest their shared second-class citizenship.

As Zena butters the remaining morsel of bread, she says, "Oh god, I'm so sorry, I've been talking about me, and we haven't said anything about you."

I summarize the day rapidly, saving the best for last. "And, finally, I slept with Daniel again last night. He said he was going to Colorado to visit his folks for ten days and he'd call me when he got back. I left the key for him. Do you think that was too pushy? Maybe it will scare him off. He didn't leave me a note." I eat the last mouthful of tofu.

Zena exclaims, "God, who knows? I remember the beginning of my affair with Pamela. I never knew if I was being too forward or not." She drains her glass.

I stare at a delicate picture on the wall, peopled with romantic figures who remind me of *Gigi*. "Sometimes I think this is 'it,' sometimes I don't even know who he is. Do you understand that?"

Zena answers, "Honey, this sounds serious. You shouldn't worry, though. If he doesn't know that you're a gem, it's his loss."

"Thanks, sweetheart." I smile at her and squeeze her shoulder. Then, pushing my plate away, I say, "Oh well, let's turn to something easy. Like, are you going to shave your legs for spring?"

"Arlene maintains it's antifeminist to shave." Zena throws her napkin on the table.

"Being a feminist is easy when you're blond. I'm going to wax them," I say defiantly.

"I already have, because I've decided that smashed hair under stockings looks ridiculous."

"What will they say at the sex club?" I tease her.

"Oh, anything goes there, I think. But, really, do you think I should go to one?" Zena asks. She tries to pour more wine, but the bottle is empty.

"Absolutely." I pat her shoulder for emphasis. "That's the only way I'm going to find out exactly what goes on in them."

Zena laughs and grabs my hand. "Oh, I wish you could come with me."

I laugh in turn. "Are you kidding? Don't you think I would be expected to join in, not just watch? I don't know, maybe it would be like the first time I went to a lesbian bar. I thought I would be raped or something, but, you know, for the first time in my life I felt that I was accepted just for who I was." As soon as I've said this, I feel as though I've made a mistake.

Zena raises one eyebrow. "Maybe you ought to try again."

"Now, look," I respond adamantly, "I thought we left guilt-tripping behind, along with the nineteen seventies."

"Except that if you wanted to do it once—oh okay, you're right, I'll back off." Zena pushes her plate aside and leans forward on folded arms. "Anyway, I always felt as free in our consciousness-raising group as you did in the bar. Every Monday night for three years."

I shrug. "Even with all the quarrels and hurt feelings? Aren't you romanticizing a little?"

"Maybe a little. Do you remember the night when we disrupted the meeting by coming in late and reading a manifesto?" Zena signals Clive to clear the table.

"What was it you said as you came in? 'We are all lesbians,' right? And then I stood up, shouting that the disruption betrayed sisterhood by being unempathic. And you shouted back that women who didn't love women in every way were the real traitors."

Zena giggles. "The beginning of a beautiful friendship, huh, honey?" She smooths my hair.

"But it never felt really secure to me until we began working together in the Pro-Choice Coalition. By the way, I heard a rumor that the Coalition is going to begin meeting again. Do you want to get involved in it?" I take the dessert menu from Clive as he hands another to Zena.

Zena wrinkles her nose. "God, I hate political groups. And talk about the lack of sisterly love. I don't want to waste a precious evening at an endless, boring meeting spent in trying to reconcile fifteen opposing points of view while all fifteen factions are battling to come out on top. I mean, I know we're going to have to fight the battle all over again now that the backlash is upon us. But who has time? It's hard enough just making a living and keeping up a relationship."

Zena opens her menu. "I'll tell you what. You go to the first meeting and tell me about it. Then I'll make up my mind. However, what we can decide on together is dessert. Should we get one and share it, or really splurge and get two?"

"Why do you think I ordered tofu? I've been waiting for dessert since we sat down to eat. Two, of course." I plunge happily into the menu.

WOMEN AS FEMINISTS

The second wave of feminism began as euphorically as a love affair. The meetings of feminist caucuses, consciousness-raising groups, and fledgling feminist political organizations soared with the wonderful freedom that fills up the room whenever women gather together. Feminists discovered what women always find when they get together without men: They no longer have to be Subject-as-Object. Free to unleash their desire, they can allow their dammed-up energies to rush out with exciting power, motivated by the sense of purpose characteristic of any convocation of like-minded people.

Empowered by the absence of men, feminism was also galvanized by the presence of a newly unearthed ethic of loyalty among women. Traditionally the glue of women's friendships and community networks, this ethic holds that women are, in distinction to men, the same and, therefore, peers, equals whose first obligation is to one another. One source of this ethic is psychological, for women's socialization toward relatedness makes them similar in behavior and psychology, sharpens their attunement to their resemblances, and obliges them to take care of each other. The second source for the ethic of loyalty is political. Women's common social position at the bottom of the gender hierarchy forges a sense of identity and therefore equality, stimulating the protective if not militant solidarity typical of the disempowered in a culture whose key is power.

Feminism sharpened the ethic of loyalty into a political tool. Although all women's groups make use of this ethic, feminist groups are particularly powerful because they fuse it with a commitment to no other interest than women's own. Unlike quilting bees, feminist groups do not exist to meet the needs of women's roles as homemakers. Unlike community-service groups or charities, they do not elaborate the definition of women as selves-in-relation whose duty it is to serve others or uphold public morality. Feminist groups are about, for, and by women, women defined by nothing other than their difference from men. Like no other group, they create the conditions for women to realize their rightful status as Subject.

However, the vital ethic of loyalty is of little help when the

differences between feminists take center stage, as they inevitably must. A product of oppression, it has the flaw of falling apart
when the common enemy disappears. The absence of the op-
pressor in feminist groups eliminates the external reason for solidarity. At this point, as in any minority group, differences and
competitive strivings show up. Feminists, divided against each
other by class, race, sexuality, and the lure of public power, often
act like crabs in a barrel while denying their wish to climb to the
top of the heap.

The first of these differences to appear in feminism was sexual. Soon after the second wave began, heterosexual and homosexual feminists, to their shock and disappointment, could no
longer talk to one another without fighting. Some heterosexual
feminists simply feared and disliked lesbians. Others worried that
issues of lesbian sexuality would divert public attention and political energy away from the matter of women's economic and
political liberation. Whatever their reasons, many straight feminists initially regarded lesbians' demands for sexual freedom and
social legitimacy as diversionary. Acrimonious battles ensued.
Lesbian feminists, mistrusting heterosexual feminists and unwilling to subordinate their basic interests, embraced a policy of sep-
aratism. The fabric of the women's liberation movement almost
disintegrated in the process.

Since then, some repair work has been done. Even though some
heterosexual feminists are still homophobic, overt homophobia
has disappeared in most of the feminist movement. In principle,
most feminists acknowledge that sexual liberation and political
freedom are mutually dependent, even if others seem at times
to forget it. Heterosexual and homosexual women have occasionally been able to align themselves in a common political cause.
Some have also been able to become friends without feeling
threatened by the other's difference.

The gay-straight split was just the tip of the iceberg. The next
differences to show up were those of race and class and, in a
new form, sexuality. In addition to variations in personality and
sexual preference, women's interests diverge depending on their
socioeconomic positions. A working-class feminist may be more
concerned with the discrimination she encounters in getting jobs
and decent wages than a middle-class feminist, be she home-
maker or career woman, whose primary complaint may be about
the restrictions placed on her by her domestic role or hindrances to

her upward mobility. While a white feminist may believe that she speaks for all women, a Third World feminist may feel that her first loyalty belongs to men and women of color. Even differences of opinion create categorical divisions within feminism. For example, the current antipornography movement, whose position fits more easily with mainstream sexual caution than that of sexual liberationists, presently has more hearing within feminism than other voices.

Because these cardinal differences confer unequal access to privilege and power, they may be expected to erupt into conflict. To put it simply, white, middle-class, educated, heterosexual feminists tend to have more money, better jobs, and greater social respect than others. As a result, they are, sadly, more likely to occupy positions of leadership and therefore have more power even within feminism itself. This inequity cannot but stimulate envy, resentment, and anger among feminists lacking privilege. At the same time, each feminist will be infected with the cultural evaluation of her position. While a feminist with privilege may, secretly or unconsciously, feel herself superior, a feminist without it may occasionally believe in her own inferiority.

The exigencies of political life allow these power differences disruptive to feminist unity to be parlayed into power outside of feminism, creating other sources of difference and conflict. Indeed, the necessity of fighting fire with fire can make equality nearly unattainable, and sometimes even obstructive, within activist feminist groups. In order to tackle public hierarchies oppressing women, feminist groups must construct hierarchies of their own. Politicians and legislators want to negotiate with accredited leaders, not with the groups they represent. Leadership, however, contradicts the ethical ideal of women's equal status, creating a sense of betrayal. Consequently, the fame achieved by feminism's spokeswomen in a culture that celebrates individuals incurs the animosity, as well as the gratitude, of rank-and-file feminists who work as members of feminist collectives. Furthermore, the alluring pleasures of power stir up competitiveness, in-fighting, and even power plays within feminist organizations. Not only the competition between mother and daughter but that between siblings for parental attention disrupts the teamwork of peers, who vie for position and for the attention and approval of feminist leaders.

That the ethic of loyalty compels a denial of such power differences accounts for much of the confusion in feminist politics, which often differs little from the ordinary course of political business in our culture. Encouraged by the women's movement to act in their own self-interest, feminists seek power in feminist politics, just as men seek power in other political arenas. Self-willed individuals, they negotiate for position using the same machinations as other politicians. They win in political meetings by talking loudly or quickly or, when everyone else is shouting, quietly and slowly; by speaking first or last; by making alliances through lobbying or manipulating; and by forming cabals or fomenting insurrections or being seductive.

Although feminist politics is, like all politics, a matter of power, of winning and losing, of competition and aggression, the ethic of loyalty couples with women's unconscious fear of differentiation and competition to emerge as a wish to play the game so that, somehow, everybody wins. The result is sometimes masquerade. Some feminists, as susceptible to the pleasures and privileges of power as anyone else, may try to get or keep it through dishonesty and opportunism. Others, whose power gives them a stake in denying differences, will coat their competitiveness in a well-meaning though somewhat saccharine sisterly concern, in order as well to protect themselves from others' retaliation. Still others may turn their aggression in on themselves, presenting themselves as victims or preening in syrupy self-deprecation over their success by putting their achievements down to luck or the gift of family circumstances.

The inability of the ethic of loyalty to dissolve the hard problems of power differences and the clash of self-willed individuals disturbs even consciousness-raising, or "CR," perhaps feminism's most unique invention. Each CR meeting is organized around a given topic or devoted to one member's personal story. It has no leaders but runs on group consensus. The only time limit is the duration of the meeting. Each woman may speak as long as she likes without fear of judgment or interruption. With this format, women have been able to discover aspects of themselves that they had not previously known, develop a sense of personal power and legitimacy, and acquire the empathic hearing and advice of women who have confronted and solved similar problems or are able to imagine how to do so. CR has in effect allowed women to take their personal histories seriously, thus in a sense giving them their collective history for the first time.

CR groups are, however, often intruded upon by public hierarchy. Sometimes they fill with friction because some people, more famous or charismatic or manipulative or original or conventional, get more attention than others who are more reserved or insecure or docile or eccentric or ahead of their time. The contradiction between CR's democratic principles and the facts of hierarchy seems often to have been resolved by groups in which the status of the members is roughly the same. CR groups are also troubled by both rivalry and primal, unconscious demands for total attention. And sometimes they wither because the ethic of loyalty may fuse with women's tendencies to merge, making differentiation not only emotionally dangerous but immoral. In consequence, feminists may replace their differing subjectivities with a conformism that finally proves deadly to the exhilarating freedom offered by feminism in the first place.

Feminism as collectivity, like individual women, now faces the challenge and dilemma of difference. That a partial reconciliation between heterosexual and homosexual women could occur suggests that other divisions can be bridged as well. The sometimes acerbic confrontations that have taken place during the last twenty years between feminists of different races, classes, and sexual orientations are discouraging. Yet, in effect, these clashes signify a primitive acknowledgment of differences. They can perhaps begin a process of determining along which facets women of different racial, class, and sexual groups might unite at the same time as they pursue their own interests. The inevitable discord arising in this process will not be betrayal but part of the creation of a more diversified, unified women's movement that recognizes its origins in the civil rights movement and its common cause with sexual liberation.

There exist divisions not only within feminism but between feminist women and nonfeminist women as well. Feminism's radical threat to the bedrock of our civilization causes many women to regard feminism, as well as other women's groups, women's friendships, and lesbianism, with suspicion and frightened contempt. Female bonding necessarily disrupts the ordinary course of events. Women's friendships crack the isolation of the conjugal nuclear family, transgressing domestic privacy. Lesbianism defies the normative, heterosexual basis of personal and social identity. Feminism challenges not only the patriarchal power that organizes public life but the individualism of our culture.

Of more strategic importance, the women's movement seems unattractive because it is easily ghetto-ized. Representing interests disdained by the cultural mainstream, its utopian politics often seem amateurish and cranky. In an ironic twist, many women, especially those who have been able to join the mainstream precisely because of feminist reforms, now find organized feminism repellent. These women who have made careers or "have it all," that is, family and career, now fear the taint of ghetto-ization. Yet there is no way that their success, such as it is and endangered by the backlash, will be sustained without a radical, ongoing feminist movement.

Women's coming together in coffee klatches, bed, and politics has been as pivotal to their personal and political power as men's bonding has been to theirs. Nor is female bonding a recent product of the women's liberation movement. "Feminism" is but the name we give in English to the most recent Western version of women's shared opposition to being defined in invidious comparison to men. Its history is deep, its cultural spread wide. It has shown up in the feisty laughter of women among the !Kung San of Botswanaland, in the women's councils found in every village among the Igbo of Nigeria, and in the nineteenth-century women's movements that undertook women's suffrage and supported the abolition of slavery in England and the United States. These are the antecedents of twentieth-century feminism, which will in turn produce generations of descendants until such time as women are no longer second-class citizens. Only then, when its *raison d'être* disappears, will feminism, too, cease to exist.

Done with our chocolate mousse and raspberry soufflé, our espresso and brandy, we pay the bill, put on our coats, and walk arm in arm into the embrace of the evening.

We stop at the corner, where I must descend to the subway to travel uptown to William's apartment.

"So, sweetheart, good luck. I wish I were going with you." I hug her and kiss her on both cheeks.

She grabs my shoulders. "Such are the joys of the free-lance life. But you're on vacation. Come on. Come for one week. I'll introduce you to Renée's roommate."

I giggle. "No, I can't. I've got my patients."

"Well, honey, you have a good time at the Devil's Delight. Why are you going there anyway?"

"Beats me."

We collapse on each other in inebriated laughter.

Looking for
Their Own Desire

(Midnight)

I climb up out of the subway into the never-ending day of Times Square. Dazzled as always by the lights, porn theaters, sex emporiums, hookers, chicken-hawks, hustlers, drug dealers and purchasers, cops, and tourists, I hold my purse close under my arm and walk briskly through the crowds toward the neighborhood once called Hell's Kitchen.

William's poor mother must worry so about him living in a place like this, whispers my own mother in shock. *And you say he washes dishes for a living? Oh dear.*

William is a permanent revolutionary. And, like all revolution-

177

aries, he's always looking for goodness in the most unlikely places. Sometimes I think that he is an extremist out of sheer perversity. And as I get older I tire more easily of his crankiness. Still, his sometimes adolescent agonizing appertains to another admirable quality, his passion for truth. He's like an old-fashioned, bohemian intellectual with whom you might sit in a café arguing into the night on some minor points of political or aesthetic doctrine, never finding an answer (and usually forgetting the question) but always soaring on the rush of ideas, dizzy with limitless horizons, mad with hope. William knows that what seems like the darker side of life usually contains at least a gleam of truth, and that's why I love him.

William chose this neighborhood not only because the rents were low but because it fascinated him. A firm disbeliever in monogamy, he's also into sexual experimentation—sex with men, sex with couples and groups, sadomasochism, God knows what else. For William, the sexual revolution was a lucky break; it made what he wanted to do anyway okay. He reads pornography and has even frequented prostitutes, something most right-thinking feminists would decapitate him for. But I get a vicarious thrill from his adventures. That's why he challenged me to go to the Devil's Delight Club last year and why I have to go through with the dare tonight.

However, the situation is a little different now—William has finally found a girlfriend who shares his tastes, whose tastes are perhaps even further out than his. Mary was a member of the Devil's Delight Club before she met him. I first met her a long time ago in a CR group, but I had not seen her often since she and the younger women splintered into their own group, claiming that their concerns were different from those of the older members. I guess they were.

I ring William's bell, and a moment later I see him leaning out the window of his sixth-floor loft. He looks around to make sure there are no passersby in the way, then throws down a key in a knotted sock. After I pick it up and extract the key to unlock the door, I mount the dim stairwell, lit by bare bulbs, and stop before a door that creaks open as I knock gently.

"If you leave your door open like that, you could get robbed or murdered," I scold, walking into the shabby living room, where magazines and books are scattered on the fraying oriental carpet. I feel instantly at home, while at the same time I consciously restrain myself from telling him to clean up.

William is sitting at his ancient, ornate desk, a gooseneck lamp spotlighting a circle on the yellow pad of lined paper on which he is writing something, probably the new short story he has been telling me about. I bend over him, cradle his face in my hands, and kiss his forehead. He's too bony, and his sandy hair has thinned too much for him to look like a teddy bear, but I still want to cuddle him.

He picks up a half-smoked joint from a hammered metal ash-tray at the far corner of the desk, lights it, and, turning around, offers it to me. "It was just because I knew you were coming up. Wanna toke?"

I take the marijuana butt, inhale, lean back on the mangy brown velveteen, inhale again, exhale, beginning to feel pleasantly cut off.

"Don't pass out, we have to go soon. I told Mary we'd meet her by midnight. But I have to change my clothes first." After he leaves the room, I open a dark-green paperback I find on the couch and begin to read at random:

> Standing at the foot of the bed, she felt her passion begin to mount, somehow intensified by the sight of the woman's legs and arms tied spread-eagled to the bedposts. Her own pussy simultaneously gave way and tightened and got very wet as she stared at the billowy body below her and felt his work-toughened hands slide roughly back down her pubic bone over her burning clit and into her slit, forcing her legs apart. He pushed her forward with the flat of his hand, then grasped her haunches. As he began to enter her from behind, she braced herself by placing her forearms on either side of the woman's hips.
>
> Once in her, he began to slide in and out with seemingly deliberate slowness, and, while he did so, she gradually bent down until her tongue could reach the aromatic wet opening in front of her. As her tongue swirled up to circle the small clitoris amidst the bristly hair, she heard the counterpointing sighs, the man slamming faster and faster against her butt and the blindfolded woman humping against the silken restraints. And then she began to suck. She sucked and sucked and sucked

very hard on the clit while twirling her tongue on its very tip until, in about ten seconds, the woman came with an astonished cry. But she kept sucking even harder and flicking her tongue even faster. The wide hips flailed around, the cries turned to screams, and the woman orgasmed again and again.

She was just about to come herself when, to her surprise, he pulled out and shifted his body so that his wet penis was nosing at her anus. He started to inch his way in, stopping occasionally to give her a chance to get used to it. Then suddenly he was all the way inside and she relaxed completely, even, to her embarrassment, letting out a fart that loosened her asshole around his thick cock. The next thing she knew, he stuck some amyl nitrate beneath her nose. Nearly blacking out from the high, she fell forward onto the woman's body, her hands trying to plunge into the big sagging breasts, her own tits squishing against the soft belly. She wished for another pair of hands to dig underneath and hold onto the massive buttocks.

And then he began to fuck. He fucked and fucked; she bucked and moaned. Her head cleared once, then she went back down under the ocean of feeling. And then her clit was straining, rubbing between the woman's legs against the silk sheet, getting more and more erect, and he kept going, and she yelped as he rocked harder and unbelievably harder. Her hips moved up and down, up and down, and she began to come in a rolling orgasm that convulsed every part of her cunt, inside and out, and lasted forever. And as it became her whole body, he became one with her, letting go and coming while his rusty cry made queerly beautiful harmony with her animal calls.

Then a petite redhead carrying a leather belt. . . .

"Which one are you reading?" William, dressed entirely in black, looks over my shoulder.

I shut the book as if my mother had come into the room and then, giggling, hold it up.

"You're blushing," he observes as I follow him into the narrow hallway.

"Well, I'm not used to reading pornography with anyone else around."

"Then this public acknowledgment of your desire is a moment of truth," he says in the half-darkness.

"Oh, William, stop being so pompous," I complain as he pulls the door closed and the police lock clicks into place.

MAKING LOVE WITH THE LIGHTS ON

In line with the general increase in sexual freedom during the twentieth century, it has become conventional in certain sectors of our society or, at least, in the media for women to play sexually. Women, freed by contraception from fear of pregnancy, are expected, and expect themselves, to separate "recreational" sex from the serious business of procreation, reveal their lust, be inventive in bed, and say frankly what they want and when they want it. No longer limited to two-person heterosexual intercourse, they feel more at liberty to explore the varieties of their sexual desire. They have experimented with new positions, partners, and preferences, tasting or making a steady diet of, for example, sex with women, sex with couples, or sadomasochism.

The marketplace offers an atmosphere and products conducive to this search for sexual freedom. Although most pornography continues to be produced for a male market, some pornographic magazines, depicting naked, supine, good-looking young men, purport to be for women. Mail-order advertisements in their back pages purvey not only frilly underwear but a large variety of sexual instruments, ranging from simple vibrators to clitoris stimulators to potions to be sniffed or applied to the genitals. Some women spend evenings in bed watching X-rated videos with their lovers. Others call up sex talk shows broadcast on radio or television. And "bachelorette" parties are even thrown for brides in which male strippers entertain them, their attendants, and friends.

However, even though a minor sexual revolution has taken place during the last two decades, the sexual playground is still far from being safe for women, and they may therefore find it hard to play. On the one hand, women, like men, are increasingly worried about contagious sexual diseases. Although cures for syphilis and gonorrhea, the banes of nineteenth-century sexual promiscuity, exist, there are none presently available for herpes and AIDS. The fear of incurable or mortal disease has quelled much of what remained of the so-called sexual revolution.

On the other hand, even though men are equally at physical

risk, women still have more reason to envision a dark alley rather than a playground when they contemplate sex. Women quite rightly continue to learn, at the impressionable age of puberty, if not earlier, that sex harbors a multitude of dangers for them. Their apprehension may be increased by uncertainty, since they do not know which, if any, of the dangers they will confront in any given sexual situation. This necessary but unsettling knowledge continues to influence their sexual feelings later on in life, even if only unconsciously.

Quite soon, girls are taught that having sex can result in accidental pregnancy, which will force them to undergo the horror, shame, and ambivalence of an abortion, or, even worse, a shotgun wedding. This fear, and its dampening of sexual ardor, continues to influence sexual attitudes among even those relatively few, fortunate, middle-class teenage girls whose parents make sure that they are supplied with contraception.

Girls learn about not only the potential reproductive consequences of sexuality but its social risks as well. They are told that boys cannot control themselves and that, therefore, rape is a constant threat. They also find out that girls who "do it" get a "reputation." Additionally, they may discover that sex makes them feel ill at ease because they are not supposed to like it even if they do. They may recoil from the messiness of sex because they are supposed to keep themselves neat and pretty. And when they go to bed with a man, they sometimes find that being so close and so naked with someone who has greater social and physical power makes them feel vulnerable and self-conscious, so that they retain one or two pieces of protective, emotional clothing.

As they come to know about the physical and social dangers of sex, girls learn to restrain their own desire. Motivated to prevent themselves from entering a situation that might prove perilous, they control their sexual fantasies. Should they have explicit sexual fantasies, they learn to be ashamed of them, a shame that persists even when, as adults, they may be aroused to orgasm by images of, say, rape, or orgies, or anonymous promiscuity, or whippings, or bestiality. Or they may succeed in shutting their sexual fantasies down by cleaning them up, eroticizing not sex but romance, love, and marriage.

Sexual excitement depends as much on fantasy, on processes of the imagination, as on physical contact. Indeed, physical arousal would be impossible without conscious or unconscious fantasy, just as fantasy would cease without the reward of physical pleasure. Sometimes sexual fantasy is conscious, often it is unconscious. Some people fantasize by deliberately selecting one among many alternative scenes that they have constructed, found reliably arousing, and filed away in their minds. For other people, fantasies automatically resume, like a temporarily interrupted movie or dream, when sexual activity begins. Intentionally or not, still others fantasize during one activity, say masturbation, but not during others, say intercourse.

Some people lack conscious fantasies altogether. Yet the sexual imagination is at work even when consciousness paints no visible pictures. Women who have no conscious sexual fantasies may still make love to a melody of desire unconsciously composed. Even though they may be unaware of the music during the actual process of lovemaking, it is arguable that somewhere in their minds play eroticized, albeit possibly prosaic, themes, such as the wish to get married and live happily ever after. Given the ideals of eternal love and familial happiness with which we all grow up in our culture, the same themes may animate heterosexual and homosexual desire equally.

Fantasy is erotic because it is an act of make-believe, conjuring up what we desire. Fantasy is the play of desire, and play is the most primitive expression of longing. Play creates something in the space between the real and the unreal, between past and present, present and future, dreams and daily life. Play breaks the crust of ordinary daily life and shatters the routines that track mind and body in the rut of the monotonous demands of work, family, and gender. It allows forbidden, childlike feelings out of adulthood's closet and provides room for the expression of culturally proscribed wishes that would otherwise be deemed disruptive of workaday life. Originating in the space between mother and child, it expresses the hope that self and other, infant and mother, can be reunited.

Even though more women are now aware that sexual fantasy enhances their sexual pleasure and that they are capable of and entitled to both, they often have difficulty fantasizing. Not only have they trained themselves to forget their fantasies, but they have trouble with playing. This is not to say that women cannot play. They can and do. Women play with their bodies by decorating them. They play with their children. And they play games of skill as well as of chance, engaging with increasing frequency in athletic contests, both professional and amateur.

But, in a fundamental way, women have difficulty playing with themselves. Their trouble begins long before adolescence, in the beginnings of selfhood and gender identity. In order to play, one must be able both to let go of and hold on to oneself. One requires a firmly established "I" who, momentarily pretending that the self is an "it," observes the self's desires and then says, "I want." This self-possessed detachment is the emotional basis on which men have traditionally pushed their bodies to the limits of endurance in the pursuit of athletic prowess as well as sexual pleasure, and which some women have begun to develop. But if, as for women, one's sense of self is split between the sense of being an "I"—a Subject who wants—and the sense of being an "it"—an Object waiting to be wanted, no "I" exists to own desire. Letting go therefore becomes psychologically dangerous. Later on, it proves socially risky as well, since to take oneself as an object, even temporarily, is to make of oneself the sex object one is generally made to embody.

Being the self-in-relation compounds the problem. Play has been likened to the relation between a nip and a bite: A nip is a bite that says, "This looks like a bite but isn't." So with "recreational" sex: Recreational sex is sex that only pretends to be love. For women far more often than for men, however, the game becomes real. The nip of lovemaking becomes the bite of love. Women get "involved." Unused to playing with themselves and accustomed to acquiring their identity through attachment to someone else, women frequently find that what has begun as play, such as the swooning of erotic caresses, has crossed the line into real life.

Although nips can become bites as easily for lesbians as for heterosexual women, the character styles ingrained in women and men by patriarchy makes the heterosexual woman vulnerable to a particularly maddening confusion when she engages in recreational sex. While her identity is residually dependent on connection to a man, his is basically connected to being a loner. Because relatedness is as uncannily familiar to her as separateness is to him, she may, to her bewilderment, merge with him, falling unwillingly in love. As a result, she is likely to find him even more elusive, because he, perceiving her involvement as uninvited, will start to pull away.

In a certain sense, however, recreational, or "casual," sex is an idea more than a practice. All sex is serious. When two people are naked together, when they cry and scream in passion, their longings for intimacy flare up, creating feelings of love or, when love is absent, at least their illusion.

To keep the sexual game going, then, people must amputate their longings for intimacy. In theory, each party can perform this surgery. In practice, however, the labor is divided. Women do the emotional housekeeping. They either fall in love or try to minimize any signs of love lest they expose themselves to disappointment. Men, in contrast, either remain emotionally inviolate or indulge themselves in the transient expression of love. Indeed, the pleasure of the pretense often leads men who engage in recreational sex to encourage women's involvement by false promises consciously or unconsciously made. A declaration of love with no grounds other than erotic euphoria, vague talk of a vacation together, an intent gaze that beams exclusivity, words that pretend to be part of an ongoing dialogue even at first meeting—these seductive moments can persuade women unconsciously seeking love to delude themselves into believing they have found it.

That women still fall in love more easily than men indicates the incompleteness of the so-called sexual revolution. Although women are now thought to be able to play at sex equally with men, they have to play according to a set of rules by which they cannot win. Once upon a time, the sexual game seemed to be simply, or crudely, about men "scoring" against women, who were holding out for marriage. But women's new license to score as well reveals the game's underlying principle: Women get involved, men do not. The social structure that makes men embody the self-as-individual who assertively wants, and women the self-for-other who dependently wants-to-be-wanted, has not changed. And the economic forces attracting women to marriage and repelling men from it keep the game alive. It is therefore only to be expected that, when the game is over, men will, often enough, feel exhilarated and women, cheapened. Hence, the "new chastity."

Even when the sex is part of intimate commitment, the crossing of personal boundaries may make women restrain and forget their desire. Although this tendency to merge heightens diffuse erotic pleasure, as the self opens to the other, hard-won autonomy may be threatened and replaced by a frightened and frightening dependency that, paradoxically, makes diffuse pleasure disorienting, if not repugnant, and therefore makes orgasm difficult to achieve. Nor are lesbians immune from this fear of regression. It is understandable, then, that sometimes women would rather sit it out, finding it too tedious, if not unnerving, to lower the emotional boundaries that have been so laboriously constructed. They thereby avoid the dangers of simple receptivity, which evokes the infantile state of despised neediness, unwelcome maternal selflessness, and the blending of the two. They also escape the risk of lust indulged, which often seems like a voluntarily self-destructive plunge into physical, psychological, or social dangers.

To enjoy making love, however, you have to own your desire, knowing not only *what* you want but *that* you want. You have to be able to make love with the lights on, if only the lights in your mind. Since women are trained to want-to-be-wanted but not to want, they may find it embarrassing to turn the lights on. Yet to turn on the lights of desire while patriarchy still reigns generates serious contradictions. As women who eagerly embraced the sexual revolution discovered, sexual liberation in the context of sexual oppression may be very exciting, but it also leads right back to objectification and exploitation.

Pornography is a central case in point. On one hand, most pornography expresses the hatred and objectification of women embedded in our culture. Images of women being beaten, chained, mutilated, raped, and even murdered reflect women's second-class status, its servility, and its attendant bad self-image. Pornography may reinforce not only misogyny but women's self-hatred. Furthermore, these often humiliating images of women produce huge profits for the sex industry by exploiting women economically.

On the other hand, many women find pornography sexually stimulating. Although relatively few women buy pornographic books or magazines, many will read them when they chance upon them. They may not go out of their way to patronize pornographic movie theaters, but many do enjoy watching "skin flicks" on cable TV or video. The conventional notion that women are not aroused by graphic sexual representation may be due not only to prejudice but to women's lack of exposure to erotica.

Women's embarrassment at the pleasure they take in pornography expresses the contradiction inherent in feminine sexuality under patriarchy. It is not unreasonable to argue that women blush because they are ashamed of being aroused by images of humiliation and pain. In order to learn to live in patriarchy, women not uncommonly come to love the parts of it that keep them in chains. Yet it is not enough to argue that women who enjoy pornography simply collude in and eroticize their own victimization. Women who giggle upon being caught with a dirty book in their hands may be reexperiencing the shame they taught themselves long ago in order to repress their desire. And they may also be flushing with pleasure upon glimpsing the unaccustomed, momentary nakedness of their own erotism.

When women read, write, and enjoy pornography, just as when they fantasize privately, they are turning on the lights. They are acknowledging to themselves and to others that they, too, like "it." They like sex and they like desire. And their resulting excitement makes sense, for wanting is what selfhood is about. Pornography may, conventionally enough, portray men who want and women who want-to-be-wanted. But it nevertheless depicts both wanting and wanting-to-be-wanted, in other words, desire in all its activity and receptivity and wanting and needing.

Given the ongoing patriarchal construction of desire, it is likely that private fantasy and public pornography will continue to portray men as Subjects and women as Objects who need Subjects to complete and elevate them. But people can identify, and empathize, across the boundaries of gender. Were this not the case, then women could read and write only about women, men only about men. Women and men could never be friends, and mothers could rear only daughters.

Pornography is private fantasy made public. Its images may be misogynist, but that is all they are—make-believe images. To equate images with actions is to misunderstand the function of fantasy in personal experience in general and sexual desire in particular. Although it is widely held that pornographic images cause men to inflict sexual violence on women, research indicates that pornography tends to reinforce men's woman-hating *attitudes* rather than to stimulate their *acts* of violence. Likewise, when women are aroused by pornographic images, they are not driven by a masochistic wish to hurl themselves into a self-destructive relationship. They are aroused, rather, because they recognize their own desire, almost as though they had never known it before.

The capacity for make-believe, play, and fantasy means that

women, like men, see more in pornography, or any image, than what is on the surface. When women get aroused by lewd stories or pictures, they are finding their own desire. They are playing with a normally forbidden part of themselves. They are toying with a conscious, public representation of their private, lustful wishes. They are entering, and allowing to flower in them, the power of desire, which, though it is tabooed because located in men, nevertheless belongs to them as well. They do what is forbidden by patriarchal law. They become the female Subject.

As William and I climb the rickety stairs to the red-doored loft of the Devil's Delight, he says, "You're going to love this party, it's a beautiful event. The costumes are wonderful. And everyone is caring. There's an amazing tenderness that comes out when everyone feels free to be and do what they want in front of everyone else."

At the door, a sign says,

MEMBERS: MALES $5, FEMALES $2.50
NONMEMBERS: MALES $10, FEMALES $5

After we pay, William buys a glass of white wine for me and a beer for himself at a table to the left of the entrance. Pretzels, potato chips, and cookies in the shapes of breasts, vulvas, penises, buttocks, and booted feet are in bowls on the table. The room is hung with crepe paper and red, yellow, and blue balloons.

We look for Mary as we stand on the edge of the crowd, whose heat makes it feel like summer. I see males, females, and indeterminates; teenagers and octagenarians; many skin colors and body types; beautiful and ugly faces; straight bodies and crippled ones.

William says, "I'm glad to see so many people here. There might not be too many more chances if the AIDS panic doesn't let up and they keep closing sex clubs down."

"But don't you think a lot of these people are just tourists?" I ask, adding, "I feel like one myself."

"I don't think of you as a tourist," he says teasingly. "I think of you as a voyeur." He laughs. "Many of us love to be watched when we're in a scene. We love voyeurs. Besides, once you walk through the door, who's to know why you came? The world will see us all the same. So at least for tonight you're an S-M freak."

Feeling a bit startled by this last remark, I turn my attention back to the crowd and gape. Like Mediterranean village families on summer evenings, people promenade, to see and be seen. A few hug and kiss in delighted greeting. Among the parade is an ethereal, ashen-haired beauty in white. Her dress drapes loosely from her shoulders; its bodice, split into two pieces that bare the inner slopes of her perfect, bell-shaped, nonsagging, size B breasts, is tucked into a wide golden belt that glints like the delicate gold chain hanging from the very thin gold pins that pierce each nipple.

"Huh!" I grab my own breasts protectively. I turn to William to point out this spectacle but am interrupted as Mary rushes up and gives him a great big kiss on the mouth. Then she hugs me, William watching with a smile and little flushes marking his cheekbones.

"Oh, I'm so glad to see you," she squeals. "You got here just in time for the costume contest." She looks very appealing herself in her full-length multicolored peasant skirt and black stomacher that bubbles her breasts up very prettily over her white scooped-neck blouse.

"How come everyone is wearing costumes?" I want to know.

"It's a celebration of the virgin potential of spring," William says enthusiastically, "a salute to joy and hope."

"How about her, is she in the contest?" Not wanting to point, I jut my chin in the direction of the one with the pierced nipples.

"Oh, isn't she fantastic? What do you think, Billy love?"

"Not as fantastic as you, Mary mine." He hugs her even more tightly.

Feeling like a supernumerary, I edge discreetly away.

Not knowing quite what to do next, I join the promenade to meander around the barnlike space as if I were doing a sociological survey. Not everyone is as exotic as the lady in white. Passing by the entrance again, I note the Hispanic bouncer's pirate garb, a black patch over one eye and a gold, silver, and blue sash adorning his vast gut, a rather prosaic costume I myself wore one Halloween when I was about nine. A bit farther along there are two men, one white, one Asian, arm in arm: The first wears a red dress and red, high-heeled sandals; the second sports just a black leather jock strap and bare feet. After them come two men and one woman; one man is costumed as Jack Kennedy and the other as Bobby, while the red-lipped, platinum-haired woman with her arms around both of them wears a white dress resembling the one that, blown upward by gusts of air from a subway grating, revealed Marilyn Monroe's delicious thighs. Following them is a pale, dark-haired woman in black stiletto heels, black fishnet stockings, and a corset of lacey black leather; she struts about in her frilly white maidservant's cap, flicking her "duster," a cat-o'-nine-tails, against her calf in a mildly titillating way.

Mary and William, holding hands, stroll up to me. "Well," I announce in what I think is a nonchalant tone of voice, "there certainly is a rather wide variety here. Although," I indicate the maid, "her costume's a bit stereotypical, wouldn't you say?"

Mary says, "Oh, no. She's the entire discourse on sexuality all by herself." Mary is a graduate student in women's studies, with an emphasis on semiotics. "*Her* used to be a *him*. She had the operation last fall and finished her electrolysis last month."

Oh.

Which entrance fee was "she" charged, asks my father sarcastically, *the one for men or the one for women?*

I follow them to a corner where others, sitting on chairs or standing, watch a black woman, about forty, comfortably built and wearing a black velvet dress, as she whips a naked white man in his sixties with a black leather paddle. His aging body in good, even athletic shape, he wears a collar, handcuffs, and clasp, and kneels with his reddened back to her. The collar, leather studded with metal, circles his neck. The handcuffs hold his wrists behind his back; they are kept tautly in place by a chain attached to the back of the collar. His teeth, finally, clench on the slack of a second chain. Locked onto the front of his collar, it pulls tightly on the metal clasp that scrunches up his genitals into one poor little mass. He seems to be shivering, and his face is pinched as if in pain.

The woman, her face calm, is now lightly caressing his back with her black leather paddle. Suddenly she smacks him with it. He shudders some more. Then her soft-skinned instrument whisks his backside like a feather and slams down again. And his tremors, which I now understand to be ecstasy, continue. Then she allows some hot wax to dribble from a black candle onto the sorer spots on his back and hits him a few times more with strokes alternately gentle and muscled. His face now registers the grimace of pain and pleasure that often accompanies orgasm.

But he doesn't seem to be coming. He probably can't get an erection with that thing on. But men can come even without a hard-on, can't they? My mind flips through the many sex books I have read since about the age of twelve. Or maybe he doesn't care about coming. That would be a role reversal, wouldn't it now?

Someone brings them some cider. She unlocks the handcuffs. He stands up, puts on his glasses, and then sits down on an empty chair. As she packs up her paraphernalia, he takes a ham sandwich out of a kit bag and eats it, chatting with her between bites. The event seems to be over. I am amazed that they now appear so ordinary and normal.

"Most of the men here are looking for dominant women," Mary explains. "In the straight world, that's hard to find."

Feeling uneasy, I ask her, "Why did they stop?"

"Well, you know, it's all usually agreed on in advance who'll do what and how long and what the safe-word is, you know, the word that means, 'Stop, I really mean it, stop.' "

"What if the person is gagged?" I ask.

"Oh, there's a safe-action."

Recalling the pornography I was reading at William's, I persist, even if it makes me look straight and square and old. "But what if someone is bound and gagged and blindfolded and . . . oh, I don't know, I guess they can wiggle their toes. But still. . . ." Suddenly, I feel a little angry. "This all doesn't seem so beautiful and honest to me. I felt so bad that that poor man had to suffer all that pain to get his pleasure, as if he thought he wasn't entitled to enjoy himself. What's the truth in this particular darkness?"

"In the war on sex, it's one of the last real holdouts for liberation, that's what," answers Mary.

"She's right. In the middle of the counterrevolution, places like this keep the faith." William waves his arms expansively. "Here, nothing has to be hidden. You can do whatever you desire."

"Well, if that's the case," I complain, "how come I'm afraid that if I look anyone in the eye, I'll feel as though I have to go home with them, or whip them, or let them tie me up?"

They seem amused. Mary puts her arm around me in a maternal sort of way and says, "Listen, you don't have to do anything you don't want to do. All you have to do is say no."

Somehow it never occurred to me.

❖

THE POLITICS OF UNCONDITIONAL LOVE

Sexuality has a special place in our culture. Construed as the prime repository of eros, it is the privileged expression of desire, of the longing to reconnect with mother that makes all later life a going forward in order to return to the safe place from which we started. Sexuality thus appears as a nonpareil source of self-realization, of personal power or the sense of effectiveness, self-determination, and authenticity for which adults yearn as they go about their daily lives. Consequently, the sexual prohibitions that influence our private lives, enforced by public law and custom, constitute a main route through which adults come to constrain their personal power. Sexuality is therefore a prism through which the structures of personal and political power in our culture may be not only experienced but appreciated.

Officially, we do not like to think that sexuality has to do with anything so crude as power. "Making love" is, rather, about pleasure, tenderness, marriage, or babies. Even recreational sex, with its hard edge of sexual politics, is viewed in a soft focus. Still less do we enjoy knowing that we may find the vicissitudes of power erotic. Yet this erotization of power explains the pervasiveness of sadomasochism in private fantasy, public media, and sexual practice.

It is useful, if not in every case appropriate, to distinguish between two kinds of sadomasochism, emotional and sexual. The first, emotional sadomasochism, entails one person's feelings of self-hate locking into another's feelings of hatred, both of these emotions being bound as well to love. The second, sexual sadomasochism, or SM, involves sexual activities that require an exchange of power, or the practice of discipline and submission, between consenting partners, some of whom regularly exchange roles.

Conventionally, women are held to be "naturally" masochistic, men sadistic. However, sadism and masochism are not innate emotions or styles. Rather, they develop in the course of maturation. The emergence of masochism and the repression of sadism in women result from the self-abnegation expected of them as self-for-other, as well as from their having to find honor in a dishonored form of self. Reciprocally, to the degree that men express sadism and repress masochism, it results from their socialization for assertiveness divorced from relatedness.

The two sorts of sadomasochism may or may not converge. Most people who are emotionally sadistic or masochistic have never entered an SM club; they may be, simply, cruel to others and/or themselves. Some people who relish giving or receiving emotional pain also eroticize physical pain. Some of these do it only at home and have never gone to a club; the point, for others, is precisely the public performance. And of those who frequent SM clubs, some are caught in the vicious and desperate cycle of emotional sadomasochism, some are not.

SM is not, perhaps, so common an activity. And the reasons any one person engages in it, like those for any individual choice of sexual partner, position, or practice, are far too complex to be summed up in a few sentences. Nevertheless, the image of one person subjugating another through discipline, bondage, humiliation, or pain is ubiquitous in individual fantasy. Many women and men arouse themselves by imagining, reading, or watching SM, whether with shameful pleasure or equanimity. Some, possibly fewer, engage in secret, sporadic, and spontaneous sadomasochistic practices. Others, probably fewer still, regularly enact ritualized sadomasochistic scenes, about which they speak only to other aficionados.

So, too, is SM the inner lining of everyday life. Men who batter their women physically or emotionally may love them all the more for their devoted suffering. Subordinates routinely treated with contempt by admired superiors may sacrifice their self-respect in servile, yet gratifying efforts to please. Politicians and other public figures are aroused by their own power, as might be inferred from Henry Kissinger's alleged observation that power is the best aphrodisiac or from the masturbation in which the late rock star Jim Morrison once indulged during a public concert. Reciprocally, people who lack public power are often aroused by those who have it. The populace was drawn to Jack Kennedy not only because of the sexual appeal that made him a "ladies' man" but because he was president. And one of the perquisites of male rock-stardom is the presence of groupies.

Eroticized power relations flood our culture and our minds. Hierarchy, which is so pervasive in the state as to define it, generates and attracts strong feelings: love for power and the powerful, hatred for weakness and the weak. These emotions permeating ordinary adult life resonate with the unconscious as well. The glamour of public power recalls the glorious omnipotence of infancy, while the personal or public failings that adults despise in themselves and others invoke infancy's terrified, angry impotence. Emotional sadism and masochism therefore represent the welding of unconscious feelings left over from childhood with the structures of public power that form the permanent scenery of twentieth-century adult life.

However, our culture, claiming equality and democracy, disguises the permanence of its public power structures and the pervasiveness of sadomasochism by coding them in the language of heterosexuality. Heterosexuality, as symbolized by the wedding-cake bride and groom, is our culture's mainstream sexual fantasy. On the surface, it envisions personal success and satisfaction through love, romance, marriage, and the family. But the bride and groom, seemingly so pure, also represent dominance and subordination. The man, possessing the phallus, is on top; the woman, lacking it, is on bottom. He is in charge; she is taken charge of. He occupies a first-class status, she a second-class one. He symbolizes the subjectivity to which all aspire, she the objectification that all wish to avoid, that she must consciously confront in everyday life, and that he inevitably faces as well. She loves him for his power; he loves her for her admiration of and submission to it. He embodies the sadist, or the "top," of SM; she, the masochist, or the "bottom."

As the embodiment of cultural values, heterosexuality makes hierarchy seem as natural as blue sky. Heterosexuality masculinizes the person who is dominant and feminizes the person who is subordinate. But since gender is equated with biological sex, and since gender hierarchy therefore seems unalterable, so, too, does hierarchy seem inevitable. Consequently, any power relations, including by implication those laced with SM, appear to be as natural and unexceptional as the joining of man and woman. The unequal relationship between males and females therefore ratifies domination and thus justifies itself.

Public SM is the counterfantasy to conventional public sex. Through a sort of "ritual of reversal," SM reveals the skeleton of power hanging in the heterosexual closet. Like Zulu planting ceremonies, in which girls wear men's clothing, carry their weapons, and do their job of herding cattle, it permits men and women to exchange roles. Like "topsy-turvy day" at summer camp, when campers rule counselors, it allows women to take charge and men to submit. Like Mardi Gras, which sanctions normally tabooed behavior, such as transvestism and extramarital flirtations, it makes public what is ordinarily private. SM's ritualized binding and whipping contradict the romantic ceremonies of engagement and marriage continually displayed in the media, stating that relations of power are as deeply embedded in normal, sexual behavior as are love and tenderness.

Through another reversal, SM transforms the critique of heterosexuality into a critique of adulthood itself, revealing the longings for tenderness and revenge, the wish for agency, and the disappointment and anger in the heart of adult life. It might seem reasonable to expect, given the masculinization of power, that everyone would rush to take up the whips and chains of dominance, to be the men, to be tops. Certainly, most people consciously want to be dominant. At a minimum, they wish to control their own lives. Since power in our society comes from controlling other people and things, wished-for autonomy in fact entails domination.

Nevertheless, the longings of most people are expressed in an SM one-liner: A department store once had a sale because there was a surplus of tops. The joke is that, among those who practice SM, there are never in fact enough tops. Among practicing sadomasochists, as well as those who simply fantasize about SM, and even those who do not, most people do not want to be on top. They prefer to be the Object and submit, to be taken charge of, taken care of, told what to do. Indeed, this yearning for passivity is the reason so many men who patronize prostitutes prefer fellatio to intercourse.

The wish for submission springs from the desire that unconsciously drives all sexuality and intimacy—the search for mother's unconditional, omnipotent love in a culture valuing people not for who they are but for what, through unremitting self-control, they do. The desire to give up control, if only for a little while, is a longing to return to those blissful moments of infancy when one was accepted for *being,* not for *doing* anything special. The yearning to reexperience being loved in all one's disorderly humanness—hate, rage, weakness, cruelty, timidity, laziness, and, as well, love, passion, fortitude, compassion, courage, initiative—attempts to restore self-esteem. The desire to yield aims to repair the damages to selfhood caused by the inevitable failures of adulthood in a culture that holds out on the economic and social omnipotence it promises and demands.

And this reparative acceptance is what the bottom unconsciously receives from the top, who, through projection, gets it in return. The bottom yields all control to the top, relinquishing the autonomous self. At the same time, the top projects all dependency onto the bottom, assuming an air of self-possession. The bottom thus gets to be like a baby, to whom the top's ministrations seem like the maternal nurturance for which the baby pines. The top gets to be like a mother, administering discipline, and sometimes punishment, for the wild baby's own good. But, through the merging of selves forged in molten erotic heat, top and bottom also change places. The top unconsciously becomes the now-cared-for baby as well; the bottom takes on the agency, the self-will and authority, of the powerful mother.

Serving as an attempt to heal, SM can, however, also cause harm. Sex takes place between two differentiated adults, not between mother and child. While the wishes of top and bottom may seem at times to converge, the top's differentiated interests must occasionally diverge. The top may, for example, discipline the bottom as a parent trains a child. However, as any parent knows, punishment can spring as much from anger as from a rational wish to instruct. Moreover, the anger itself may depend less on the child than on some other trouble in the parent's love life or work life.

Nor is the top's rage solely a reincarnation of the parent's irrationalities. The top, identifying with the bottom, becomes the furious baby retaliating for mother's cruel absences. And, by projection, the bottom participates in this sweetly vengeful recouping of the weakness we have all felt during our childhood and hate during our maturity. SM's risk, then, is that the wild passions of infancy, filtered through the irrationalities of full-grown adults, will escape conscious control, bringing more pain than pleasure.

The possible abuse of a practice is no reason to proclaim it unmitigatedly dangerous. Were this the case, one would have to call for the reinstitution of Prohibition or, given the frequency of wife beating, the elimination of heterosexual marriage. But it is very hard to see how SM can, in the ordinary course of events, be entirely divorced from the unconscious hatred and despair underlying emotional sadomasochism. In one key way, emotional sadomasochism and SM operate on an identical wavelength, the oscillation between severity and gentleness. An essential ingredient in SM's ritual beatings is the delectable alternation between soft caresses and vicious blows. Cycles of love and hate define emotional sadomasochism, as demonstrated by women who repeatedly return to husbands who beat them and, in fewer instances, by battered men who similarly forgive their vicious wives. In each case, the alternation between abuse and benevolence murmurs with the miserable hatred felt by the powerless infant when mother is gone and the melting gratitude when she returns to kiss the rageful tears away. There is no relief sweeter or more addictive than the return of the loved one who, having been cruel, now offers tenderness.

Even though it is true, then, that all you have to do is say yes or no, you may not always be fully conscious of that to which you are giving or withholding consent. You can do whatever you want in any sexual encounter, but wanting is attached to needing. In speaking to another person, one is also in conversation with unconscious and social forces that exist beyond one's will. Consequently, in the same way that many women, straight or gay, may slip unintentionally into a cycle of emotional sadomasochism with their lovers, so in SM one may find oneself having said yes to something to which one would rather have said no.

Nevertheless, whatever the emotional and physical dangers of SM, the condemnation it receives is due not only to caution. Like non-procreational sex, or sex-for-pleasure, in the nineteenth century, and homosexuality a generation ago, SM is castigated because it defies taboos and, in so doing, tells us what we do not want to know. SM releases the child's desire locked away in the adult mind, and tells the truth that, in our culture, the marrow of desire is structured by power. And, like homosexuality or any sexual practice other than contraceptionless, missionary-position, penis-in-vagina intercourse, SM sets off moral false alarms because it bluntly announces that people like sex. People have sex not because it is a divine duty in the interests of procreation or an instrumental one in the service of the survival of the human species. They have sex because they want to.

And if they can do what they want in bed, then they can do what they want elsewhere. Although they may quash their desire in order to fit into orderly adult life, they can, at any time, rebel. Any sexual activity recalling the explosive passions for love, care, and personal power, which, properly harnessed, can overthrow the repressive, hierarchical social order in which we must live, is therefore politically dangerous. The feeling-statement "I want" may amount to little more than solipsism in a consumerist society like ours. But, in circumstances of political protest it could be, and must always have been, one with the breath of life.

The movement for free sexual expression is one of the most important social movements of modern life. Fundamentally, it protests not only current arrangements for sexuality but those for desire altogether. It is a rebellious voice in an ongoing cultural conversation. As such, however, it never escapes the limits against which it strains. All of its "thou shalts" are not simply positive assertions of desire, but arguments against the "thou shalt nots" of culture.

Nevertheless, while sexual liberation struggles against bondage as much as it reaches for freedom, it proclaims that everyone wants what women want—to own their own desire. Women's sexual desire bears the marks of the oppression in whose context it develops. But so does men's. Although men are, for example, permitted by convention and training to enjoy pornography, they nevertheless buy their books and magazines and see their movies on the sly. Indeed, the stealth becomes part of the pleasure, for men, too, learn to eroticize the chains on their desire.

What women want is to say plainly, freely, and confidently, "I want." Their desire to desire represents the return of the repressed in all adults—their longing to realize the power of their desire, to be endowed not with the right to dominate but with the right simply to be who they are and who they might become.

I feel as though I'm about to pass out. "Listen, I'm OD-ing. I have to go home."

William opens his mouth to speak, then looks at Mary and says, "Let's take her home."

She pecks him on the cheek. "Look, Billy love, I want to watch the end of the costume contest, so why don't you two just go."

I interject, "No, I can go by myself, really, don't worry."

William says to Mary, "I'll see her home and then come back for you."

"You don't need to," Mary half-turns away, her arms folded.

William's jaw is getting that stubborn molar-grinding look. "I want to." He grabs her shoulder, busses her cheek as she just barely keeps herself from pulling her head away.

Once outside, I suddenly relax, my fatigue now more like soft sleepiness than the high-wire exhaustion it was just moments ago. As we walk to the main avenue to find a taxi, I regard with interest the exotic sexual creatures who populate the 3:00 A.M. streets— people whose feathers are bedraggled from the evening before, people whose flight is just beginning, people who play at being what they are and are not. I cringe, too, at the risks they run as they live out their nighttime fantasies.

In the cab, William puts his arm around me.

I ask tentatively, "What's going on with you and Mary?"

He is silent for a long while, then says, "I always feel when I leave a woman in the morning that she'll feel bad, that I'm disappointing someone."

I pull away. "That's very paternalistic of you."

"Fuck you."

Oh boy, we're at it again. I try to make up. "I mean, I can see that it's also sweet of you. I mean, you don't . . ." I pull my thoughts together. "Listen, either you're jealous of Mary or you miss her or you just don't want to sleep alone. Whichever it is, it's playing havoc with your ideals of nonmonogamy, which is why you're going back to get her."

"You're always taking the side of freedom, but really you're arguing for imprisonment," he replies.

"So are you, only you don't know it, and it's not imprisonment," I retort. "There is a darkness in you. There's a darkness in that scene at the club. There's something left out, there has to be. Nothing ever tells the whole story, no theory, no movie, no book. There's a missing truth for you, too. I don't think you know what you want. But you're not trying to figure it out."

"How can I when everyone else thinks they have the answer?" he says wildly. "Trying to figure these things out alone is like trying to build socialism in one country. It can't be done."

"You're exactly like the rest of us. You want someone you love to love you in exactly the way you want," I answer, thinking that maybe we're both right.

He doesn't answer. But I know we will continue the fight on the phone tomorrow and, eventually, make it all up.

The cab drops me at the corner. After I wave good-bye, I decide impulsively to get a pack of cigarettes from the all-night deli, even though I quit smoking more than a year ago.

As I walk home on the sidewalk opposite my own with a lit cigarette in my hand, I see the man who hangs out most of the day on my corner.

"Good evening," he says to me.

"Good evening," I say, jerking my head back, the corners of my mouth forking automatically into a good-girl smile.

We walk two steps more.

"And how are you?" he asks.

Confused by this oddly timed question that seems appropriate for day but not for the middle of the night, I slow to let him pass, contemplating a leap into the street should he make the smallest move in my direction.

"Don't be afraid," he says, gesturing for me to continue to precede him. "I'm a good person," he adds, putting his key in the front lock of his apartment building, two doors away from my own.

Epilogue/On the Road
(Dreamtime)

*I*n my dreams, the roads are often under construction. Or they are slippery with mud, snow, ice. Occasionally I am on foot. Usually I am driving a car. Most often, I am frightened.

In my analysis, my analyst and I interpreted the cars as me, my armor, my defenses, my hopes. One of the first cars I remember dreaming about was a Porsche—fancy car, fancy hopes. Then a Volkswagen; I seemed to have come down to earth. Once there was even a fuel truck, on whose door I slammed, macho-style, as I drove past the house where I spent my miserable adolescence. Later there was the Saab I shared with my husband.

More recently, it is the Honda I bought myself. Married and divorced, my most recent cars are competent, sturdy, serviceable.

But now, I am thinking about the roads, not about the cars. Sometimes it is a dirt road, twisting dangerously in its ascent to an Alpine village. Sometimes, the pavement of the road I travel is being repaired, and a monstrous machine chews up the ground right under my wheels, threatening to drop me to the center of the earth—or perhaps to China. At other times, it is a city street, a road across a bridge, a highway ramp slick with ice. And on occasion, the road is under construction and unfinished.

But all the roads are exciting. When I lived in the suburbs, I drove around in waking hours, letting myself get lost, hoping to discover a new road that would lead to a town I'd never heard of before. Now, when I am driving and spot a sign that says, ROAD UNDER CONSTRUCTION, PROCEED AT YOUR OWN RISK, I feel a thrill that impels me to travel it. Usually I resist. It is likely, after all, to lead to a suburban development, and all I would find there would be some model homes, replicas of the one my parents bought when I was a child.

But I could be wrong.

The road in my dreams is the path of my life. Unknown, frightening, exhilarating, if only I dare to take it. It would be satisfying if there were always at least one unpaved road to travel.

POINT OF DEPARTURE

Patriarchy is, first and last, a system of domination. Grounded in political hierarchy, it, like all forms of domination, inclines us, men as well as women, to lose our sense of personal authority by playing on our doubts about the reality and validity of our selves, perceptions, and values. But patriarchy differs from other kinds of domination, whether racism, class structure, or colonialism, because it goes directly for the jugular of social life and personal integrity—desire. Patriarchy, or sexism, attacks desire by reducing it to sex and then defining sex in the limited terms of gender.

In our culture, the diffuse, messy wildness of desire is called sex. Only in sex is incoherence culturally permissible, acceptable, even celebrated; inebriation cannot hold a candle to it. In contrast to desire's indefiniteness, sex can be named, managed, packaged, and sold. While infants delight in boundary-less pleasure, adults and their sexual preferences are classified as straight and gay, normal and perverse, legal and criminal. The rules for chastity, heterosexuality, monogamy, love, and marriage create channels within which desire may flow and which define its overflow. Concentrated in sex is all the erotic pleasure meant to compensate for the disappointments of public life. Marketed like any other leisure-time commodity, sexual pleasure is simultaneously glamorized and drained of its specialness. Still we prize it, because it is the cultural voice of desire, of bittersweet memories of youth's limitless possibility.

Gender, chief among the channels for desire, conveys domination as well. Gender identity, based on both identification with one's own gender and the contrast between male and female, subsumes the definition of self and therefore the primal differentiation between self and other. However, the rooting of gender identity in patriarchy transforms a simple difference, self/other, into an unambiguous relation of power, male/female. By symbolizing both difference and hierarchy, the phallus disguises all relations of power as mere relations of difference.

This symbolic confounding of difference and hierarchy is no accident. In our culture, all relations of difference, not just those between women and men, tend to evolve into actual relations of power. Although our democratic ideals contain a claim to tolerate differences, we honor the "melting pot" meant to make them disappear. On the one hand, we believe that, despite their differences, individuals are equal and ought therefore to be treated according to the same standard. And it is true that universal, abstract standards of excellence, rather than particularistic ones of personal connection or divine right, have permitted many people to be upwardly mobile. Yet, on the other hand, it is equally true that people who are "different" are stigmatized by their difference, required by it to live up to a definition of themselves that they did not create.

"Difference" is not a neutral concept. The differences our culture is proud to ignore emerge by contrast with an ideal, average person, an "Everyman," a person without a personality, as it were. Yet this homogenized person, against whose economic opportunities and political rights those of everyone else are measured, really does have a persona. The Everyman from whom all differences flow is the white, heterosexual, Anglo-Saxon, Protestant male, a variety of human being from which most people differ. Although sameness, or identity, and equality are dissimilar qualities, our social ideals assimilate them to one another. Therefore, any difference from this Everyman comes to signify, and indeed to bring about, inequity. While some differences can be camouflaged, others resist disguise. Jewish or Catholic white men can sometimes pass for the straight, male WASP. But no man of color, nor any woman no matter what her color, can. The stigmatization of the flesh guarantees social inequality, and at the same time strips people of their personal power.

The stigma of femininity, of women's cardinal and second-class difference from "man," is the chief means by which the state dominates women and, thereby, everyone. The state's control is indirect. Its power rests ultimately on coercive force, on its singular right to restrain people physically, by jailing or even killing them. However, the conduct of ordinary life submits to much subtler controls. Put simply, the state does not place armed guards at every door. Nor do they stand at mother's knee. Rather, people conform to social institutions, countering their best interests not because they are spineless but because, through quite ordinary and therefore nearly unnoticeable activities, the power of the state reappears in their minds.

The state captures hearts and minds through patriarchy. It attempts to control the bodies—and so the sexuality, and so the desire—of women and thereby of the children they rear and of the men and other women for whom they are nurturers and symbols of want and need. The most fertile source of power over personal identity and elemental social relations is in the linked matters of sexuality, procreation, and gender. And the most accessible route to this source of power passes through women because they give birth. Birth is not only a biological event with a beginning and an end. It is the birth of a person and the birth of a social relationship. The state exercises control over birth, people, and relationships by controlling the material and symbolic bases of sex and reproduction, and therefore women's bodies and minds.

The state's judgment on these "repro-sexual" matters defines women and thereby fashions an individuality susceptible to domination. It makes women into beings whose rights to their selves—to their bodies and minds—are less than the rights others have to them. It creates them as the Subject-as-Object whose desire is alienated from her. This social deformation of women's desire indelibly marks their psyches because it sets in when they are most psychologically vulnerable—when gender identity forms, when adult consciousness begins to take shape during puberty, when they are pregnant, and when they are rearing their precious young.

Insofar as children receive their earliest nurturing from a person whose subjectivity is a battle between her desire to create herself and society's truncation of her desire, their earliest image of self must be one of domination. This image of domination, spread out on billboards, television commercials, and magazine ads, repeats itself in later, adult consciousness *ad infinitum*, like an Andy Warhol silk screen. Thus is a veil of glamour drawn over the adult condition, in which, for at least forty hours a week and in some ways for a lifetime, one is supposed to be another's creature yet also retain a conviction and appearance of self-will.

THE ODYSSEY

If the way to society's mind is through woman's desire, so does woman's desire point a way to resistance. While the conventional Odyssean journey belongs to the lone self, the journey to domination's end, for women as for everyone, will be a doubled, ambiguous one. It will be simultaneously individual and collective, in the service of society as well as of desire, self-for-other as well as self-for-individual. While the masculinized odyssey terminates in a known place, in a home with wife and family, the end of women's odyssey, like the end of domination, remains to be created as the journey proceeds; indeed, will be created by the voyage itself. While Odysseus traveled through the strange, fantastic land of the Other to find the Self, women, like other second-class citizens, are the Others making their journey on utterly familiar soil. They will find their selves only by digging up the very ground of Self on which they walk to get through the day.

Resolving sexual contradictions requires tolerating the ambiguity of dwelling in their midst. Despite the Western mind/body dualism that assimilates women to the body and men to the mind, women have minds as well as bodies, inhabiting the ambiguity of having both. They strive to realize their own desire even as their society militates against them. When they cohabit with their superiors, or refuse to, it is as much out of will and passion as from compulsion. And, like men, they are expected to be authorities of their own desire, even while they are also objectified into the image of desire's irrationality disdainfully dismissed from the routine of public life. It is this subjectivity, tolerant of the ambiguity hidden in the contradiction of the Subject-as-Object, that preserves the spark of desire. Women may incarnate domination for everyone. But if they are people who can, with will, capitulate to hierarchy, then they are people who can, with equal will, refuse.

Feminism is the political expression of this refusal. Born of the patriarchy that stigmatizes femininity, feminism is simultaneously a political and a cultural movement. It attempts to redress the balance of power between men and women so that equality for everyone can be realized. And it tries to redefine femininity even as patriarchy endures, in the hope of eliminating once and for all the domination that everyone experiences. Feminism's battles, victories, and losses are like a winding road that often doubles back on itself. Each achievement, like any social change short of total revolution, is vulnerable to being drawn back into the patriarchy threatening to reclaim and destroy it. Each reversal is a new beginning.

At first, feminism tried to restructure women's lives by questioning the validity of the distinction between "femininity" and "masculinity." Refusing the gender dichotomy as well as the gender hierarchy, the second wave of feminism began by asserting a fundamental identity of desire among men and women. Women were not inherently second-class but as innately intelligent, capable, and lustful as men. On the basis of this assertion, feminists claimed women's right to equal economic opportunity and to equal treatment before the law. Furthermore, feminists argued that women's and men's erotic longings and their general psychological potential were not only equal in strength and value but identical. The politics of androgyny ratified women's longings to act on their own desires, whether by getting a job or demanding a raise, by forming political groups that fought for publicly funded child care centers or abortion rights, by revolutionizing scholarship, or by exploring the varieties of their lust.

As feminists entered the marketplace, took on political antagonists, and plunged into the sexual revolution, however, the utopian assertion of unisex desire hit the wall of reality. Given the incalculable effects of socialization and the doggedness of patriarchy, the politics of androgyny seemed to reach its limits. Purely emancipationist goals, in the absence of a broader political critique of the very hierarchies to whose tops women wished to climb, could, and did, lead straight back to patriarchy. For some women, feminism came to mean nothing more than "career feminism." Now, as then, many women are primarily interested in their individual rights to enter the public domain, especially to secure footholds on corporate and financial ladders. They are only secondarily, if at all, concerned with the second-class status common to women of all classes that galvanized feminism in the first place.

Likewise, while it was essential to insist on a fundamental androgyny of sexual desire, men's desire was as highly structured, and impaired, as women's. Although men were privileged to enjoy their bodies, monogamously and promiscuously, without fear or blame, still their eroticism suffered the limitations of a culture that makes sex a commodity and an opiate and defines it by the absence of intimacy and reproductive responsibility. Without a woman-centered sexual politics, a simple liberationist position, it soon appeared, would leave women where they began, in missionary position, and on the bottom at that.

The androgynist position contained a hidden contradiction that soon emerged to birth a more woman-centered politics. Sameness of desire and equality before the law did not mean that women's interests were identical to men's. In particular, it became immediately evident that women's capacity to bear children necessitated a politics of reproductive freedom. The reproductive-rights movement, beginning in the struggle to decriminalize abortion, later expanded to extend that right to women of all classes by combatting government efforts to exclude it from welfare coverage.

At the same time, women, by insisting on the validity of their own sexual desire, began to articulate its differences from men's. Many, encouraged as well by the gay liberation movement, acknowledged their homosexual feelings. In the process, a separate, lesbian subcommunity grew up within the larger one of feminism to become the social basis for the formation of a feminist counterculture. In this intellectual and political counterculture incorporating straight as well as gay women, feminists began to rediscover, understand, and value the culturally mandated psychological and behavioral styles of intimacy, emotionality, and relatedness that differentiated women from men. They began as well to try to institutionalize these qualities in the groups in which they lived, loved, and worked.

Yet woman-centered, or "cultural," feminism as it has now come to be called, threatens to return us to the beginning of our journey. In the course of legitimating women's desire, cultural feminism has somehow elevated it over men's. Thus stigmatizing men rather than women, it simply recycles Western dualistic thinking. Vague on the origin of gender differences, cultural feminism effectively argues for innate differences in men and women, siding with our original enemy, biological determinism. It also includes, notably, a strong critique not only of male violence but of pornography and other forms of sexuality that it deems "male," as against the wish for reciprocity and intimacy that it characterizes as "female." Cultural feminism therefore returns sexuality to the fold of gender, leaving the field of women's desire where it has always been, in patriarchal hands.

No politics can escape the soil in which it grows. Cultural feminism is as rooted in and therefore as vulnerable to patriarchy's sway as the politics of androgyny. It was essential to assert an identity of desire. And great personal and political benefits derive from conceptualizing "woman" as still unexplored terrain that promises delights and passions yet unimaginable within the confines of patriarchal, procreational sex. But "woman" remains a cultural category meaningful in opposition to "man." It necessarily partakes of all the qualities, positive and negative, with which it has been conventionally endowed by patriarchy.

Having gotten this far on our journey, as confused and divided as we are at this juncture, it is nevertheless time to go on that long, winding road again. We have to start where we began, guided by the great deal that we have learned. What we have discovered, overall, is really common, anthropological sense: Each of us is in some ways like all other people, in other ways like some other people, and in still other ways like no one else. While an androgyny of desire does exist, desires also differ from social group to social group and from individual to individual. The contradiction that we face is that, although feminism is about all women, different women have different interests.

Feminist politics must resolve this contradiction. Assuming that primal desire is the same in all of us, we must also recognize that it begins to be shaped almost as quickly by subculture—class, race, religion, sexuality—as by gender. All women share a material existence, social experience, and consciousness patterned by the fact that they are women as opposed to the other gender. At the same time, their individual wants and needs take their shape from the systematically differing social conditions that concretely inform not only women's lives but the lives of the men of their social group. And, finally, the desires of each individual woman emerge from the dense weave of her inborn temperament, the family and subculture into which she is born, and the social significance of her gender. We must therefore determine how to create a movement that expresses both the desire of all women and the differentiated desires of different women.

The centerpiece of our activism must continue to be women's common desire for political and economic emancipation. Living in the heart of contradictions, we must now regard as ongoing, routine parts of our lives efforts to institutionalize the goals with which, thanks to feminism, the general populace now agrees—equal pay; political office; abortion rights; organized child care; shared parenthood; shared domestic work; the right to management positions; equal access to amateur and professional athletics; legal punishment for rape, spouse battering, and sexual harassment; and the Equal Rights Amendment.

At the same time, we must not forget that the feminist goals enabling women's success in the public domain can be, and have been, co-opted by an economy in which most adult women work for wages not simply because they want to but because, as single individuals, single parents, and even wives living in what can never again be one-income families, they have to. In some ways, feminism serves as a justification and incentive to get women to want to do what the economy exacts of them. It may also deepen existing class and status divisions among women.

In this co-opting context, more controversial goals become even more crucial. While most people give lip service to women's emancipation in public life, they are less enthusiastic about women's complete sexual freedom. One of our most urgent tasks is therefore to safeguard our control over our bodies, presently under siege from right-wing political groups and a government antagonistic to abortion rights, this control lies in reproductive freedom, for which we must continue to struggle: not only legal abortion, but safe and aesthetic contraception, voluntary sterilization, day care, and a guaranteed annual income enabling our children to have the opportunity to live a decent life.

However, the control of reproduction belongs only to women. Ideally, a society without gender hierarchy would recognize that its best interests lay in women's reproductive autonomy, so that there would be no moral friction between cultural tradition and women's wishes as regards reproduction. Ideally, because reproductive responsibility would belong to society as a whole, women could turn to a solid base of accumulated cultural wisdom to disentangle the ambiguities of reproductive decisions, both those to bear children and those to terminate pregnancies. They could share their decisions with kin and friends without fear of overt or covert coercion.

However, until children, childrearing, and relatedness in general are as central to our culture as rescuing bankrupt corporations and building nuclear weapons are to our present government, reproductive power belongs entirely in women's hands. As long as women are made to bear the full burden of reproductive ambiguity, they must have the right to execute their decisions according to their own counsel, choosing whom, if anyone, to consult as they make their decisions.

Still, reproductive freedom is necessary but not sufficient for women's discovery of their own desire. The search for women's sexual liberation, like the search for genuine equality for all, demands a new round of utopian, feminist thinking about society, self, and sex. As women, whose stigmatized difference from men prevents us from realizing our desires, we must, first, imagine a society where difference cannot be a nucleus for hierarchy. Such a society would have to include both economic and political equality. In it, class differences would no longer exist and differences of gender, race, ethnicity, religion, and sexuality would no longer be transformable into those of wealth and power. A feminism that does not include some version of socialism is no feminism at all.

Neither is a feminism lacking a touch of anarchism worthy of the name. Our utopian visions must also include social institutions that, replacing the state, allow each unique personal voice to have political import. In order to envision a utopia in which difference is genuinely prized, we must turn our society not upside down but inside out. We must picture ways to remove the capacities for relatedness and empathy from their domestic closet and situate them at the heart of public life. This does not mean to replace masculinized values with feminized ones. Rather, the two should be integrated in the hope that genuinely new, androgynous, human ones will result. If each person were equally as

interested in the well-being of the other as of the self, then objectification, exploitation, and domination would be impossible.
This mutuality of interest would, in turn, be realizable only when
social institutions would guarantee that both self-for-other and
self-for-individual as personal styles and cultural goals were equally
valued and equally available for men and women, according to
their own, differentiated predilections.

At the same time, we have to conjure up a society that values
sexual pleasure as an end in itself. As the tide rises against civil
rights and as a sex panic over AIDS sets in, the only liberating
position is pro-sex. Progressive political periods, such as that of
the last twenty-five years, are usually followed by reactionary
sentiment and legislation. Sexual puritanism is always key to the
reaction, as during the 1950s, when mass opinion held homosexuality to lead automatically to child molesting, and, as presently,
when pornography is thought with equal certainty to cause rape.

Feminism must therefore transcend what is currently a bitter
internal debate between the antipornography movement and the
lesbian sadomasochist movement. Their dispute must be regarded not as the end but as the beginning of a genuinely feminist discussion about sex and freedom. While we must incorporate
the woman-centered reevaluation and derepression of female desire, we must also recognize that feminism has not yet produced
an authentic, female sexual Subject.

We must therefore envision social institutions that treasure the
variousness of desire and resist the temptation to erase difference. Desire is not everywhere constructed the same. We have to
understand the diversity of desire as it emerges in different subcultures—races, ethnicities, and sexualities. Yet we must also insist on sexual pleasure as a socially valued end in itself. We must
heed the various voices of women's desire—heterosexual, lesbian, outlaw. We have to imagine a society in which promiscuity
of desire as well as sex is women's prerogative equally with men,
in which intimacy with self and other becomes as much a part of
masculinity as it has been of femininity.

Breaking the mold of desirelessness into which women have
traditionally been cast breaks sexual molds altogether. Imagining
this, we might be able to dream up a society that, including all
presently known sexual choices, would be receptive to new ones
as well. Since we still lack a general understanding of the origins
of individual sexual choice, we must expect that the social insti-

tutions of sex, as well as individual preference, will evolve. We require a society sufficiently flexible to encompass the variety of erotic desire typifying any individual life—from the polymorphous perversity of infancy to the changes of our juvenile, adolescent, and adult years to the shifts in preference for partner or pleasure during adulthood. Our lives should be able to incorporate both the self-interested promiscuity that streaks through sexual desire and the longings for intimacy that seek to re-create the mother-child merger in enduring, loyal, monogamous relationships.

Were sexuality no longer cast in a monolithic mold, perhaps we could sweeten the bread-and-butter of our life with some of the eros now reserved for sex alone. We might then be able to reconstruct and redistribute desire in places in which it might be but presently is not, or in which it usually appears but fleetingly: not only the bearing but the rearing of children, work, the management of public life, contemplation, care of the earth. If we start to picture how to provide room for desire's multiplicity, then perhaps we can accord sexuality a new place, one that does not overload it with the responsibility of realizing all desire and that can therefore provide more, and more certain, enjoyment.

In the course of this utopian thinking, we ought to do some serious thinking about the relationship between sexuality, childhood, and adulthood. As teenage girls continue to get pregnant before they are sufficiently autonomous to mother as well as they might wish, we have to plan how to educate our children about sexuality early enough to counsel them, yet not so early as to frighten them into mistrusting their sexual passion. Children require sexual knowledge when they are young enough not to be harmed by their own desires or those of adults who might take advantage of them, and when they are old enough to experience the autonomy of their desires. Especially when some proponents of sexual liberation call for the legalization of sex between men and boys, and given the ambiguities of sexual desire, other sexual liberationists have to examine the question of "consent." We have to rethink the conventional line between childhood and adulthood in such a way that empowers children who are ready for sex sooner than many of us were thought to be in our own youth, but protects those who cannot yet know the ramifications of what they are consenting to.

Finally, as part of our thinking about sexual variety, we must also consider whether gender, which has been the secular state's primary means of constricting desire, need exist at all. If sexuality is about desire and pleasure rather than about procreation; if desire and pleasure originate in experience before gender does; and if sexual desire varies cross-culturally as well as in the course of individual lifetimes—then gender may be unnecessary. Although a genderless psyche and a gender-free society might be impossible to achieve, it is important to imagine what they might be like in order to stretch our minds and escape the hold of gender on our desires.

We might begin by trying to imagine ourselves without the character styles assigned to women and men. In a gender-free society, women would not be restricted to relatedness nor men to individualizing. Required to be neither self-for-other nor self-as-individual, women and men could live in a creative tension between these two extremes. Women would no longer risk loss of self in order to mature, men would not tend toward emotional isolation. Rather, each would have access to a far greater range of experience, so that each life would be a journey of discovery, not a disappointing telescoping of possibility.

Imagining ourselves without gender, we might begin to think of ourselves and each other in more fluid, accurate, and authentic ways. Were people thought to have sex with individuals rather than genders, and were acts, rather than people or preferences, labeled as homosexual or heterosexual or bisexual, we might have a chance to be more simply ourselves. We might fear less the inevitable flight of our desire beyond the borders of sexual categories. Indeed, we might discover that gender disguises commonalities of specifically sexual desire of which we have been unaware, as asserted by those feminist homosexuals and sadomasochists who say they have found more in common with men who share their sexual preferences than with women who do not.

We might then be able to construct our intimacies on a different basis. Without gender, sex discrimination in the workplace would be impossible, and household work could not be stigmatized as feminine. Men and women would no longer have to unite in couples or families on the basis of women's need for men's earning power, nor men's dependence on women's domesticity. Nor would heterosexual intimacy be marked by the sometimes antagonistic passion in which each person imagines that the other contains a missing, primal, omnipotent portion of self.

Coming closer to Self and Other in this imaginary genderless society, we might be able to dispense with the Otherness that makes difference alien. Were Self and Other to meet unaided or unhindered by gender, we might discover that our selves were not homogeneous, isolated wholes, but composed of the joinings and disjunctures between multiple selves and others.

The idea of wholeness is right, the timing wrong. One cannot be all of oneself all at once because *be* is, by itself, an inadequate word for human existence. One "becomes" as well as "be's." Wholeness is not a thing to be accomplished and done with. It is a process. To look for wholeness as an accomplished fact is to seek finality. But the relation between mind and culture looks more like infinity. Wholeness goes on and does not end, because who one is, and what a culture is, emerges not from a static place but from continual engagement with a world full of contradictions.

Imagining a society in which hierarchy cannot encrust difference and that welcomes desire in all its variety is, however, connected to imagining a political movement where differences are valued equally with uniformities. Our imagination must be informed by diverse utopias constructed not by applying theory to data like paint to a wall but by allowing theory as living thought and life as thoughtfully lived to inform each other. If the process of building theory involves examining the actual living of daily life, then the resulting theory about women will necessarily take differences among women into account. So far, the feminist vision has been most profoundly shaped by white, middle-class women's critiques of housewifery and the double standards for sexuality and beauty. Equally important, but less visible, has been the leftist, feminist linking of patriarchy with capitalism and the state.

Yet there are other, even less publicly recognized, feminist starting points for the analysis of domination and the imagination of freedom. Lesbian utopian visions begin with a critique of compulsory heterosexuality. Some women of color see the differences between races and ethnicities as the primary cutting edge, and those between gender as a secondary one. For sadomasochists and other sexual liberationists, the points of departure are sexuality and power. As a movement with twin origins in social emancipation and sexual liberation, feminism must therefore determine how to gather new energy from the sparks set off by the charged differences of these varying visions of freedom. Only then will we be able to begin imagining a movement and a society in which variety will be the spice of life rather than simply an ingredient to be melted down into one homogeneous mass.

If we can do this, we will have proceeded some of the way toward a principal, utopian promise of feminism: The struggle for women's equality means equality for *all* women at *all* levels of society—white women and women of color, women of all classes, lesbians and heterosexual women and sexual outlaws, women of all ages, ethnicities, and religions. However, equality across hierarchies is oxymoronic. If it should come to pass that all women at all points on all hierarchies were equal, then it would mean that hierarchy had disappeared altogether, that being different meant difference and no more, that equality for all had become the reality of all. In other words, the struggle for women's liberation is indissolubly connected to the liberation struggles of all oppressed people.

Sexuality is not the route to revolution. But it is a prime shaper of desire, and constraint of desire leads directly to self-betrayal and social bad faith. We suffer not from too much desire but from too little. One reason we fail to rebel, or have incomplete revolutions, is that our hopes have been truncated, especially by sexual oppression, whose core is the repression of desire. We must therefore desire all we can, no matter how much it hurts or how foolish it seems. We may not be able to get everything we want, but only by wanting everything we can imagine can we get everything we need.

Bibliographical Discussion

*I*n the course of offering some suggestions for further reading, I would like here both to indicate the specific sources from which some of my ideas have come and to discuss the literature in general on which I have depended to write this book. The discussion proceeds by chapters. When articles have been reprinted in anthologies, I have tried to refer to them there so as to provide access to the widest possible sampling of the literature.

AUTHOR TO READER

There are some useful introductions and overviews for the major perspectives that inform the commentary. For anthropology, and the concepts of "culture" and "society" as well, see Muriel Dimen-Schein, *The Anthropological Imagination* (New York: McGraw-Hill, 1977). The classic introduction to orthodox psychoanalytic theory is Sigmund Freud, "Introductory Lectures to Psychoanalysis," *The Standard Edition of the Complete Psychological Works of Sigmund Freud*, vols. 15–16 (London: The Hogarth Press, 1961, 1963). An important American version of psychoanalysis is the Interpersonalist School, founded by Harry Stack Sullivan; see his *The Interpersonal Theory of Psychiatry* (New York: Norton, 1953). An object-relations approach to psychoanalysis is Harry Guntrip, *Psychoanalytic Theory, Therapy, and the Self* (New York: Basic Books, 1971).

It is not possible to offer a single introduction to feminist thinking, since this is such a new and diverse field of scholarship. Among those feminists examining socioeconomic conditions, there are the Marxist-feminists—for example, Annette Kuhn and Annemarie Wolpe, *Feminism and Materialism* (London: Routledge and Kegan Paul, 1978)—and the socialist-feminist—for example, Zillah Eisenstein, *Capitalist Patriarchy and the Case for Socialist Feminism* (New York: Monthly Review Press, 1979), and Batya Weinbaum, *The Curious Courtship of Women's Liberation and Socialism* (Boston: South End Press, 1978). Among cultural feminists, those who emphasize the inner life, personal experience, and spirituality, one might look at Mary Daly, *Gyn/Ecology: The Metaethics of Radical Feminism* (Boston: Beacon Press, 1978), and Susan Griffin, *Woman and Nature: The Roaring Inside Her* (New York: Harper and Row, 1978). Joan Cocks, "Wordless Emotions," *Politics and Society* 13 (1984): 27–57 responds to both cultural and Marxist-feminists from a socialist position. There are, of course, those who fall between camps, for example, the Freudo-Marxists, as well as, for example, Kate Millett, *Sexual Politics* (Garden City, N.Y.: Doubleday, 1970).

Feminism is a complicated issue among black, Latina, and Third World women, appealing to women's desires for personal and political emancipation but sometimes conflicting with primary loyalties to race and culture. Among the growing literature are bell hooks, *Ain't I a Woman: Black Women and Feminism* (Boston: South End Press, 1981); Diane K. Lewis, "A Response to Inequality: Black Women, Racism, and Sexism," *Signs* 3 (1977): 339–61; Cherrié Moraga and Gloria Anzaldúa, eds., *This Bridge Called My Back: Writings by Radical Women of Color*, 2nd ed. (New York:

Kitchen Table, Women of Color Press, 1983); Robin Morgan's collection *Sisterhood Is Global: The International Women's Movement Anthology* (New York: Anchor, 1984); and Barbara Smith, ed., *Home Girls: A Black Feminist Anthology* (New York: Kitchen Table, Women of Color Press, 1983).

The French feminists are influenced by psychoanalytic as well as Marxist thinking. See Elaine Marks and Isabelle de Courtivron, eds., *New French Feminisms: An Anthology* (New York: Schocken, 1981).

On the concept of the "state," central to Marxist theory, see Friedrich Engels, *The Origin of the Family, Private Property, and the State*, edited by Eleanor Burke Leacock (New York: International Publishers, 1973), the editor's introduction to which is very enlightening. A good review essay is Ben Jessop, "Recent Theories of the Capitalist State," *Cambridge Journal of Economics* 1 (1977): 353–73. See also James O'Conner, *Accumulation Crisis* (New York: Basil Blackwell, 1984), chap. 7.

To my knowledge, the first appearance in print of the sentence *the personal is political* was in 1969, in an article by Carol Hanisch, "The Personal Is Political," *Notes from the Second Year* (New York: Radical Feminists, 1969), pp. 76–78, reprinted in Redstockings of the Women's Liberation Movement, eds., *Feminist Revolution, An Abridged Edition with Additional Writings* (New York: Random House, 1978), pp. 204–205. Counterculturalists and feminists were not the first to point to the scholarly and existential significance of this idea. C. Wright Mills, in *The Sociological Imagination* (New York: Oxford University Press, 1959), argues that sociology must in the last analysis be an intersection of biography and history. Jean-Paul Sartre makes a similar argument about investigating human experience in *Search for a Method* (New York: Vintage, 1968), especially chaps. 2 and 3. However the counterculture and feminism were the first to recognize the political significance of *autobiography*.

The idea that slogan represents therefore has a history. As an intellectual pursuit, it emerges from the confluence of two great nineteenth-century intellectual traditions, Marxism and psychoanalysis. Their influence on twentieth-century thinking is as important as that of the theories of evolution and relativity, for they set the terms for all further discussion on their subjects. Marxism is the central and most comprehensive theory of society and social inequality presently available; see Karl Marx, *Capital:*

A Critique of Political Economy (New York: International Publishers, 1967); Engels, *op. cit.*; and Karl Marx and Friedrich Engels, *The German Ideology* (New York: International Publishers, 1970). And psychoanalysis, the product of Sigmund Freud and his adherents, is that of the mind and the person; see Freud, *op. cit.* But, curiously, each addresses the other's subject matter using common and smart, but often unexamined, sense. The contrast, in each, between sophistication on its own turf and naiveté on the other's, seems to call out for their union.

Many thinkers, situating themselves in the Freudo-Marx nexus, have tried to do just that. The most important of the first to do so belonged to the Frankfurt School. They included among them Max Horkheimer (see *Critical Theory: Selected Essays* [New York: Seabury Press, 1972]); Herbert Marcuse (see *Eros and Civilization* [Boston: Beacon Press, 1955]), and Wilhelm Reich (see *The Mass Psychology of Fascism* [New York: Farrar, Straus & Giroux, 1970]). A good introduction to this school of thinking is Martin Jay, *The Dialectical Imagination: A History of the Frankfurt School and the Institute of Social Research, 1923–1950* (Boston: Little, Brown, 1973). Norman O. Brown, in *Life Against Death* (Middletown, Conn.: Wesleyan University Press, 1959), takes up similar themes from a non-Marxist position.

These writings had a profound influence on the more recent group of New Left writers, those leftists disillusioned with the economism of Marxist theory and practice and stirred by the counterculture's expansion of consciousness and emphasis on the concreteness of personal experience in everyday life, in contrast to the abstractness of theory. See, for example, Stanley Aronowitz, *False Promises* (New York: McGraw-Hill, 1974); Jessica Benjamin, "Authority and the Family Revisited: A World Without Fathers," *New German Critique* 4 (Winter 1978): 35–57; and Joel Kovel, *The Age of Desire: Notes of a Radical Psychoanalyst* (New York: Pantheon, 1981).

Among the New Leftists were feminists, whose effect was significant because women are, as Myra Jehlen has pointed out in "Against Human Wholeness: A Suggestion for a Feminist Epistemology," unpublished paper-in-progress presented at the Columbia University Seminar on Women and Society, December 17, 1984, the "Other" in the paradigms of each of these two great intellectual currents. In other words, Marxism skips over women's traditional place, the domestic domain, assuming that all private relations of intimacy, sexuality, and maturation somehow take place automatically as reflexive responses to the economic process. Engels, *op. cit.*, notably attempts to consider the position of women and the evolution of sexual life, but his theory's lack of a psychology dooms his attempt to the same fate. Psychoanalysis, of course, has a lot to say about women, but many of its comments on them—such as its observations about the biological inevitability of penis envy—seem in fact to be uncritical reformulations of a little boy's ideas about little girls, as Karen Horney observes in "The Flight from Womanhood," in her *Feminine Psychology* (New York: Norton, 1967), pp. 54–70. Perhaps more importantly, "woman" in psychoanalytic theory is less often the "subject" than its "object." Women's experience is frequently used as a platform on which to work out other ideas; see, for example, Freud's theory of masochism, "The Economic Problem of Masochism," *The Standard Edition of the Complete Psychological Works of Sigmund Freud*, vol. 19, pp. 157–70; or Jacques Lacan's theory of the symbolic construction of the psyche, "Guiding Remarks for a Congress on Feminine Sexuality," in Juliet Mitchell, ed., and Jacqueline Rose, ed. and trans., *Feminine Sexuality: Jacques Lacan and the École Freudienne* (New York: Norton, 1982), pp. 86–98.

Still, Marxism and psychoanalysis are potentially friendly to feminism, the first as explanation for women's socioeconomic conditions, the second to shed light on the sexual, the internal, and the interpersonal, things with which women in our culture share the same symbolic space, as Joan Cocks put it, *op. cit.* However, to the extent to which feminist thinkers bring their "otherness" into these disciplines, they must inevitably transform them. Where once there was a confluence, there will have to be a new river. There are several feminist works that are part of this new formation. Two that analyze experience from the inside as much as from its social origins are Jessica Benjamin, *op. cit.*, and Nancy Chodorow, *The Reproduction of Mothering: Psychoanalysis and the Sociology of Gender* (Berkeley, Calif.: University of California Press, 1978). Other feminist accounts, also deeply embedded in social theory, focus more on psychoanalytic theory than on the experiences to which it applies: Shulamith Firestone, *The Dialectic of Sex* (New York: Bantam, 1970); Juliet Mitchell, *Psychoanalysis and Feminism* (New York: Vintage, 1975); Gayle Rubin, "The Traffic in Women: Notes on the Political Economy of Sex," in

Rayna Reiter, ed., *Toward an Anthropology of Women* (New York: Monthly Review Press, 1975), pp. 157–210; and Eli Zaretsky, *Capitalism, the Family, and Personal Life* (New York: Harper and Row, 1976). This volume is part of this tradition-in-gestation.

Freud's "The Psychopathology of Everyday Life," *The Standard Edition of the Complete Psychological Works of Sigmund Freud,* vol. 6 (1966) establishes the rationale for examining ordinary behavior through a psychoanalytic lens.

A recent and provocative discussion of the "woman's voice" is Elaine Showalter, "Women Who Write Are Women," *New York Times Book Review,* December 16, 1984.

The original cross-cultural studies of sex and gender are Margaret Mead's *Sex and Temperament in Three Primitive Societies* (New York: William Morrow, 1935) and *Male and Female: A Study of the Sexes in a Changing World* (New York: Mentor, 1949), to which feminist theory is indebted for providing the first published empirical evidence for the cultural, as opposed to the biological, basis for gender.

Simone de Beauvoir's *The Second Sex* (New York: Vintage Books, 1974) is the starting point for every discussion in this contemporary second wave of feminism.

PROLOGUE

My phrase, "two millennia of women writing about women," refers, of course, to Sappho. See Sarah B. Pomeroy, *Goddesses, Whores, Wives and Slaves* (New York: Schocken Books, 1975), pp. 52–56.

Meredith Tax, "Woman and Her Mind," in Anne Koedt, Ellen Levine, and Anita Rapone, eds., *Radical Feminism* (New York: Quadrangle Books, 1973), pp. 23–35, tells a story similar to that which opens this chapter; my account differs in its emphasis on the subjectivity that accompanies the objectification. Another, more recent discussion of street-hassling is Pam McAllister, "Wolf Whistles and Warnings," *Heresies,* vol. 2, no. 2, issue 6, *On Women and Violence* (Summer 1978): 37–39. Ingrid Bengis's courageous *Combat in the Erogenous Zone* (New York: Bantam, 1972), the story of a woman wandering through the sexual maze, shook a lot of us up, and loose. Another important personalized discussion of women's ordinary experience is Germaine Greer, *The Female Eunuch* (New York: McGraw-Hill, 1970).

The discourse on "desire" is generated by the French psychoanalyst Jacques Lacan, most of whose writings are fairly impenetrable. One might look at *Écrits, A Selection* (New York: Norton, 1977). A good introduction, especially from the perspective of the present discussion, is Juliet Mitchell, ed., and Jacqueline Rose, ed. and trans., *Feminine Sexuality: Jacques Lacan and the École Freudienne* (New York: Norton, 1982).; see especially the editors' introductions. It is evident that I disagree with the Lacanian notion of desire as divorced from need.

Any feminist writing on women and psychoanalysis must acknowledge Juliet Mitchell's reconsideration of classic psychoanalytic theory from a feminist perspective in order to clarify its utility for the feminist project and for women, *Psychoanalysis and Feminism* (New York: Vintage, 1975).

I take the conception of "Man" as "wanting" and "Woman" as "wanting-to-be-wanted" from Jessica Benjamin, "Woman's Desire," delivered at the Symposium on Psychoanalysis and Feminism, New York University Postdoctoral Program in Psychotherapy and Psychoanalysis, October 1, 1982; see also her *The Bonds of Love* (New York: Pantheon, forthcoming). My notion of the Subject-as-Object was inspired by Sherry Ortner, "Is Female to Male as Nature Is to Culture?" in Michelle Z. Rosaldo and Louise Lamphere, *Woman, Culture, and Society* (Stanford, Calif.: Stanford University Press, 1974), pp. 67–89, in which she makes the point that women's knowledge and acknowledgment of their own devaluation is evidence for their consciousness, their membership in culture, and their humanity. On women's doubled consciousness, see Joan Kelly, "Feminism and Doubled Consciousness," *Feminist Studies* 5 (Spring 1979): 216–27 (reprinted in *Women, History and Theory: The Essays of Joan Kelly* [Chicago, Ill.: University of Chicago Press, 1984]). On women's perpetual awareness of being the watched watching the watcher, see John Berger, *Ways of Seeing* (London: British Broadcasting Corporation and Penguin Books, 1972).

Finally, the sense of being split from one's own experience, which, I argue, is the principal condition of the Subject-as-Object, may be said to be that of alienation. Bertell Ollman's *Alienation: Marx's Conception of Man in Capitalist Society*, 2nd ed. (New York: Cambridge University Press, 1976) is a good introduction to the basic Marxist concept of alienation, as well as several other psychological concepts. There are two good but different sorts of psychological discussion about "the divided self," both of which try to locate the inner experience of alienation in the social conditions that bring it about. One is R. D. Laing's *The Divided Self* (New York: Penguin, 1965), a psychoanalytic investigation of a type of psychopathology in our society. The other is a sociological treatise that deals with this intrapsychic division not as pathology but as a normal concomitant of alienation; it is by Richard Sennet and Michael Cobb, *The Hidden Injuries of Class* (New York: Vintage, 1972).

Ricki Levenson, "Loyal Ghosts: An Exploration of Women's Difficulties in Thinking," paper presented at the Women's Therapy Center, New York, February 3, 1984, reviews the psychoanalytic literature on the differential rearing of sons and daughters by fathers and mothers. The differential response of parents to sons and daughters is also discussed by Nancy Chodorow, "Gender, Relation, and Difference in Psychoanalytic Perspective," in Hester Eisenstein and Alice Jardine, eds., *The Future of Difference* (Boston: G. K. Hall, 1980), pp. 3–19. See also Dorothy Dinnerstein, *The Mermaid and the Minotaur: Sexual Arrangements and Human Malaise* (New York: Harper and Row, 1978), p. 68.

Georg Groddeck, *The Book of the It* (New York: Mentor, 1961) writes of the unconscious as the "it," the genderless source of psychic life.

IN PASSION'S WAKE (6:00 A.M.)

Early infantile experience, centrally informative of sexuality, is a subject for much excited discussion, in part because, given that babies cannot talk, it can only, like the prehistory of human culture, be imagined. In general, I follow the object-relations school of psychoanalytic thought; see Harry Guntrip, *Psychoanalytic Theory, Therapy, and the Self* (New York: Basic Books, 1971). In addition, I am influenced by Ernst Schachtel, *Metamorphosis: On the Development of Affect, Attention, and Memory* (New York: Basic Books, 1959), especially his chapter "On Memory and Childhood Amnesia," pp. 279–323, which provides key insights about the relation between adult language and childhood experience and sensation.

Freud writes of disgust as the inversion of pleasure in "Letter 75," *The Standard Edition of the Complete Psychological Works of Sigmund Freud*, vol. 1 (London: The Hogarth Press, 1966), pp. 268ff.

My understanding of cultural symbolism owes a great deal to Clifford Geertz, *The Interpretation of Cultures* (New York: Basic Books, 1973). The anthropologist Mary Douglas, in *Purity and Danger* (New York: Pelican, 1970), discusses the cultural imperative to keep things orderly, to separate the impure, such as menstrual blood, from the pure. The anthropologist Victor Turner analyzes the function of rituals for human culture in *The Ritual Process* (Chicago: Aldine, 1969).

On Káfe rituals, see Elizabeth Faithorn, "The Concept of Pollution among the Káfe of the Papua New Guinea Highlands," in Rayna Reiter, ed., *Toward an Anthropology of Women* (New York: Monthly Review Press, 1975), pp. 127–40.

Discussions of women's concerns about physical beauty fill the feminist literature from its inception. Two are Susan Brownmiller's *Femininity* (New York: Linden, 1983) and Kim Chernin, *The Obsession: Reflections on the Tyranny of Slenderness* (New York: Harper and Row, 1981). A report on women legislators, "State Legislators: Center Stage for Women," by Nadine Brozan, appeared on the Style page of *The New York Times* on November 18, 1985, p. B8.

On the relations among nature, culture, and women, see Sherry Ortner, "Is Female to Male as Nature Is to Culture?" in Michelle Z. Rosaldo and Louise Lamphere, *Woman, Culture, and Society* (Stanford, Calif.: Stanford University Press, 1974), pp. 67–89.

Doris Lessing, in her novel *The Golden Notebook* (New York: Ballantine, 1962), wrote what many of her readers see as a feminist manifesto about the experience of a twentieth-century woman.

As Elsa First put it in "A Great Psychiatrist," *The New York Review of Books*, August 17, 1978, p. 32, D. W. Winnicott tells us the meaning of the teddy bear: It is what he calls a "transitional object," which symbolizes, unconsciously, both the separation and the connectedness between child and parent; as such, the internalization of the transitional object is essential in the passage from infancy to adulthood. See his *The Piggle: An Account of a Psychoanalytic Treatment of a Little Girl* (New York: International Universities Press, 1977); *Playing and Reality* (New York: Penguin, 1980); and *The Maturational Processes and The Facilitating Environment* (New York: International Universities Press, 1965).

❖

THE STRANGE RELATIONSHIP BETWEEN SEX
AND REPRODUCTION (7:30 A.M.)

Anyone interested in a classic male story of sex and gender should read J. P. Donleavy, *The Ginger Man* (New York: Delacorte Press, 1965). Anyone familiar with the beats knows Jack Kerouac's *On the Road* (New York: Viking, 1957). Those both attracted and repelled by both should read Diane di Prima's *Memoirs of a Beatnik* (New York: Olympia Press, 1959).

More recent novels taking women as their protagonists are: Rita Mae Brown, *Rubyfruit Jungle* (New York: Daughters Publishing Co., 1933); Erica Jong, *Fear of Flying* (New York: Holt, Rinehart, and Winston, 1973); Maxine Hong Kingston, *Woman Warrior: Memoirs of a Girlhood Among Ghosts* (New York: Knopf, 1976); Gloria Naylor, *The Women of Brewster Place* (New York: Penguin, 1980); Judith Rossner, *Looking for Mr. Goodbar* (New York: Simon and Schuster, 1975); and Alice Walker, *The Color Purple* (New York: Harcourt, Brace, Jovanovich, 1982).

One of the most important concepts to arise from feminist theory is the distinction between "public" and "private," codified by Michelle Z. Rosaldo, "Woman, Culture, and Society: A Theoretical Overview," in Michelle Z. Rosaldo and Louise Lamphere, *Women, Culture, and Society* (Stanford, Calif.: Stanford University Press, 1974), pp. 17–42.

The edition of Homer's *Odyssey* I use is the translation by Robert Fitzgerald (New York: Anchor, 1963).

Clifford Geertz, *The Interpretation of Cultures* (New York: Basic Books, 1973) offers the seminal insight that myth and ceremony serve as both descriptions of and prescriptions for culture.

Nancy Chodorow, *The Reproduction of Mothering: Psychoanalysis and the Sociology of Gender* (Berkeley, Calif: University of California Press, 1978), makes the crucial distinction, to which all feminist thinking is indebted, between the permeable self-boundaries engendered by socialization in women and the clear-cut ones similarly instilled in men.

The importance I attribute to reproductivity is not unusual in feminist scholarship, although my definition of it is, I believe, new. The most impressive attempt to theorize about reproductivity is Shulamith Firestone's utopian work, *The Dialectic of Sex* (New York: Bantam, 1970).

All discussions of the "double day" in European and American society must take off from Juliet Mitchell's *Woman's Estate* (London: Penguin, 1971), which, though weak on sexuality, states the case on production and paves the way for the analysis of reproduction. But the way that women handle the double day varies with social stratification. My heroine is clearly sufficiently well-to-do that she could probably afford household help were she a mother. On extended-family arrangements among poor black women, see Carol Stack, *All Our Kin* (New York: Harper and Row, 1974). On white working-class women, see Lillian Rubin, *Worlds of Pain* (New York: Basic Books, 1976). On the different arrangements for production and reproduction among Third World women, see, for example, Ester Boserup, *Women's Role in Economic Development* (New York: St. Martin's Press, 1970); and Mona Etienne and Eleanor Leacock, eds., *Women and Colonialization: Anthropological Perspectives* (New York: Praeger, 1980). Natalie Sokoloff, *Between Money and Love: The Dialectics of Women's Home and Market Work* (New York: Praeger, 1980), provides data on women's paid labor. Karl Marx, in *Capital: A Critique of Political Economy* (New York: International Publishers, 1967), notes, on p. 671, that in 1855 in Brussels women's wages were about 57 percent of men's.

Sherry Ortner and Harriet Whitehead, in their introduction to their co-edited *Sexual Meanings* (New York: Cambridge University Press, 1981), discuss cross-cultural variation in the meanings of "woman"; see also Jane Collier and Michelle Rosaldo, "Politics and Gender in Simple Societies," *ibid.*, pp. 275–329. Karen Sacks, *Sisters and Wives* (Urbana, Ill.: University of Illinois Press, 1982), analyzes the different economic causes and social consequences for women of these kinship statuses in African societies.

Margaret Benston discusses the role of women's work in the capitalist economy in "The Political Economy of Women's Liberation," *Monthly Review* 21 (September 1969): 13–27. The argument for pay for housework was put forth by Mariarosa dalla Costa, "Woman and the Subversion of the Community," *Radical America* 6 (January/February 1972). Carol Ascher's critique, "Women and Pay for Housework," in Edith Hoshino Altbach, *From Feminism to Liberation* (Cambridge, Mass.: Schenkman, 1980), pp. 263–70, makes the point about the domestic domain as women's refuge for autonomy and authenticity.

The feminist appreciation of housewifery itself has undergone an evolution. It begins with Betty Friedan's critique, *The Feminine Mystique* (New York: Dell, 1963). See Pat Mainardi, "The Politics of Housework," in Robin Morgan, ed., *Sisterhood Is Powerful* (New York: Random House, 1970), pp. 447–54, for the classic feminist complaint. Feminist scholarship has attempted to develop a theory of housework's role in consumption. See Carol Ascher (under the name of Carol Lopate), "The Rise of Ms. Consumer," *College English* (April 1977); also relevant here is her idea, *ibid.*, that housework is neither production nor consumption. Batya Weinbaum and Amy Bridges, "The Other Side of the Paycheck: Monopoly Capital and the Structure of Consumption," in Zillah Eisenstein, *Capitalist Patriarchy and the Case for Socialist Feminism* (Boston: South End Press, 1978), pp. 190–205, is a definitive statement on the services that housewives provide for capitalist employers. Wanda Minge-Klevana, in "Does Labor-Time Decrease with Industrialization? A Survey of Time-Allocation Studies," *Current Anthropology* 21 (June 1980): 279–98, comes up with some interesting statistics on the increase of the housewife's labor time during the twentieth century and offers suggestions as to its political function. Maxine Margolis, *Mothers and Such* (Berkeley, Calif.: University of California Press, 1984), gives a cultural-materialist view of changes in housework in United States history.

On the history of the apparent split between public and private and its implications for subjectivity, see Eli Zaretsky, *Capitalism, the Family, and Personal Life* (New York: Harper and Row, 1976), which I found very influential.

On men's role in families, see Peter J. Stein, "Men in Families," in Beth B. Hess and Marvin B. Sussman, eds., *Women and the Family: Two Decades of Change, Marriage and Family Review*, vol. 7, nos. 3–4 (Fall/Winter 1984): 143–62.

The Boston Women's Health Collective, *Our Bodies/Our Selves* (New York: Simon and Schuster, 1971) is the ground-breaking discussion of women's health and sexuality emblematic of the success of the women's health movement. A very useful handbook on reproductive rights is Committee for Abortion Rights and Against Sterilization Abuse, *Women Under Attack* (New York, 1979). Rosalind Pollack Petchesky, *Abortion and Women's Choice: The State, Sexuality, and Reproductive Freedom* (Boston: Northeastern University Press, 1985), is a passionate, thorough, and partisan discussion of the moral and political philosophy of reproductive rights. Beverly W. Harrison provides an important discussion of Christian ethics of reproductive freedom in *On the*

Right to Choose: Toward a New Ethic of Abortion (Boston: Beacon Press, 1983). See also Kathleen McDonnell, *Not an Easy Choice: A Feminist Re-examines Abortion* (Boston: South End Press, 1984.)

MONKEYS, APES, AND THE MYTH OF THE EVERY-READY FEMALE (9:00 A.M.)

I am indebted to Alison M. Jaggar's perception that, where human nature is concerned, there is no line between nature and culture, so that, as she put it in her paper, "Human Biology and Feminist Politics" at the American Political Science Association, New York City, November 2, 1981, for human beings the line between nature and culture "is not so much false as incoherent." This idea and others developed in her *Feminist Politics and Human Nature* (Totowa, N.J.: Rowman and Allenheld, 1984), a brilliant elucidation of the epistemologies of major feminist theories.

The late Lila Leibowitz, in *Females, Males, Families* (North Scituate, Mass.: Duxbury Press, 1978), wrote an exceptionally readable book that contains an informed discussion of sex in nonhuman nature as well as an overview of a materialist anthropological approach to gender and the family.

John Money and Anke Erhardt's *Man and Woman, Boy and Girl* (Baltimore, Md.: The Johns Hopkins University Press, 1972) is the volume to consult on gender difference in human biological sexuality.

See M. Kay Martin and Barbara Voorhies, *Female of the Species* (New York: Columbia University Press, 1975), on Navaho sex/gender variation.

Edgar Gregerson provides an encyclopedic view of human sexuality in *Sexual Practices: The Story of Human Sexuality* (New York: Franklin Watts, 1983).

Biological determinism is a particularly crucial issue for women and anyone else whose biology has been held to be the cause of their character or fate. It merits and has merited careful study and critique by feminists. There are many varieties of biological determinism. For examples of deterministic theories proposing the instinctuality of gender roles, see Robert Ardrey, *African Genesis* (New York: Dell, 1961), and Lionel Tiger and Robin Fox, *Man, the Imperial Animal* (New York: Holt, Rinehart, and Winston, 1971).

The most recent incarnation of biological determinism is "sociobiology," a school of thought that would reduce sexual and intimate behavior to the reproduction of genes. It assumes that there exists between males and females an atmosphere of genetically based mutual distrust, not because of any psychological or cultural factors but because of the survival of the species: Male and female have opposed goals, he more sex, she more parental care, in the absence of either of which biological reproduction could not take place. What sociobiologists do not seem to have noticed is that sexuality and nurturance are mutually exclusive only because of culture, not biology. Edmund O. Wilson's *Sociobiology* (Cambridge, Mass.: Harvard University Press, 1975) sets forth the principles of sociobiology. For a biologist's critique of sociobiology, see Stephen J. Gould, "Genes on the Brain," *The New York Review of Books*, June 30, 1983, pp. 5–10.

For a critique of this and other biological determinisms in anthropology, see Alexander Alland, Jr., *The Human Imperative* (New York: Columbia University Press, 1972). For a Marxist-feminist response to biological determinism, see Donna Harraway, "Animal Sociology and a Natural Economy of the Body Politic 2. The Past Is the Contested Zone: Human Nature and Theories of Production and Reproduction in Primate Behavior Studies," *Signs* 4 (1978): 37–50. See, as well, two critiques of the sociobiological interpretation of human sexuality: J. Patrick Gray and Linda D. Wolfe, "Human Female Sexual Cycles and the Concealment of the Ovulation Problem," *Journal of Social and Biological Structures* 6 (1983): 345–52, discuss "concealed ovulation," which is the basis for the cultural myth of "the ever-ready female." Mina Davis Caulfield, "Sexuality in Human Evolution: What Is Natural in Sex?" *Feminist Studies* 11 (1985): 342–64, systematically analyzes sociobiology's bias toward Western patriarchal sexual and social forms and presents an interpretation of human female sexuality in terms of the adaptive significance of group life in human evolution. An article suggesting the necessity of periodic receptivity to male potency is Richard P. Michael and Doris Zumpe, "Potency in Male Rhesus Monkeys: Effects of Continuously Receptive Females, *Science*, April 28, 1978, pp. 451–52. For an example of how the notion of permanent receptivity is used in anthropology, see Marvin Harris, *Culture, People, Nature* (New York: Harper and Row, 1980), p. 34, an otherwise stimulating textbook from the cultural-materialist point of view.

An excellent demonstration of the cultural basis of human nature is Lucien Malson, *Wolf Children and the Problem of Human*

Nature (New York: Monthly Review Press, 1972); it includes the classic, *The Wild Boy of Aveyron*, by Jean-Marc-Gaspard Itard, the story of an eighteenth-century doctor's attempt to teach a feral child to speak.

In offering ethnographic examples, I wish to convey the range of women's experience cross-culturally. I do not want to suggest, romantically, that other societies are necessarily better off, although it can be said that in some ways anthropology is in search of a more humane opposite to its own culture; see Stanley Diamond, *In Search of the Primitive: A Critique of Civilization* (New Brunswick, N.J.: Transaction Books, 1974).

The original, classic study of the Trobriand Islanders is Bronislaw Malinowski, *Argonauts of the Western Pacific* (New York: E. P. Dutton, 1961). Annette Wiener's important re-study, *Women of Value, Men of Renown* (Austin, Tex.: University of Texas Press, 1976), makes up for the earlier silence on women's central social place in this matrilineal society. Data on the Tuken are from Bonnie Kettel, personal communication; see also Bonnie and David Kettel, "The Tuken of Western Kenya Highlands," *Cultural Source Materials for Population Planning in Eastern Africa* (Nairobi: East African Publishing House, 1972), pp. 354–427.

The best general survey of gender and primates that also demonstrates the relevance of the data for humans is Sara Blaffer Hrdy, *The Woman That Never Evolved* (Cambridge, Mass.: Harvard University Press, 1981); she offers a not entirely convincing argument about the usefulness of sociobiology to feminist scholarship but does provide important information about aggression among nonhuman primate females. Nancy Tanner's *Becoming Human* (New York: Cambridge University Press, 1981) interprets the human and nonhuman primate fossil record to provide novel and provocative hypotheses about the role of females in human biological and cultural evolution. See, as well, the review essay by Adrienne E. Zihlman, "Gathering Stories for Hunting Human Nature," *Feminist Studies* 11 (Summer 1985): 365–78.

The data I have used on nonhuman primates have been gathered from various sources. I am indebted to Linda D. Wolfe, personal communication, for information on langur, macaque, and hamadryas baboon gender relations. On rhesus, see her "Female Rank and Reproductive Success Among Arashimyama B Japanese Macaques *(Macaca fuscata)*," *International Journal of Primatology* 5 (1984): 133–43. On Harry Harlow's experiments with rhesus sexuality and parenting, see Leibowitz, *op. cit.* On nonhuman primate erotism, see Ronald D. Nadler, "Sexual Cyclicity in Captive Lowland Gorillas," *Science,* September 5, 1975, pp. 813–14.

There are many new, important feminist histories of women. On women in America, see Gerda Lerner, ed., *The Woman in American History* (Reading, Mass.: 1971) and Gerda Lerner, ed., *Black Women in White America: A Documentary History* (New York: Vintage, 1973). On women in Europe, see Renate Bridenthal and Claudia Koonz, eds., *Becoming Visible: Women in European History,* 2nd ed., rev. (New York: Houghton Mifflin, 1986), and Bonnie S. Anderson and Judith P. Zinsser, *Europe's Women* (New York: Harper and Row, forthcoming). On women in ancient Greece and Rome, see Sarah B. Pomeroy, *Goddesses, Whores, Wives, and Slaves: Women in Classical Antiquity* (New York: Schocken, 1975). The late Joan Kelly had a profound influence on feminist history; see her *Women, History, and Theory, Collected Papers* (Chicago, Ill.: University of Chicago Press, 1984).

Rayna Reiter, ed., *Toward an Anthropology of Women* (New York: Monthly Review Press, 1975), and Michelle A. Rosaldo and Louise Lamphere, *Women, Culture, and Society* (Stanford, Calif.: Stanford University Press, 1974), are two good anthologies, collected from different points of view, for feminist anthropology. The question of the universality of gender hierarchy is under debate within feminist anthropology. Some theorists hold that patriarchy and rape are the result of capitalism and are therefore absent in pre-capitalist societies; see, for example, Eleanor Burke Leacock, *Myths of Male Dominance, Collected Articles on Women Cross-Culturally* (New York: Monthly Review Press, 1981). Karen Sacks, *Sisters and Wives* (Urbana, Ill.: University of Illinois Press, 1982), takes a related but modified position, arguing against the theory of universal subordination. So does Peggy Reeves Sanday, *Female Power and Male Dominance: On the Origins of Sexual Inequality* (New York: Cambridge University Press, 1981), who attempts to demonstrate the range of women's "power" and its erosion as industrial, state society is neared in the course of evolution. One primary problem with the case against universal subordination is the assumption of an unblemished egalitarianism in hunter/gatherer society; for a critique of this Engelsian position, see Muriel Schein and Carol Lopate, "On Engels and the Liberation of Women," *Liberation* 16 (February 1972):4–9.

New feminist psychological accounts of women making use of

psychoanalytic theory include Jessica Benjamin, whose "The Bonds of Love: The Roots of Rational Violence," in Hester Eisenstein and Alice Jardine, eds., *The Future of Difference* (Boston: G. K. Hall, 1980), pp. 40–70, and *The Bonds of Love* (New York: Pantheon, forthcoming) link women's psychology to patriarchy and social domination. Nancy Chodorow, *The Reproduction of Mothering: Psychoanalysis and the Sociology of Gender* (Berkeley, Calif.: University of California Press, 1978), and Dorothy Dinnerstein, *The Mermaid and the Minotaur: Sexual Arrangements and Human Malaise* (New York: Harper and Row, 1976), discuss the way in which the experience of female mothering creates not only male and female psychologies but problems in heterosexual intimacy and consequent dilemmas for our culture. Jean Baker Miller, *Toward a New Psychology of Women* (Boston: Beacon Press, 1976), suggests that women may have a different intrapsychic structure than men and reevaluates the traditional derogation of feminine character by perceiving strengths in traits previously regarded as limitations.

Carol Gilligan, *In a Different Voice: Psychological Theory and Women's Development* (Cambridge, Mass.: Harvard University Press, 1983), elaborates on the foregoing accounts with a developmentalist discussion to propose a new, critical theory of moral development. This theory holds that men are trained toward one, culturally dominant course of moral thought, and women toward a second, culturally inferiorized one; the combination of the two, she argues, would be better not only for individuals but for our society as a whole.

A path-finding feminist biography utilizing "the personal is political" to new effect is Carol Ascher, *Simone de Beauvoir: A Life of Freedom* (Boston: Beacon Press, 1981). See the essay by Elizabeth Kammarch Minnich, "Friendship Between Women: The Act of Feminist Biography," *Feminist Studies* 11 (Summer 1985): 287–306, reviewing Ascher, as well as Ruth First and Ann Scott, *Olive Schreiner: A Biography* (New York: Schocken Books, 1980), and Elizabeth Young-Bruehl, *Hannah Arendt: For Love of the World* (New Haven, Conn.: Yale University Press, 1982).

The twentieth-century consideration of scientific method and canons of truth has a very large literature, to which feminist scholarship is now adding. Thomas Kuhn's *The Structure of Scientific Revolutions* (Chicago: University of Chicago Press, 1970) critiques the social construction of science. Paul Feyerabend, in *Against Method* (London: Verso, 1978), presents a radical critique of objectivity in scientific research. Ruth Benedict's *Patterns of Culture* (New York: Houghton Mifflin, 1934) situates Western science in its cultural context.

Among the feminist critiques of science, the most important and the one to which I am most indebted is Evelyn Fox Keller, *Reflections on Gender and Science* (New Haven, Conn.: Yale University Press, 1985). Keller, a mathematical biologist who trained initially as a physicist, combines historical studies of science, a psychoanalytic interpretation of the relation between gender and scientific theory and method, and reevaluations of particular scientific theories, to produce a new vision of a continuously evolving scientific truth. A feminist epistemology, criticizing, among other concepts, the dichotomy between subjectivity and objectivity, is in gestation; see Alison M. Jaggar, *Feminist Politics and Human Nature* (Totowa, N.J.: Rowman and Allenheld, 1984); Sandra Harding and Meryl Hintikka, *Discovering Reality* (Dordrecht, Holland: D. Reidel, 1983); and Nancy Jay, "Gender and Dichotomy," *Feminist Studies* 7 (Spring 1981): 38–56.

The title of Evelyn Keller's biography of Barbara McClintock, *A Feeling for the Organism: The Life and Work of Barbara McClintock* (San Francisco: W. H. Freeman, 1983), reveals McClintock's uniquely conceived approach to her work.

For a man approaching science in a nontraditional way, see Fritjof Capra, *The Tao of Physics: An Exploration of the Parallels Between Modern Physics and Eastern Mysticism* (New York: Bantam, 1977).

Attitudes toward sexuality among the !Kung San are reported in Marjorie Shostak, *Nisa* (New York: Random House, 1981). Yolanda Murphy and Robert F. Murphy describe sexuality for the Mundurucú in *Women of the Forest* (New York: Columbia University Press, 1974). Rape among the Cheyenne is discussed by E. A. Hoebel, *The Cheyenne* (New York: Holt, Rinehart, and Winston, 1960).

The feminist classic on rape is Susan Brownmiller, *Against Our Will: Men, Women, and Rape* (New York: Simon and Schuster, 1975), whose extensive survey is informed by the doubtful theory that rapists are universally driven by an innate wish for power. Paula Webster makes the case, with which I agree, that, since rape is universal, so is gender hierarchy; see her "The Politics of Rape in Primitive Society," *Heresies*, vol. 2, no. 2, issue 6, *On Women and Violence* (Summer 1978): 16–22.

"A New Recognition of the Realities of Date Rape," by Beth Sherman, appeared in *The New York Times* on October 23, 1985, p. C17.

POWER AND SEX (11:00 A.M.)

A biography of Sojourner Truth is Hertha Pandi, *Her Name Was Sojourner Truth* (New York: Appleton-Century-Crofts, 1962).

The assignment of newswomen to the "Spouses' [i.e., Wives'] Program" at the National Association of Broadcasters was reported in *The Village Voice*, p. 8, April 30, 1985.

Pamela Fishman discusses how men's and women's conversational styles carry out and reinforce gender hierarchy in "Interaction: The Work Women Do," in Barrie Thorne, Chris Kramarai, and Nancy Henley, eds., *Language, Gender and Society* (Rowley, Mass.: Newbury House Publishers, 1983), pp. 89–101.

My approach to the state derives from anthropological as well as socialist and anarchist theory; see Marvin Harris, *Culture, People, Nature* (New York: Harper and Row, 1980), for an example of an important anthropological view of the state.

Deborah Fallows, *A Mother's Work* (Boston: Houghton Mifflin, 1985), documents middle-class women's recent discovery of the fundamental joylessness of public life and the guilt they feel about their children, although she couches her story in a backlash prescription that women ought to return home to their children.

My experience in teaching working-class women, often black and Hispanic but white as well, reveals a rising feminist sentiment among them.

Germaine Greer, *The Female Eunuch* (New York: McGraw-Hill, 1970), was among the first to propose that women's culturally created styles and values offer ways that would revolutionize the ordinary treadmill of public life.

DEPENDENCY AND EMPATHY, OR AUTONOMY'S BETTER HALF (2:30 P.M.)

It is difficult to find a good general discussion of the technique of psychotherapy, since there are so many varieties. Frieda Fromm-

Reichman, *Techniques of Intensive Psychotherapy* (Chicago: University of Chicago Press, 1950), is a classic. See also Harry Guntrip, *Psychoanalytic Theory, Therapy, and the Self* (New York: Basic Books, 1971). On women's experience of psychotherapy, and on women therapists working with women patients, see Luise Eichenbaum and Susie Orbach, *Understanding Women: A Feminist Psychoanalytic Approach* (New York: Basic Books, 1982), for a simplified object-relational approach; Miriam Greenspan, *A New Approach to Women and Therapy* (New York: McGraw-Hill, 1983), which emphasizes the "here and now" of women and their relations with other women; and Judie Alpert, ed., *Psychoanalysis of Women* (New York: The Analytic Press, forthcoming). An excellent overview of therapy is Joel Kovel's *A Complete Guide to Psychotherapy: From Psychoanalysis to Behavior Modification* (New York: Pantheon, 1976). The classic discussion of psychoanalytic "cure" is Freud's "Analysis: Terminable and Interminable," *Standard Edition*, vol. 23 (London: The Hogarth Press, 1966), pp. 216–53. See also M. Masud R. Khan's "The Becoming of a Psycho-Analyst," in his *The Privacy of the Self* (New York: International Universities Press, 1974), pp. 112–28.

Phyllis Chesler's *Women and Madness* (New York: Avon Books, 1972) was the first to document women's disproportionate participation as patients in the business of psychotherapy. Greenspan, *op. cit.*, updates Chesler's figures. As a confirmatory note, it is interesting that all eleven of the schizophrenic patients described in R. D. Laing and A. Esterson, *Sanity, Madness, and the Family* (London: Tavistock, 1964), are women.

Betty Friedan, *The Feminine Mystique* (New York: Dell, 1963), was the first book of the second wave of feminism to argue for a female identity independent of connections to others, especially men and children.

Middle-class single motherhood is only now beginning to be studied. Jean Renvoize, *Going Solo: Single Mothers by Choice* (London: Routledge and Kegan Paul, 1985), interviews several such single mothers and analyzes the history and results of their choices. The brief psychoanalytic paper by Phima Engelstein, Maxine Antell-Buckley, and Phyllis Urman-Klein, "Single Women Who Elect to Bear a Child," in Barbara L. Blum, ed., *Psychological Aspects of Pregnancy, Birthing, and Bonding*, vol. 4, New Directions in Psychotherapy Series (New York: Human Sciences Press, 1980), pp. 102–119, is an interesting intrapsychic study, but it unfortunately pathologizes the subjects' choices. For sociological discussions, see Beth B. Hess and Marvin B. Sussman, eds., *Women and the Family: Two Decades of Change, Marriage and Family Review*, vol. 7, nos. 3–4 (Fall/Winter 1984): 143–62. Carol Stack, *All Our Kin* (New York: Harper and Row, 1974), discusses the history and survival strategies of black single-motherhood. Barbara Ehrenreich, *The Hearts of Men: American Dreams and the Flight from Commitment* (New York: Doubleday, 1984), analyzes the economic and social causes driving middle-class men from the traditional breadwinner role toward bachelorhood. See Jessica Benjamin, "The Bonds of Love: The Roots of Rational Violence," in Hester Eisenstein and Alice Jardine, eds., *The Future of Difference* (Boston: G. K. Hall, 1980), pp. 40–70, for her argument that they are driven away as well by the "partnership ideology," a product of feminism that amplifies men's domestic responsibility.

A lot of people have a lot to say about mothering. Among psychoanalysts, D. W. Winnicott is extraordinarily useful and humane; see his discussion, important despite its slight pathologizing tone, of the empathy necessary for mothering, "Primary Maternal Preoccupation," *Collected Papers: Through Paediatrics to Psycho-Analysis* (New York: Basic Books, 1958); also enlightening, and relieving, is his paper on the conflicts mothers might feel about their children, "Hate in the Counter-Transference," *ibid.* His analysis of the "potential space" between mother and child as crucial to the child's development is found in his *Playing and Reality* (New York: Penguin, 1980).

There are several essential feminist discussions of mothering. I have drawn much of my discussion from Nancy Chodorow's path-breaking analysis of how it is that women's ease with dependency, merging, and empathy leads them to want to mother, *The Reproduction of Mothering: Psychoanalysis and the Sociology of Gender* (Berkeley, Calif.: University of California Press, 1978). Equally important, but with a greater emphasis on the psychoanalysis of culture, is Dorothy Dinnerstein, *The Mermaid and the Minotaur: Sexual Arrangements and Human Malaise* (New York: Harper and Row, 1976). Sara Ruddick's "Maternal Thinking," *Feminist Studies* 6 (Summer 1980): 342–67, addresses mothering from the point of view of a philosopher concerned with demonstrating the specificity of maternal thought processes. In addition, see Adrienne Rich, *Of Woman Born: Motherhood as Experience and Institution* (New York: Norton, 1976).

The discussion of mothering and its psychological concomitants bears on the discussion of women's psychology in general. Naomi Weisstein's "Psychology Constructs the Female, or The Fantasy Life of a Male Psychologist (with some attention to the fantasies of his friends, the male biologist and the male anthropologist)," in Anne Koedt, Ellen Levine, and Anita Rapone, eds., *Radical Feminism* (New York: Quadrangle Books, 1973), pp. 178–97, is an early feminist critique of conventional academic and clinical psychological views of women as sick and weak. See also Benjamin, *op. cit.*; Chodorow, *op. cit.*; Carol Gilligan, *In a Different Voice: Psychological Theory and Women's Development* (Cambridge, Mass.: Harvard University Press, 1983); and Jean Baker Miller, *Toward a New Psychology of Women* (Boston: Beacon Press, 1976). A sampling from current psychoanalytic thinking is Harold P. Blum, ed., *Female Psychology: Contemporary Psychoanalytic Views* (New York: International Universities Press, 1977).

On women as daughters, see Lucy Gilbert and Paula Webster, *Bound by Love: The Sweet Trap of Daughterhood* (Boston: Beacon Press, 1982).

My discussion of the emergence of selfhood out of infantile diffuseness through separation/individuation depends on Margaret S. Mahler, Fred Pine, and Anni Bergman, *The Psychological Birth of the Human Infant* (London: Hutchinson, 1975).

My view of autonomy and dependency as mutually enhancing comes from Miller, *op. cit.* It is influenced as well by the idea that, while men's dependency needs are culturally legitimate, women's are not, as expounded in Luise Eichenbaum and Susie Orbach, *What Do Women Want: Exploding the Myth of Dependency* (New York: Coward-McCann, 1983). The psychoanalyst W. Ronald D. Fairbairn discusses a notion of "mature dependency" in *Psychoanalytic Studies of the Personality* (London: Routledge and Kegan Paul, 1953), pp. 34–35, and *passim*.

The phrase *life is with people* is the title of the classic ethnography of European Jews by Mark Zborowski and Elizabeth Herzog, *Life Is with People: The Jewish Little Town in Eastern Europe* (New York: International Universities Press, 1952).

Lenore J. Weitzman, *The Divorce Revolution: The Unexpected Social and Economic Consequences for Women and Children in America* (New York: Free Press, 1985), documents the unexpected inequities arising from the bad mix of a still-patriarchal social structure and feminist-inspired reforms in divorce laws.

NORMAL ENVY (5:15 P.M.)

Dorothy Dinnerstein, *The Mermaid and the Minotaur: Sexual Arrangements and Human Malaise* (New York: Harper and Row, 1976), evokes the relation between misogyny and maternal power more powerfully than any other feminist work.

Melanie Klein, the Freudian from whose work the object-relations school of thought emerged, establishes the importance of infantile envy, although I disagree with her conception of it as primarily destructive. For an introduction to her often obscure writings, see Hannan Segal, *An Introduction to the Work of Melanie Klein* (New York: Basic Books, 1973).

Penis envy, according to classical psychoanalytic theory, is the essential feminine dilemma, but not according to other thinkers. Donna Bassin, "Woman's Images of Inner Space: Data Towards Expanded Interpretive Categories," *International Review of Psychoanalysis* 9 (1982): 191–203, summarizes the Freudian position, reviews criticisms of it, and proposes that women's experience would be better understood by an expansion of our notions of inner space. One might consult also Harriet F. Lerner, "Parental Mislabeling of Female Genitals as a Determinant of Penis Envy and Learning Inhibitions in Women," in Harold P. Blum, ed., *Female Psychology: Contemporary Psychoanalytic Views* (New York: International Universities Press, 1977), pp. 269–84. Janine Chasseguet-Smirgel makes the point that the penis is desirable because it is the means to acquire maternal omnipotence; she adds that men have penis envy, too; see "Feminine Guilt and the Oedipus Complex," in Janine Chasseguet-Smirgel, ed., *Female Sexuality: New Psychoanalytic Views* (Ann Arbor, Mich.: University of Michigan Press, 1970), pp. 97–134. See also Jessica Benjamin's insight that, if girls want to be boys, what boys want is to be more so, in "The Oedipal Riddle," in John Diggins and Mark Kann, eds., *The Problem of Authority in America* (Philadelphia: Temple University Press, 1981), pp. 195–224.

On women's relation to what I call the continuum between activity, assertion, anger, and aggression, see Teresa Bernardez-Bonesatti, "Women and Anger: Conflicts with Aggression in Contemporary Women," presented at the American Psychiatric Association Annual Meeting, Toronto, Canada, May 4, 1977. See also Harriet Goldhor Lerner, *The Dance of Anger: A Woman's Guide to Intimate Relationships* (New York: Harper and Row, 1985).

Few studies presently exist on fathers and their behavior with their children, though more are in process. See the psychoanalytic compendium by Michael Lamb, ed., *The Role of the Father in Child Development* (New York: Wiley, 1976). Ernst Abelin, *Self-Image, Gender Identity, and the Early Triangulations* (unpublished manuscript, 1978) is a study of great weight whose anecdotal evidence is therefore less convincing. For feminist accounts, see Lucy Gilbert and Paula Webster, *Bound by Love: The Sweet Trap of Daughterhood* (Boston: Beacon Press, 1982), as well as Judith Lewis Herman's angry critique, *Father-Daughter Incest* (Cambridge, Mass.: Harvard University Press, 1981). A more personal, if wandering, memoir-cum-analysis is Signe Hammer, *Passionate Attachments: Fathers and Daughters in America Today* (New York: Rawson Associates, 1982).

Sherry Ortner's "The Virgin and the State," *Michigan Discussions in Anthropology* 2 (1976): 1–16, as I and others suggest, argues that most men occupy a rather juvenilized position in the state and do not in fact represent the authority of society in social fact, even though they might in the infant's mind.

Feminist appreciations and critiques of the Lacanian notion of the phallus as signifier of difference include Juliet Mitchell, ed., and Jacqueline Rose, ed. and trans., *Feminine Sexuality: Jacques Lacan and the École Freudienne* (New York: Norton, 1982) and Jane Gallop, *The Daughter's Seduction: Feminism and Psychoanalysis* (Ithaca, N.Y.: Cornell University Press, 1982).

The incest taboo is a topic of great interest in many, although not all, cultures. Some anthropologists make it central to their theory of culture; see Claude Lévi-Strauss, *Structural Anthropology*, Claire Jacobson and Brooke Grundfest Schoepf, trans. (New York: Basic Books, 1963). Through the formulation of the Oedipus complex, Freud, of course, makes it the cornerstone of his theory of neurosis and civilization; see, for example, "Civilization and Its Discontents," *The Standard Edition of the Complete Psychological Works of Sigmund Freud,* vol. 21 (London: The Hogarth Press, 1961), pp. 59–149. Not all anthropologists believe, however, that the Oedipus complex is universal; see Bronislaw Malinowski, *Sex and Repression in Savage Society* (New York: Meridian Books, 1955), for the classic claim for a "matrilineal complex." Anne Parsons offers the most thoughtful consideration I know of for the universality of the Oedipus complex, in her "Is the Oedipus Complex Universal? The Jones-Malinowski Debate

Revisited and a South Italian Nuclear Complex," in Warner Muensterberger, ed., *Man and His Culture: Psychoanalytic Anthropology after 'Totem and Taboo'* (New York: Taplinger, 1970), pp. 331–84.

On Venus figurines, see T. G. E. Powell, *Prehistoric Art* (New York: Praeger, 1966), and Peter J. Ucko and Andrée Rosenfeld, *Palaeolithic Cave Art* (New York: McGraw-Hill, 1967). On the symbolism of the Olmec jaguar, see Elizabeth P. Benson, ed., *Dumbarton Oaks Conference on the Olmec, October 28th and 29th, 1967* (Washington, D.C.: Dumbarton Oaks Research Library and Collection, 1968), especially articles by Kent V. Flannery, Peter T. Furst, and David C. Grove.

WOMEN ALONE (6:45 P.M.)

On the quality of present public life, see Eli Zaretsky, *Capitalism, the Family, and Personal Life* (New York: Harper and Row, 1976), and Harry Braverman, *Labor and Monopoly Capital: The Degradation of Work in the Twentieth Century* (New York: Monthly Review Press, 1975).

For psychoanalytic views of menarche, see Teresa Benedict, *Studies in Psychosomatic Medicine: Psychosexual Functions in Women* (New York: Ronald Press, 1952), who traces hormonal changes in relation to psychoanalytic material. One of Judith Kestenberg's many studies on the subject is "Menarche," in Sandor Lorand and H. I. Schneer, eds., *Adolescents* (New York: Hoeber Press, 1950). Finally, the standard Freudian, but wrongheadedly biologistic, work is Helene Deutsch, *Psychology of Women*, vol. 1 (New York: Grune and Stratton, 1944).

The discussion of the state's role in creating personal life is complex, and the subject is poorly understood. According to Marx, the "social reproduction" of personal relations takes place automatically as a part of the process of production; see *Grundrisse* (London: Penguin Books, 1973). But a careful reading of *Capital: A Critique of Political Economy* (New York: International Publishers, 1967) reveals inner contradictions in this theory. Antonio Gramsci, *Selections from the Prison Notebooks* (New York: International Publishers, 1971), furthers the discussion by pointing to the role of the state, education, and the media in creating the person. So do the Frankfurt School theorists; see, for example, Max Horkheimer, "Authority and the Family," in *Critical Theory:*

Selected Essays (New York: Seabury Press, 1972), pp. 47–128.

Feminists have a different, and interested, eye on this process. Some have sought to understand it as something that both constructs and constrains women's role. Rayna Rapp, Ellen Ross, and Renate Bridenthal, "Examining Family History," *Feminist Studies* 5 (1979), pp. 174–200, is an illuminating study of the evolution of the family. Virginia Goldner, "Remarriage Family: Structure, System, Future," in Lilian Messenger, ed., *Therapy with Remarriage Families* (Rockville, Md.: Aspen Press, 1982), pp. 187–206, offers a psychoanalytic and social history of what she calls the "Ozzie and Harriet" family. On the relation between family, class, and economy, see Rayna Rapp's "Family and Class in Contemporary America," *Science and Society* 42 (1978), pp. 278–300. See also Zaretsky, *op. cit.*, and Ellen Willis, *Beginning to See the Light* (New York: Knopf, 1983).

Other feminists are interested in the dialectical process by which women are transformed and transform others by their work; see, for example, Anne Foreman, *Femininity as Alienation: Women and the Family in Marxism and Psychoanalysis* (London: Pluto Press, 1977), which analyzes how the transformation of money into love and then, in effect, love into money leads ineluctably to the housewife's alienation. Annette Kuhn, "Structures of Patriarchy and Capital in the Family," in Annette Kuhn and Annemarie Wolpe, *Feminism and Materialism* (London: Routledge and Kegan Paul, 1978), pp. 42–68, makes a related analysis in her Althusserian formulation of the "relative autonomy" of patriarchy.

Other New Left writings have had an influence on my discussion. Barbara and John Ehrenreich, "The Professional-Managerial Class," reprinted in and made the subject for a book of critiques in Pat Walker, ed., *Between Labor and Capital* (Boston: South End Press, 1979, pp. 5–49), conceptualize a third class between bourgeoisie and workers whose job it is to shape personal experience. Like others of its kind, however, this formulation does not link this class to the domestic domain. Joel Kovel's notion of "the administration of mind," in *The Age of Desire: Notes of a Radical Psychoanalyst* (New York: Pantheon, 1981), touches on the issue of the state's role in this area but does not take into account the place of women in this administration and its feminization. See Kathy Ferguson, *The Feminist Case Against Bureaucracy* (Philadelphia: Temple University Press, 1984), for an approach that does. Bertell Ollman's "The Marxism of Wilhelm Reich: On the Social

Function of Sexual Repression," in his *Social and Sexual Revolution: Essays on Marx and Reich* (Boston: South End Press, 1979), tries out the concept of "relations of maturation" to further this analysis of the relation between mind and society. Finally, Jacques Donzelot's *The Policing of Families* (New York: Pantheon, 1979) is suggestive but requires translation from the French context that birthed it in order to be useful for the state's shaping of the person in our own society.

On the family among the !Kung San, an especially well-studied egalitarian society, see Marjorie Shostak, *Nisa* (New York: Random House, 1981). The most complete ethnography is Richard B. Lee, *The !Kung San: Men, Women, and Work in a Foraging Society* (New York: Cambridge University Press, 1979).

Peter J. Stein, ed., *Unmarried Adults in Social Context* (New York: St. Martin's Press, 1981), has compiled the major collection of sociological writings on the single life. See also his "Singlehood," in Eleanor D. Macklin and Roger H. Rubin, eds., *Contemporary Families and Alternative Lifestyles* (Beverly Hills, Calif.: Sage Publications, 1983), pp. 27–47. *The New York Times,* November 24, 1985, gives statistics on the proportions of single people in the population.

Nancy Chodorow, *The Reproduction of Mothering: Psychoanalysis and the Sociology of Gender* (Berkeley, Calif.: University of California Press, 1978), pp. 191–98, discusses the ways in which a heterosexual union may be a different relationship for men than it is for women. Shulamith Firestone, *The Dialectic of Sex* (New York: Bantam, 1970), was the first to point out that the ideology of love serves to disguise the inequity between men and women.

WOMEN TOGETHER (9:00 P.M.)

On women's friendships, Lillian Faderman's classic, *Surpassing the Love of Men: Romantic Friendship and Love Between Women from the Renaissance to the Present* (New York: William Morrow, 1981), reveals the hidden history of women's friendship, offering a glimpse of a range of intimacies excluded by the sharp dichotomy between sex and love in our culture. See also Lillian B. Rubin, *Just Friends: The Role of Friendship in Our Lives* (New York: Harper and Row, 1985). A very insightful and funny article on women's intimate conversations appeared in *The Village Voice,* "Cool Narratives About Hot Stuff," by Elizabeth Stone, August 25, 1977, p. 31.

Most contemporary psychoanalytic writings are careful to avoid blatantly imposing a male model on female sexuality. But it is always there by implication. See Mary Jane Sherfey's comprehensive *The Nature and Evolution of Female Sexuality* (New York: Random House, 1966). Feminist critiques of orgasm theory begin with Anne Koedt, "The Myth of the Vaginal Orgasm," in Anne Koedt, Ellen Levine, and Anita Rapone, eds., *Radical Feminism* (New York: Quadrangle Books, 1973), pp. 198–207. *The G-Spot, and Other Recent Discoveries About Human Sexuality*, by Alice Kahn Ladis, Beverly Whipple, and John D. Perry (New York: Holt, Rinehart, and Winston, 1982), gives physiological and biochemical evidence for vaginal orgasm, or perhaps a third "kind" of orgasm.

For recent feminist scholarship on women's sexuality, see the two special issues of *Signs* on *Women—Sex and Sexuality*, vol. 5, no. 4 and vol. 6, no. 1. Also see *Heresies* vol. 3, no. 4, issue 12, "The Sex Issue" (1981); Ann Snitow, Christine Stansell, and Sharon Thompson, eds., *Powers of Desire: The Politics of Sexuality* (New York: Monthly Review Press, 1983); and Carole Vance, ed., *Pleasure and Danger: Exploring Female Sexuality* (London: Routledge and Kegan Paul, 1984). An instant classic on heterosexism was Adrienne Rich's "Compulsory Heterosexuality and Lesbian Experience," *Signs* 5, pp. 631–60, and reprinted in Snitow, *op. cit.*, pp. 177–205.

I have borrowed heavily from John D'Emilio's succinct historical and sociological analysis of the origin of twentieth-century homosexuality as a social and personal identity in "Capitalism and Gay Identity," in Snitow, *op. cit.*, pp. 100–116.

Joyce P. Lindenbaum analyzes the solutions to fear of merger in the relationships of some lesbian couples whom she treated in couples therapy, in "The Shattering of an Illusion: The Problem of Competition in Lesbian Relationships," *Feminist Studies* 11 (Spring 1985): 85–103.

Joan Nestle gives a personal and historical account of butch/femme roles in "The Fem Question," in Vance, *op. cit.*, pp. 232–41.

Audré Lorde called for a "dialectric" of difference in feminism as long ago as "The Second Sex—Thirty Years Later: Conference on Feminist Theory," New York City, September 29, 1979. Juliet Mitchell, speaking on "Psychoanalysis and Feminism" at Barnard College on November 12, 1985, also argued for the necessity of feminists to come to terms with differences of race and class, not mentioning, however, the equal centrality of sexual difference.

There are several useful discussions of the Igbo. Victor C. Uchendu's ethnography, *The Igbo of Southeast Nigeria* (New York: Holt, Rinehart, and Winston, 1965), is informed by the author's membership in this culture. Peggy Reeves Sanday, *Female Power and Male Dominance: On the Origins of Sexual Inequality* (New York: Cambridge University Press, 1981), provides data on several different sections of the large Igbo nation. Karen Sacks, *Sisters and Wives* (Urbana, Ill.: University of Illinois Press, 1982), supplements these two works with specific information on the solidarity provided to married women by their councils.

LOOKING FOR THEIR OWN DESIRE (MIDNIGHT)

Although I disagree with his conclusion that sexuality is primarily based on hostility, Robert J. Stoller's *Sexual Excitement: Dynamics of Erotic Life* (New York: Pantheon, 1979) offers an interesting discussion of fantasy and sexuality.

Both Herbert Marcuse, *Eros and Civilization* (Boston: Beacon Press, 1955), and Norman O. Brown, *Life After Death* (Middletown, Conn.: Wesleyan University Press, 1959), see play as vital to human thriving. Stanley Aronowitz, *False Promises* (New York: McGraw-Hill, 1974), discusses the importance and colonization of play in late capitalism. Géza Roheim, the psychoanalyst and anthropologist, sees it as essential to human life, in *The Origin and Function of Culture* (New York: Anchor, 1971). D. W. Winnicott, in *Playing and Reality* (New York: Penguin, 1980), discusses the developmental importance of play in the "potential space." The limitations on this space, and therefore on playfulness, that women experience because of the tendency of mothers and daughters to merge was suggested to me by psychologist Donna Bassin in conversation.

The brilliant conception of play as the difference between a nip and a bite is Gregory Bateson's, in his *Steps Toward an Ecology of Mind* (New York: Ballantine Books, 1972).

The feminist debate on pornography is heated. Andrea

Dworkin, *Woman Hating* (New York: E. P. Dutton, 1974), links pornography directly to violence against women. Susan Griffin, *Pornography and Silence* (New York: Harper and Row, 1981), contributes other key arguments about its destructive effects on women's social and personal presence. Three volumes—*Heresies* vol. 3, no. 4, issue 12, "The Sex Issue" (1981); Ann Snitow, Christine Stansell, and Sharon Thompson, eds., *Powers of Desire: The Politics of Sexuality* (New York: Monthly Review Press, 1983); and Carol Vance, ed., *Pleasure and Danger: Exploring Female Sexuality* (London: Routledge and Kegan Paul, 1984)—take an opposing view; see especially the editors' introductions to each volume, which collectively make the point that it is dangerous for women not to explore their own sexuality, even if some of it seems to converge with a patriarchal model. Of the proposition that women are aroused more by romance than explicit sexual imagery, Ann Snitow's "Mass Market Romance: Pornography for Women Is Different," in Snitow, *op. cit.*, pp. 245–63 (originally published in *Radical History Review*, Special Issue 20 [Spring/ Summer 1979]), is the definitive study.

Lonnie Barbach, *Pleasures: Who Writes Erotica* (New York: Harper and Row, 1984), offers recent soft-core and hard-core pornography by women. But women have written pornography before. See Pauline Réage, *The Story of O* (New York: Grove Press, 1965), and, more recently, Kathy Acker, *Kathy Goes to Haiti* (Toronto: Rumour Publications, 1978), and *Coming to Power: Writings and Graphics on Lesbian S/M,* edited by members of SAMOIS, a lesbian/feminist S/M organization (Palo Alto, Calif.: Up Press, 1981).

Mary Daly, *Gyn/Ecology: The Metaethics of Radical Feminism* (Boston: Beacon Press, 1978), pp. 107–312, argues that sadomasochism constitutes the heart of patriarchy itself. See also Dworkin, *op. cit.* That sexual relations are transformed into power relations through the metaphor of heterosexuality was pointed out first by Kate Millett, *Sexual Politics* (Garden City, N.Y.: Doubleday, 1970), pp. 336ff.

Ethnographic discussions of rituals of reversal are found in Max Gluckman, *Rituals of Rebellion in South-East Africa* (Manchester, Eng.: Manchester University Press, 1954), and James George Frazer, *The Golden Bough: A Study in Magic and Religion* (New York: Macmillan, 1951).

The feminist debate on sexual sadomasochism is as fiery as the one on pornography, if more underground. Two anthologies of prose, poetry, and theory are representative. On the side of advocacy is *Coming to Power, op. cit.* See also Dorothy Allison, "Erotic Blasphemy," *N.Y. Native* (January 1982), and Vance, *op. cit.* On the opposing side is Robin Ruth Linden et al., eds., *Against Sadomasochism: A Radical Feminist Analysis* (East Palo Alto, Calif.: Frog In The Well Press, 1982). Ann Ferguson, "Pleasure Power and the Porn Wars," *Women's Review of Books,* Vol. III, No. 8, May 1986, pp. 11–13, tries to define a third position.

My thinking on emotional and sexual sadomasochism is influenced very strongly by the object-relational discussions in Jessica Benjamin, "The Bonds of Love: The Roots of Rational Violence," in Hester Eisenstein and Alice Jardine, eds., *The Future of Difference* (Boston: G. K. Hall, 1980), pp. 40–70; and M. Masud R. Khan, "From Masochism to Psychic Pain" and "Pornography and the Politics of Rage and Subversion," in his *Alienation and Perversions* (New York: International Universities Press, 1979), pp. 210–18, 219–26. Their argument, that sexual sadomasochism acts as an attempted cure of damaged self-boundaries and is powered by the longing for unconditional love, are particularly telling against Helene Deutsch's assertion of "normal" female masochism, *Psychology of Women,* vol. 1 (New York: Grune and Stratton, 1944).

According to Michel Foucault, *The History of Sexuality, Volume 1: An Introduction* (New York: Vintage, 1980), the place of sexuality in the Euro-American tradition is as a discourse on a particular aspect of desire by means of which oppression takes hold. The state, he argues, commands us to speak, or not to speak, of sexuality, and by means of this our souls can be controlled. I agree, but to his formulation must be added a glaring omission: the feminist discourse on sexuality, including the particular oppression women face in contemporary sexual arrangements. Anthropological investigation could, however, demonstrate the validity of his argument by exploring the construction of desire in other cultures. From this point of view, an interesting study of lust as but a subtype of desire, not its prototype, is John Kirkpatrick's "Lust and Marquesan Personhood," paper presented at the American Anthropological Association, Chicago, November 20, 1983. See also Muriel Dimen, "Notes Toward the Reconstruction of Sexuality," *Social Text* 6 (Fall 1982): 22–30;

and "Variety Is the Spice of Life," *Heresies* vol. 3, no. 4, issue 12, "The Sex Issue" (1981), pp. 66–70.

EPILOGUE

The concept of "domination" is formulated and discussed by the Frankfurt School of social theorists; see Martin Jay, *The Dialectical Imagination: A History of the Frankfurt School and the Institute of Social Research, 1923–1950* (Boston: Little, Brown, 1973).

For a cross-cultural survey of sexual customs and values, see Ellen Ross and Rayna Rapp, "Sex and Society: A Research Note from Social History and Anthropology," in Ann Snitow, Christine Stansell, and Sharon Thompson, eds., *Powers of Desire: The Politics of Sexuality* (New York: Monthly Review Press, 1981), pp. 51–73. On the variability of sex, see Muriel Dimen, "Variety Is the Spice of Life," *Heresies* vol. 3, no. 4, issue 12, "The Sex Issue" (1981) pp. 66–70. On the commodification of sex, see Muriel Dimen, "Notes for the Reconstruction of Sexuality," *Social Text* 6 (Fall 1982): 22–30.

Alison M. Jaggar, *Feminist Politics and Human Nature* (Totowa, N.J.: Rowman and Allenheld, 1984), discusses the "abstract individual," including its eighteenth-century origins and its present place in liberal political philosophy, particularly its obscuring of the issue of gender.

The quintessential discussion of stigma is Erving Goffman, *Stigma: Notes on the Management of Spoiled Identity* (Englewood Cliffs, N.J.: Prentice-Hall, 1963). Richard Sennet and Michael Cobb, *The Hidden Injuries of Class* (New York: Vintage, 1972), using another set of terms, investigate the internalization of class stigma among blue-collar workers.

I have developed further a theory of the state's control of minds through the system of "regenesis," in my "The Family, Social Reproduction, and the State," *Science and Society* (forthcoming).

On feminist interpretations of images of women in the media, see Gaye Tuchman, Arlene Kaplan Daniels, James Benét, eds., *Hearth and Home: Images of Women in the Mass Media* (New York: Oxford University Press, 1978), and the more recent Annette Kuhn, *The Power of the Image: Essays on Representation and Sexuality* (London: Routledge and Kegan Paul, 1984).

I had written this epilogue before I had read Hester Eisenstein's wonderful intellectual history of the last twenty years of feminist thinking, *Contemporary Feminist Thought* (Boston: G. K. Hall, 1983). How gratifying, then, to discover that independently we had, first, conceptualized the evolution of feminist thinking in the same way, as beginning in an androgynist position and emerging into a woman-centered one, and, second, suggested the same solution to the present apparent stalemate in the clash of differences among feminists, that is, a new round of feminist utopian thinking.

My choice to speak of "androgynist" versus "cultural" feminism is partly a matter of spatial limitations. However, the contrast I employ seems useful as well because it underscores the initial questions of similarity and difference between women and men that we have not yet answered. In any event, there are many ways to cut the pie. One of these is Jaggar's fruitful distinction between liberal, Marxist, radical, and socialist feminists, *op. cit.*, and in her classic text, with Paula Rothenberg, *Feminist Frameworks: Alternate Theoretical Accounts of the Relations Between Women and Men* (New York: McGraw-Hill, 1978). Others, like me, would want to distinguish betweeen radical feminists and cultural feminists. Still others might as well divide materialist feminists from psychoanalytic feminists.

The anthropologist Robert Redfield made the acute observation that each person is like all other people, some other people, and no one else, in "The Universally Human and the Culturally Variable," *Journal of General Education* 10 (1957): 150–60.

Gloria Steinem, "Feminism: 20 Years Down, 80 Years to Go," *Cosmopolitan*, November 1984, pp. 344–45, evaluates feminism's achievements and unfinished tasks. It is evident that I do not hold with Betty Friedan's proposal that feminism turn to solving the problems of men and families, as put forth in *The Second Stage* (New York: Summit Books, 1981), although her article in *The New York Times*, November 3, 1985, seems to retreat from that position and take up sounder issues.

Representative feminists against pornography are Andrea Dworkin, *Woman Hating* (New York: E. P. Dutton, 1974) and Susan Griffin, *Pornography and Silence* (New York: Harper and Row, 1981). For a rebuttal, see Lisa Duggan, "Censorship in the Name of Feminism," *The Village Voice*, November 16, 1984, p. 11. Pro-sex discussions may be found in *Heresies*, vol. 3, no. 4, issue 12, "The Sex Issue" (1981); and Carol Vance, ed., *Pleasure and Dan-*

ger: Exploring Female Sexuality (London: Routledge and Kegan Paul, 1984).

On the elimination of gender, see my "Notes for the Reconstruction of Sexuality," *op. cit.*

Esther Newton and Shirley Walton demonstrate, through personal accounts, the confusion eliminated and clarity achieved by categorizing acts, rather than people or preference, by their sexual characteristics, in "The Misunderstanding: Toward a More Precise Sexual Vocabulary," in Carol Vance, *Pleasure and Danger: Exploring Female Sexuality* (London: Routledge and Kegan Paul, 1984), pp. 242–50.

Kate Millett offers a serious discussion of children and sexual liberation in "Beyond Politics? Children and Sexuality," in Vance, *op. cit.*, pp. 217–24.

Index

A

Abortion, 45, 46–51, 95, 96, 140, 182, 207, 209
Adoption, 94, 110
Adulthood, male vs. female passage to, 34–37
Aggression, 124, 129–131, 159
  feminist, 173
  nonhuman primate, 63
  and rape, 69–70, 72
AIDS, 181, 211
Alcoholism, 87
Ambiguous nature of sex, 67, 69–71, 205
Amniocentesis, 47
Androgyny, politics of, 206–208
Anorexia, 28–29

Anthropology, 62
Antipornography movement, 172, 211
Apes, sexual behavior of, 60–63, 67
Appearance, physical, 116, 120, 138
  and femininity, 18–30
  of working women, 75, 77
  See also Fashion
Artificial insemination, 94
Assertiveness, 122–126, 129–131
  sexual, 124–126
Authority, women's use of, 82–89
Autonomy vs. dependence, in parent-child relationships, 103–111, 118

B

Baboons, 62
Biological clock, 94
Biological determinism, 61, 67, 70, 98, 208
Birth control. *See* Contraception
Birth control pill, 37, 46, 47
Blacks, 109
    and single-motherhood, 95–97
Body care, and femininity, 18–30
Body hair, 19, 20, 24–25

C

Career vs. domestic work, 39–44
Cervical cap, 46
Childbirth, 46, 49
Child care, 209
Childhood, 22–25, 27, 212
    gender patterns learned in, 7–9
    memories of, 141–142
Childlessness, 99
Child molesting, 211
Childrearing, 209, 210
    dependency vs. autonomy in, 103–111, 118
    mother-daughter relationship, 98–101, 118, 158–159
    nonhuman primate, 98–99
    See also Daughter-father relationship; Daughter-mother relationship; Family; Father; Motherhood
Child support, 50
Chimpanzees, 63
Class, 6–7, 77, 78

discrimination, 78
    and feminism, 171–172
Clitoris, 18, 165
Clothing. *See* Fashion
Condoms, 37
Contraception, 30, 37, 46–51, 96, 140, 181, 182, 209
    and myth of female freedom, 46–51
    See also specific forms
Cosmetics, 19
CR groups, 173–174
Cultural definitions of gender, 6–12
Cultural feminism, 208
Cultural patterns for sexual practice, 56–57, 58, 67, 69–72
Custody laws, 50

D

Darwin, Charles, 60–61
Daughter-father relationship, 123–124, 130
Daughter-mother relationship, 98–101, 118, 158–159
    rivalry over father, 158–159
Dependency, 28, 91–112
    vs. autonomy, in parent-child relationship, 99–101, 103–111, 118
Desire, sexual, 7, 9, 12, 23, 28, 56, 58, 186–188, 198, 202, 215
    and myth of the ever-ready female, 70–72
    See also Sex and sexuality
Diaphragm, 37, 46, 47
Diets, 19, 27
Divorce, 50, 110, 142
Domestic help, 144
Domestic vs. career work, 39–44

Domination, desire for, 202, 203, 205. *See also* Male domination
Double day, 39–44
"Dyke" stereotype, 164–165, 167

E

Ejaculation, 70
Emotional sadomasochism, 192–193, 196–197
Empathy, in parent-child relationship, 103–111
Envy, 116–120, 130
    between women, 158
    penis, 119–120, 131
Equal Rights Amendment, 209
Erection, 125–126
Estrus, 67, 71
Ethnicity, 47, 77, 78, 95
Ever-ready female, myth of, 70–72

F

Family, 57, 110, 117–118, 140–146
    evolution of, 140–146
    minority, 95–96
    nonhuman primate, 62, 63
    nuclear, 142–144
    recent developments in, 110, 143–145
    and single-motherhood, 95–97
    See also Childrearing; Father; Motherhood
Fantasies, sexual, 182–184, 187–188, 194
Fashion, 5, 19–21, 75, 116, 138
Father:

-daughter relationship, 123–124, 130
    mother-daughter rivalry over, 158–159
    myths of, 117–119, 123–124, 128–129, 130
    and patriarchal stereotypes of gender, 64, 72, 86, 88, 119–120, 131, 202–203, 208
    single, 95
Fear, 130
Femininity, 204
    acceptance of, 137–138
    and body care, 18–30
    and lesbianism, 164–165
Feminism, 5, 51, 88, 170–175, 206–207
    and class, 171–172
    cultural, 208
    and ethic of loyalty, 170–174
    future of, 208–215
    lesbian vs. straight, 171, 174
    and nonhuman primate research, 62–63, 67
    power struggles in, 172–173
    and race, 171, 172
    and single-motherhood, 94–95
Feminist scholarship, 62–67
Fertility, 136
Flextime, 95
Friends, 145
    women as, 157–160
Future of feminism, 208–215

G

Gang rape, 69
Gay liberation movement, 163, 207

Gender, 6–12, 203
-free society, 213–214
hierarchy, 75–90, 111, 131, 194, 203, 206
and homosexuality, 162–168
interaction of biological, cultural, and psychological factors in, 55–58, 64–65, 67
and male vs. female self-realization processes, 34–37, 42, 85–88, 118–119, 123–124, 184
patriarchal stereotypes of, 64, 72, 86, 88, 119–120, 131, 202–203, 208
patterns learned by children, 7–9
Genetics, 57, 61–62
Gibbons, 63
Gonorrhea, 181
Government services, 147–149, 152
Grandparents, 96
Guilt, 48
Gynecologists, 46

H

Hair, body, 19, 20, 24–25
Harassment, sexual, 43, 77, 209
Health clubs, 145
Hermaphroditic genitals, 56–57
Herpes, 181
Hierarchy, gender, 75–90, 111, 131, 194, 203, 206
Hispanics, and single-motherhood, 95–97
Homosexuality, 37, 58, 67, 94, 95, 110, 137, 162–168, 211
and discrimination, 163
history of, 162–163
stereotypes of, 164–165
See also Lesbianism
Hormones, 57, 61, 136
Housework vs. career, 39–44

I

Impotence, 125
Income levels of working women, 7, 40, 42–43, 49, 209
Individualism, 147, 148, 151
Individualization, male vs. female processes of, 34–37, 42, 85–88, 118–119, 123–124, 184
Infancy, 22, 23, 27, 99
dependency in, 100, 104, 107, 108
Intimacy, 149–151, 167
in female friendships, 157–160
lesbian, 164–168
and sexual game, 185
Intuition, 41–42
IUD, 37, 46, 47

K

Kinship networks, 143–144, 147

L

Lesbianism, 37, 77, 78, 94, 95, 137, 162–168, 184, 207, 214
"butch-femme" roles, 166
"dyke" stereotype, 164–165, 167
and feminist movement, 171
See also Homosexuality
Loneliness, 148–149, 151, 152

M

Male domination, 194, 195, 202
  in nonhuman primate
    groups, 62–63
  and rape, 72
  See also Patriarchal stereo-
    types of gender
Male vs. female individualization
  processes, 34–37, 42, 85–88,
  118–119, 123–124, 184
Manipulation, women's use of,
  78–80
Marriage, 185, 194, 195
Masturbation, 67, 124, 167, 183
Maternity leave, 95
Menopause, 136
Menstruation, 25, 136–138
Midwives, 46
Minorities, and single-motherhood, 95–97
Monkeys:
  childrearing behavior of, 98–
    99
  sexual behavior of, 60–63, 67
Monogamy, 61, 150
  in nonhuman primates, 63
Motherhood, 22–23, 36, 40, 41,
  117–118, 195–196
  cultural worship of, 107, 109
  dependency vs. autonomy in,
    103–111, 118
  and divorce laws, 50
  and empathy, 103–111
  mother-daughter relation-
    ship, 98–101, 118, 158–
    159
  self-worth undermined by, 9,
    99, 101
  single, 94–97, 110, 143, 209
  unexpected, 48–49

  and working women, 110
Mythology, 34, 35

N

Natural childbirth, 46
Navaho culture, 56–57
New Guinean Káfe culture, 21–
  22
No-fault divorce, 50
Nonhuman primate groups:
  childrearing behavior in, 98–
    99
  sexual behavior in, 60–63, 67
Nuclear weapons, 27
Nurturing vs. authoritative ten-
  dencies in women, 82–84

O

Open marriage, 144
Orangutans, 63
Orgasm, 36, 125, 165
Ovulation, 70

P

Passivity, female, 125, 126
Paternity leave, 95
Patriarchal stereotypes of gen-
  der, 64, 72, 86, 88, 119–120,
  131, 202–203, 208
Penis envy, 119–120, 131
Personal ads, 145
Personal and political power, re-
  lationship between, 6–12, 58,
  84–88, 126, 129–132, 138, 175
Physics, 64–66
Pornography, 172, 181, 186–188,
  198, 211
Poverty, 95, 96

Power, 6–12, 203
  and feminism, 172–173
  personal and political relationship between, 6–12, 58, 84–88, 126, 129–132, 138, 175
  and sex, 73–90, 192–198
  and women's use of manipulation, 78–80
Prostitution, 195
Psychological factors of sex, 57–58, 67, 69–72
Puberty, 124, 136–138
Purification rituals, female, 17–25

R

Race, 6, 47, 77, 78, 95, 214
  discrimination, 78, 95, 96
  and feminism, 171, 172
Rape, 5, 63, 69–72, 182, 209, 211
Recreational sex, 184–185, 192
Religion, 57, 77–80
Reproduction, 61, 207
  and biological clock, 94
  and contraception, 46–51
  and sex, 34–52, 56, 58, 61, 67, 164, 182, 209–210
  and single motherhood, 94–95

S

Sadomasochism, 181, 192–198
  emotional, 192–193, 196–197
Scholarship, feminist, 62–67
Science, cultural and gender biases in, 64–66
Secretaries, 84
Self-esteem:
  and body care, 18–19, 26, 27, 28–30
  and gender, 9
Self-realization, male vs. female processes of, 34–37, 42, 85–88, 118–119, 123–124, 184
Semen, 18, 22, 24
Separation anxiety, 159
Sex and sexuality, 16, 56, 181–198, 202–203
  ambiguous nature of, 67, 69–71, 205
  and assertiveness, 124–216
  and contraception, 46–51, 182
  fantasies, 182–184, 187–188, 194
  and female purification rituals, 17–25
  future of, 211–213
  interaction of biological, cultural, and psychological factors in, 55–58, 67, 69–72
  in nonhuman primates, 60–63, 67
  and power, 73–90, 192–198
  recreational, 184–185, 192
  and reproduction, 34–52, 56, 58, 61, 67, 164, 182, 209–210
  teenage, 47, 212
  See also Desire, sexual; Homosexuality; Lesbianism; Reproduction; Sadomasochism
Sexual harassment, 43, 77, 209
Single adulthood, 144–145
Single fatherhood, 95
Single motherhood, 94–97, 110, 143, 209

Sociobiology, 61
Spermicidal foam, 46
Spouse battering, 209
Stepfamily, 110
Sterilization, 46, 47–48, 50
Street hassling, 1–4, 10–12, 72
Submission, desire for, 195–196
Syphilis, 181

T

Teenage sex, 47, 212
Three-gender systems, 56–57
Tuken tribe (Kenya), sexual activity in, 57
Two-gender systems, 56–57

V

Vagina, 18
    as cultural symbol, 18

and ever-ready female myth, 71
Venereal diseases, 46, 181
Vibrators, 181

W

Weight loss, 19, 27
Welfare, 47, 96, 143
Widows, 145
Working women, 63–64, 143, 207
    appearance of, 75, 77
    assertiveness of, 130–131
    domestic chores of, 39–44
    and gender hierarchy, 75–90, 131
    income levels of, 7, 40, 42–43, 49, 209
    and motherhood, 110
    occupations of, 43
    and pregnancy, 49
    sexual harassment of, 43, 77, 209